Metaphysics and Music in Adorno and Heidegger

Metaphysics and Music in Adorno and Heidegger

Wesley Phillips
Independent Scholar, UK

palgrave
macmillan

First published 2015 by
PALGRAVE MACMILLAN

Palgrave Macmillan in the UK is an imprint of Macmillan Publishers Limited, registered in England, company number 785998, of Houndmills, Basingstoke, Hampshire RG21 6XS.

Palgrave Macmillan in the US is a division of St Martin's Press LLC, 175 Fifth Avenue, New York, NY 10010.

Palgrave Macmillan is the global academic imprint of the above companies and has companies and representatives throughout the world.

Palgrave® and Macmillan® are registered trademarks in the United States, the United Kingdom, Europe and other countries.

ISBN: 978–1–137–48724–7

This book is printed on paper suitable for recycling and made from fully managed and sustained forest sources. Logging, pulping and manufacturing processes are expected to conform to the environmental regulations of the country of origin.

A catalogue record for this book is available from the British Library.

Library of Congress Cataloging-in-Publication Data

Phillips, Wesley, 1976–
Metaphysics and music in Adorno and Heidegger / Wesley Phillips.
pages cm
Includes bibliographical references and index.
ISBN 978–1–137–48724–7
1. Music – Philosophy and aesthetics. 2. Adorno, Theodor W., 1903–1969 – Criticism and interpretation. 3. Heidegger, Martin, 1889–1976 – Criticism and interpretation. 4. Wagner, Richard, 1813–1883 – Criticism and interpretation. I. Title.

ML3800.P455 2015
781.1′7—dc23 2015004273

For Alban

Contents

Preface

For various reasons, the current book was a long time in the making, and the author's research focus has evolved over this time. For an indication of other research undertaken in recent years, a list of the author's publications may be found in the Bibliography section towards the end of this book.

Three subsections have appeared elsewhere in different forms. An earlier version of part of Chapter 1 appeared as, 'Melancholy Science? German Idealism and Critical Theory Reconsidered', in *Telos,* 157 (2011). A musicologically and historically elaborated version of material relating to Luigi Nono, here represented in the third and fourth chapters, appeared as, 'Spaces of Resistance: The Adorno–Nono Complex', in *Twentieth Century Music,* 9 (2012).

All translations into English are by the author unless stated otherwise in the notes.

Acknowledgements

For their critical responses to earlier drafts of this book, I am grateful to both Peter Osborne and Peter Hallward. I also wish to thank Charles Wilson for his invaluable musicological advice and editorial support. I am grateful to my editor and reviewer for their helpful comments and suggestions. Finally, for encouraging me to write this book and for her general support, I remain infinitely grateful to Yaiza.

Introduction

Continental philosophy is an umbrella term covering a plurality of philosophical traditions that have historically emanated from the continent of Europe towards the English-speaking world (an emanation that is now bi- and multi-directional, rendering the appellation 'Continental' at best nominal). Indeed, Continental philosophy has never been so plural, for the number of these traditions has accumulated since its emergence in the 1970s. The question of what unifies the Continental umbrella lies beyond the scope of this introduction. No doubt, it would be simpler to define Continental philosophy in the manner that its detractors originally coined it: *not* analytic philosophy.[1] Nevertheless, any positive attempt to define the idiom would have to proceed politically as well as philosophically – that is to say, in its post-1968 context. What was required was a philosophy that would change the world and not merely interpret it. In this respect, that which has unified these traditions concerns, on the one hand, a recognition of the limitations of an academic philosophy that disingenuously duplicates the 'rigour' of the positive sciences; and, on the other hand, an attempt to think beyond these limitations, to bring philosophy into contact with the world both as it is and as it ought to be. In order to respond to this 'ought', philosophy is compelled to engage with that which positivist philosophy rejected: metaphysics, understood as the question of the whole.

A central motivation behind this book is a sense that this moment of engagement with the problem of metaphysics remains the problem of Continental philosophy – a problem that has nevertheless slipped from its grasp over recent years. It could be said that the discourse has lurched from a postmodern rejection of metaphysics into a premodern affirmation of it. In some cases, this affirmation has abandoned the political 'project' altogether (strands of speculative realism being a notable example); and in other cases, metaphysics has been used to ground a political orientation, but the metaphysics in question has remained somewhat precritical (whether in terms of mathematical ontology or certain forms of Spinozism).[2] This antinomy is symptomatic of the need for a contemporary debate. A discourse is nothing without a debate – it is not guaranteed by the proliferation of traditions alone.

An earlier form of this debate – one that has not been fully appreciated to date – took place, in the middle third of the twentieth century, between two German philosophers. The political divergence between Theodor W. Adorno and Martin Heidegger will not be concealed in this book. However, these fathers of Continental philosophy (most obviously, Heidegger) share an attempt to renew philosophy by avoiding the three pitfalls that lay before them, and which in many respects continue to lie before us today. Firstly, in contemporary vitalism, both thinkers identified a protest against reification that became complicit with reification. Secondly, each rejected absolute idealism, implicit during the 1920s and 30s in both transcendental phenomenology and neo-Kantianism (in spite of the latter's attempt to de-transcendentalise Kant). Such metaphysical absolutes could no longer be tolerated in the context of modernity. But thirdly, positivism's rejection of metaphysics as such was equally unproductive, ultimately, since it relinquished the problem and possibility of value altogether. The three tendencies could be found in combination. Hence, by partitioning out the problems of value and validity, neo-Kantianism could be said to have blended a metaphysical absolute with a positivist concession to value-free science. And the sociologist Georg Simmel could incorporate a neo-Kantian methodology into his vitalistic life-philosophy. The three tendencies arguably come together, negatively, in Adorno's and Heidegger's critique of the prevailing philosophies of history.

The problem of the philosophy of history comes to the forefront of these thinkers' respective projects because confronting the history of metaphysics means engaging with the history of philosophy *and* because the possibility of historical change requires a 'logic' of such change – an alternative to the Hegelian ruse of reason. In his lecture 'On the Idea of Natural History' (1932) Adorno acknowledged Heidegger's *attempt* to construct a systematic yet non-idealist philosophy of historical 'facticity'. In his inaugural lecture on 'The Actuality of Philosophy' (1931), Adorno had even described Heidegger as 'One of the most powerful academic philosophers of the present' – although 'powerful' could well signify *influential*.[3] This influence was to become pernicious for Adorno – not coincidentally, following Heidegger's Nazi-backed rectorship of the

University of Freiburg in 1933. Heidegger would resign in 1934, but Adorno's engagement, following his exile to England in the same year, was thereafter characterised by polemical negativity. Heidegger's reactionary modernism became the model for the wrong path of contemporary philosophy. It was thus the *competing* nature of Heidegger's philosophy that motivated Adorno to engage with it in his polemics: in the 'Relation to Ontology' section of *Negative Dialectics* (1966) and its 'propaedeutic', *The Jargon of Authenticity* (1964). There was a 'need' for ontology, but this need was 'false'.[4]

Before summarising the content of this polemical negativity, it is worth introducing the parallels (a term used in the editorial introduction to a recent and rare collection of essays on the two figures).[5] Adorno and Heidegger share a number of concerns, alongside their critiques of vitalism, idealism and positivism: the significance of art; the philosophy of language; the critique of reification; the critique of the image; the above-mentioned philosophy of history after Hegel; and, most importantly, a confrontation with an avowedly European tradition of metaphysics. The problem of metaphysics is in both cases understood historically and culturally. For Adorno, the metaphysical tradition falls into disrepute 'after Auschwitz'. For Heidegger, metaphysics culminates in the passive nihilism of 'modern technology' (according to which, notoriously, the death camps are but one instantiation alongside industrial agriculture). Following Adorno's cue, Heidegger's archaism must be shown for what it is. The question of Heidegger's relation to Nazism will receive less attention in this book, for two reasons. Firstly, as Adorno repeatedly suggests, Heidegger's reactionary archaism is inseparable from his seduction by the Nazi movement: a critique of the former is already a critique of the latter. Secondly, there already exists a substantial literature on these issues, increasingly coming to show Heidegger's many shortcomings. When attempting to show what remains productive in Heidegger, there is much to write against. There has to be a lot to gain in order for the enterprise to be worthwhile in the first place.

Adorno's own critique of Heidegger focuses in on several themes. Heidegger's 'jargon' is archaic and authoritarian. As we shall see, this does not merely amount to a critique of Heidegger's style of writing: for Adorno, language is 'immanent to' the idea of philosophy. Adorno's second fundamental criticism is that, in securing a dualism of being(s) and Being, Heidegger idealises Being into a resurrected absolute (in the sense of an idealism after the end of idealism). Adorno does not follow the ways in which this relationship might not be dualistic in the earlier Heidegger, most likely because Adorno strategically decides not to follow the arguments of Heidegger's texts, pursuing polemic instead of criticism. Or rather, for Adorno, Heidegger presents few arguments that can be criticised. Adorno's charge rings truer of the later Heidegger than of *Being and Time*, where Adorno could well have followed and criticised Heidegger's concept of, for example, the temporalisation of possibility (of course, 'authenticity' gets its due, but it is treated as a slogan of the 'German ideology' as a whole). Indeed, a major problem in reading Adorno's Heidegger-critique is that Adorno translates Heidegger's concepts into a terminology that Heidegger had sought to avoid: subject, object, concept, abstraction, and so on. In a certain sense, even when Adorno is right, he does not lay a glove on the texts themselves. Adorno's engagement with Heidegger is in this sense transcendent, not immanent critique. For his part, Heidegger is reported as saying dismissively of Adorno, 'I have read nothing by him.'[6] Thus, any critical comparison of the two cannot proceed solely textually. In what follows, much of Adorno's polemic will be upheld. But this polemic overlooks important concepts in Heidegger, concepts that might in fact constitute an Adorno critique.

The theme of Adorno and Heidegger goes further, however. Their respective characterisation of *and* response to the problem of metaphysics includes at its heart a concept of waiting. In his 'Meditations on Metaphysics', Adorno writes of the possibility of 'metaphysical experience' today:

> Unmistakably, pure metaphysical experience becomes paler and more desultory in the process of secularisation, and this softens the substantiality of its older form. It conducts itself negatively in the question, 'Is that all?', and comes closest to being realised [*aktualisiert*] as waiting in vain. Art has demonstrated this – in *Wozzeck*, Alban Berg ranked those bars the highest which expressed waiting in vain, as music alone can, quoting its harmony in the decisive caesuras and ending of *Lulu*.[7]

The case for 'waiting in vain' is stated more positively in the contemporaneous lectures on metaphysics: it is 'no doubt the form [*Gestalt*] in which metaphysical experience manifests itself most strongly to us.'[8] This study will attempt to define 'waiting in vain' as 'music alone can' express beyond Adorno's outline definition by examining the author's writings on music (constituting around half of his writings). But this interpretation will equally seek to situate this expression beyond 'music alone', such that we may speak of a 'musical' expression. Just as Adorno's and Heidegger's critiques of metaphysics constitute an account of modernity, so will modernity be taken to possess a certain musical character.

If Adorno has the answer to the problem of metaphysics then 'why Heidegger?' – since the latter offers no theory of contemporary modernity as dominated by the forms of capital. The answer to this question is twofold. The first reason is that Heidegger's '*Destruktion*' of metaphysics goes beyond Adorno's structurally more conservative response to the quandary.[9] Adorno often seems to take on a discredited metaphysical tradition with resources from that same tradition – notably, Kant. Heidegger's account of metaphysical modernity conversely remains ineffectual to the extent that it includes no theorisation of capitalism – that which dominates our global modernity today – such as is to be found, to some extent, in Adorno. The 'lament over reification', to which both Adorno and Heidegger were party, concerns the fact that the commodity form is a social form.[10] The second reason for Heidegger, however, is that, like Adorno, he thinks the response to the problem of metaphysics in terms of a concept (or rather, concepts) of waiting. In the Heidegger of the late 1920s we find a phenomenology of waiting and boredom as 'the fundamental attunement of our contemporary *Dasein*'. This turn to the contemporary marks the beginning of a transition from a phenomenology of waiting to a philosophy of historical waiting – a quasi-messianic history of (the forgetting of) Being. Such is our immersion in the forgetting that its alternative requires not only a thinking of that alternative but equally a new comportment of that thinking and acting. At present, 'we can at most awaken the readiness of expectation'.[11] This thought – that the representational willing of utopia blocks utopia – is to be found in both thinkers, as is the notion of a waiting-expression as constituting the sublation of representational willing on the one hand and passive-nihilist non-willing on the other. Indeed, we are already living the utopia, secured by the will to identity (Adorno) or the will to domination (Heidegger). It should, however, be stated at the outset that what is sought here is not a balanced appraisal of the two thinkers, but rather – to use Heidegger's description of his own *Kantbuch* – a 'violent' interpretation of each in relation to a historical materialist problematic that, of the two men, only ostensibly concerned Adorno.[12] Of course, such an interpretation of Heidegger would not be the first 'progressive' appropriation (from Marcuse onwards). The historical materialist problematic asks: what is the *promise* of historical materialism, given that it must sublate – cancel *and* include – a metaphysical tradition so as to make a speculative claim on the whole that is not yet?

The charge of quietism will be acknowledged in the work of both thinkers. Waiting normally signifies inactivity, although it is true that, in the Spanish *esperar* for example, waiting can also mean hope. At the same time, waiting waits for activity, an act or event that is awaited in advance. When waiting, we wait for something in the absence of that something, a something that is nevertheless made present as that which is awaited. In waiting, we have and do not have what we are waiting for, at the same time. It is on account of this perpetual contradiction that waiting is often described in terms of a privation – whether as boredom, forbearance or patience. Following Simone Weil, Maurice Blanchot drew a connection within his French language between waiting and attention. Waiting is thus a comportment of activity. But waiting equally remains a privation from the act: 'Attention, waiting. Waiting, affliction [*L'attention, l'attente. L'attente, le malheur*]'.[13] Waiting perpetuates the existing world since patience always pays the price of forbearance and suffering, the price of which can never be too high. Patience can wait forever. Adorno's response to this criticism would be to accept it, only to radically distinguish waiting in vain from its *expression*. And it is this activity that promises to challenge and overcome the quietism and fatalism of the later Heidegger also, in spite of his attempted deconstruction of the opposition between theory and practice.

But waiting is not expectation. Expectation is characteristic of, for example, dialectical materialism. Neither does what is sought in this book quite match the strong forms of messianism on offer within Continental philosophy, according to which radical change is absolutely contingent and could come at any moment. The concept of waiting-expression offers to mediate nihilist boredom on the one side and messianic hope on the other.

* * *

The means for staging the above philosophical drama is music. This may seem arbitrary, but there is a long tradition of philosophising with music. The tradition has been motivated by three affinities between metaphysics and music, the order of which has changed historically: form, language and affect. The *idea* of music in modern philosophy has often comprised a mimesis of ancient ideas of *mousike* (from the muses, *mousa*, and their divinities, the *mousai*). By virtue of its unification of the muses, the Presocratic *mousike* was synonymous with what was then understood to constitute philosophy itself.[14] In Plato, it meant education, *paideia*.[15] These two ideas of music, as unity and as education, reappear in early German romanticism, and, it will be argued, in Walter Benjamin's Goethean concept of '*das Musische*'.[16] Indeed, the mimesis of *mousike* had to be modern on account of the fragmentary nature of the ancient models. *Mousike* is in fact contested *within* Plato and his dialogues, the word receiving no stable meaning (in the *Republic, mousike* refers to both education and music alone). The modern philosophical inventions exploit this equivocation, fuelled at the end of the eighteenth century by the contemporaneous rise of 'absolute music'. Philosophical ideas of music meant the invention of a musical tradition, often in the absence of real music: *the harmony of the spheres*. In the *Timaeus*, Plato described an original, harmonious attunement between the cosmic soul and body. The intervallic ratios uncovered by Pythagoras – upon comparing pitches heard from a blacksmith's anvil – were to be the measure of this attunement.[17] Neoplatonism developed this idea via neo-Pythagorean Platonism and bequeathed it to modern philosophy – the harmony of the spheres was repeated in the rationalist systems, the pantheism controversies of German idealism, and in romanticism and after, as we shall see.

For Adorno, philosophy 'is truly the sibling of music'.[18] He thus seems to follow in the above tradition of 'philosophy and music'. But Adorno remains counter-traditional for two reasons. Firstly, his idea of music is informed by an experience of music (there are other historical exceptions: Johannes Kepler based his *Harmonice Mundi* [1619] on the polyphony of Orlando di Lassus).[19] Secondly, Adorno inverts and interrupts the tradition of the harmony of the spheres with a concept of dissonance. Music is less obviously integral to Heidegger's work. But a notion of music appears at two decisive moments. As in Adorno, both of these moments are connected to a thinking of the whole in relation to modernity. The first moment corresponds to an attempt to ground philosophy in a 'fundamental attunement'. In his 1929–30 lecture course, *The Fundamental Concepts of Metaphysics*, Heidegger draws upon the musical connotations of *Stimmung*, which can mean mood or tuning:

> An attunement is a way, not merely a form or mode, but a way [*Weise*] – in the sense of a melody that does not merely hover over the so-called proper being of man, but that sets the tone for such being, i.e., attunes and determines the manner and way [*Art und Wie*] of his being.[20]

This sense of attunement recalls the Neoplatonic tradition. But a reason why Heidegger is not necessarily Neoplatonic here is that, as in Adorno, the relating attunement remains non-harmonious, moving from vibration into becoming, nature into history. In light of a shared tradition of melancholy science from Schelling, both Adorno and Heidegger can be seen to offer a notion of *Stimmung* as both mood and inter-relation.

Heidegger's second musical moment concerns his suggestion that music occupies the height of Western metaphysical subjectivity, only to hint that its nihilism is to be 'twisted free' of, at and out of this musical height.

The assessments of music in Adorno and Heidegger were prompted by a German musical culture that, for the most part, is no longer a cultural or political force; as was Thomas Mann's assessment of German music in *Doctor Faustus* (1946). For Mann, modern music allegorised a specifically German will to destruction (the composer, Adrian Leverkühn, buys his musical genius with his soul). It is perhaps surprising that Mann's musical advisor for the novel – he who forbade poetry after Auschwitz – has relatively little to say about the sadistic use of 'classical' music in the camps. It was left to a poet and survivor – one who took exception to Adorno's literal ban by honouring it in spirit – to articulate this dialectic of enlightenment in the land of Bach. And is not Celan's *Todesfuge* a work of dissonance?[21] In spite of the relative distance of the problems surrounding German historical memory (from a global perspective at least), the old musical debates remain strangely timely, given the success of music as a commodity since the war. For Jacques Attali, 'we must not forget that music remains a very unique commodity' (Adorno had already made this claim in the 1930s).[22] Music crosses borders, those of space, language and culture, more readily than other cultural forms, almost as if mimicking the movement of exchange itself. Music seems to impinge upon the meaning of globalisation *and* of utopia by way of its temporal and spatial ambiguity. In his 'philosophical biography' of Nietzsche, Rüdiger Safranski comments that music:

> has become the acoustic backdrop of our entire existence ... A substantial portion of the population between the ages of thirteen and thirty now lives in the extralinguistic and prelinguistic Dionysian spheres of rock and pop. The inundation of music knows no bounds.[23]

Though the musical cultures of Adorno's and Heidegger's day are now marginal, another culture of music is has become central, making their musical reflections strangely pertinent.

It might then seem strange that the example of an expression of waiting in vain that we shall encounter will be a composer who worked in the idiom of what is currently and confusingly termed 'classical music'. The fact that Luigi Nono worked against his medium offers a partial response. Nevertheless, works such as *Prometeo: Tragedia dell'Ascolto* (1984) will serve to elucidate the spatiotemporal meaning of an expression of waiting in vain. This example is complicated and enriched by the fact that its text was compiled by a philosopher well versed in Benjamin and Heidegger (if not Adorno). Massimo Cacciari's writings will be discussed. But it is Nono who provides this study with an authority on modern music that is external to Adorno and Heidegger. Nono takes music in a direction that Adorno did not *quite* foresee, opening up a critique of Adorno's expression of waiting in vain.

Other, non-musical examples of artworks could have been examined here – examples of time-based practices, including film and theatre. There is, notably, a philosophical literature coming from both materialist and existentialist traditions on Samuel Beckett, who knew a thing or two about waiting. If Beckett were to be examined, the example would be *Endgame* and not *Waiting for Godot*. For Adorno, the latter remained within the idiom of post-war existentialism, the jargon of which became the object of *Endgame*'s ridicule[24] (Heidegger himself, upon seeing *Godot*, commented dryly: 'That man must have read Heidegger').[25]

Each of the five chapters proceeds by way of particular readings of Adorno and Heidegger, each one revolving around the issues of metaphysics and waiting. As such, aside from the final chapter (which addresses the issue head on) there is no fixed sequential order but rather, it is hoped, a constellation of materials. In Chapter 1, an attempt is made to respond to the issue of a regressively infinite task (as waiting in vain) in Adorno's melancholy science by showing how his philosophy of language and music is informed by Benjamin's early work on language and melancholy. Benjamin's work in turn bears several affinities to Schelling's *post*-Kantian system of freedom. Rather than disavowing the problem of the system, Adorno signals an interruption of the idealist harmony of the spheres with a dissonant systematicity. In Chapter 2, a parallel is drawn between Adorno's and Heidegger's critiques of representational willing as a nihilistic form of subjectivity. This comparison is made by way of Richard Wagner, who offers a point of philological and philosophical contact. Adorno's 'ambivalent' stance towards the composer is radicalised in the first part of Chapter 2 in order to bring out a theory of dialectical nominalism. Resonating with the later Benjamin, distraction, boredom and the decentring of the ego turn out to be not only the mark of decay but also of progress. In the second part of Chapter 2, Heidegger's situating of Wagner at the height of metaphysics is read according to his notion of its 'twisting free'. Relating this to the concept of *Aufhebung*, it is shown that twisting free bears a necessarily musical character.

Chapters 3 and 4 address the temporal and spatial character of the expression of waiting in vain respectively, each one turning to the example of Nono. Adorno's statement that the 'two spheres of music', modern music and commodity music, 'must be thought of together' is explained in the context of his concern with reification and experience within and without music, and with the theory that progress might be possible by way of a mimesis of detemporalisation. This mimesis is connected to Benjamin's concept of the dialectical image, on the basis of specific affinities – superficially going against Adorno – between music and the image. Prompted by Nono and his philosophical collaborator, Chapter 4 relates Cacciari's philosophy of 'the metropolis' to the spatial peculiarity of *Prometeo*. This is articulated according to a comparison between Cacciari's negative thought and Adorno's negative dialectic, on the grounds of concepts of the tragic. This leads to a consideration of the utopian character of the artwork with regard to its relationship to notions of place and non-place. The final chapter returns to the overarching question about waiting in vain in relation to the promise of metaphysics, on the basis of the findings of the previous chapters. Specifically, a notion of interrupted anticipation is drawn out of both thinkers in relation to boredom, waiting and futurity.

1
Melancholy Science as Dissonant System

Resignation and the infinite task

Ever since Adorno was reproached by his students in the late 1960s, Frankfurt School critical theory has been accused of resignation.[1] By determining contemporary society as totally reified, the charge goes, Adorno's critical theory thereby denies its own agency for social change (to reify means to turn subjectivity into a thing). Adorno had already defined his project as 'the melancholy science', the only possible philosophy amidst conditions of 'damaged life' – and does not melancholy suggest resignation?[2] Adorno's more recent detractors have included Italian radical thinkers. For Antonio Negri (writing with Michael Hardt), Adorno's critical theory represents a form of 'deconstruction' at a time when what is required is 'constructing, in the non-place, a new place.'[3] And for Giorgio Agamben, 'negative dialectics is an absolutely non-messianic form of thought, closer to the emotional tonality of Jean Améry than that of Benjamin.'[4] What these statements share is the old charge of a decisive abstraction of theory from practice, understood here as construction and messianic event respectively.

It took a careful reader of Adorno to see that this problem in his thought was a consequence of the influence of neo-Kantian philosophy on many German theorists at the beginning of the twentieth century. In her *Melancholy Science* (1978), Gillian Rose offered what is still the most detailed – though by no means apologetic – introduction to Adorno's thought. But by the time of *Hegel Contra Sociology* (1981), Rose would fault a turn away from the speculative whole in Adorno and others. Adorno's underlying philosophical motivation remained neo-Kantian, Rose suggests there and in subsequent essays, in its affirmation of the unrealisability of the whole by way of its regressively infinite deferral.[5]

In spite of the under-examined nature of Rose's categorisation of Adorno under 'neo-Kantian Marxism', supporting evidence for her verdict can indeed be found in the critical theorist's most openly philosophical work, *Negative Dialectics* (1966).[6] Adorno concedes from the outset that 'praxis' is 'postponed indefinitely'.[7] Praxis is not thereby ruled out. But that praxis is postponed indefinitely raises the problem of the infinite task, a maxim of much neo-Kantianism. Is the infinite task a possible task, or is it rather a form of waiting in vain? If the melancholy science involves an infinite task then it invites those problems associated with the Kantian antinomy of reason, later replicated in neo-Kantianism under different circumstances to those of Kant himself.

Rose reassured her reader that the 'melancholy science is not resigned, quiescent or pessimistic.'[8] But by the time of her Hegel study, she seemed to uphold a more traditional and denigrating association of melancholy with sickness, without examining the nature of this sickness. Freud distinguished 'melancholia', the masochistic displacement of the ego for the lost beloved, from 'mourning [*Trauer*]', which works through the loss of the beloved. When 'completed the ego becomes free and uninhibited again.'[9] Freud's distinction serves to indicate that melancholy is not one-dimensional in philosophy as in psychoanalysis. The disavowal of the whole is the philosophical counterpart to the disavowal of the lost object, masochistically enjoyed and thus constantly reaffirmed. Rose was right to raise the problem of neo-Kantianism in Adorno and contemporary radical thought. But her turn against Adorno can equally be understood as a consequence of her previous under-examination of melancholy.[10] As Rose would have known, the melancholy science translates *die traurige Wissenschaft* – hence, *Trauer* and not *Melancholia*.[11] Following Rose's cue, but resisting her conclusions (Hegel alone), this chapter will situate Adorno within a tradition of melancholy scientists as a way of rescuing him from the flames of the regressively infinite task. In particular, Adorno's ongoing appropriation of Benjamin's early reflections on language prove fundamental to Adorno's understanding of metaphysics and experience. This appropriation is often filtered through Adorno's writings on music.

Neo-Kantianism emerged in Germany in the latter half of the nineteenth century as a symptom of and response to both the decline of idealism and the rise of the natural sciences. Neo-Kantianism attempted to read Kant scientifically by formally separating out the questions of the 'is' and the 'ought' – the Marburg and Baden schools tending to follow these two concerns respectively – and by reading Kant's metaphysically derived transcendental deduction empirically. For Rose, this drastic division of philosophical labour into 'validity' and 'value' not only signalled the demise of any speculative interest in the whole – a philosophical prerequisite for historical materialism – but also gave rise to a generation of thinkers that tended to approach their object as something already given, only to become preoccupied by questions of method.[12] Since Rose's critique is Hegelian (the early, Jena Hegel), many of her criticisms are equally applicable to Kant's own transcendental idealism. Indeed, Rose could have said in *Hegel Contra Sociology* that the neo-Kantian dualism of value and validity is set up in Kant's failure to mediate his theoretical and practical projects. The *Critique of Pure Reason* uncritically required the subsequent critiques to ground its concept of freedom, the unconditioned (this is why the German idealists always read Kant backwards). In the first *Critique*, reason is set out as the uniquely rational task arising from its antinomical structure. The critique of pure reason shows the task of reason to be critique, the pursuit of knowledge. This has justifiably been termed Kant's 'intellectual categorical imperative.'[13] Upholding the principle of sufficient reason, Kant conceives of the task of reason in terms of the pursuit of knowledge 'conditions [*Bedingungen*]'. If 'the conditioned is given', states Kant, 'then the whole sum of conditions, and hence the absolutely unconditioned, is also given, through which alone the conditioned was possible.'[14] Kant uses 'given' in two opposing senses here. The conditioned is given in experience, as appearance – whereas the sum of conditions, which is (the) unconditioned, is given as an 'idea', not in experience. As with the thing-in-itself, the unconditioned is the necessary ground of appearance ('through which alone the conditioned was possible'), yet this metaphysical realm is not available to experience itself. Since the unconditioned can only be known in this way, each of the four antinomies refer to the question of whether the unconditioned is finite or infinite – that is to say, effectively, whether the unconditioned *is* or *is not*. The problem is that the antinomies are answers, not questions. Hence Adorno writes of the third antinomy that, 'each thesis and antithesis is developed as non-contradictory in itself. To that extent, the antinomy is by no means comfortably dismissed, but rather its inevitability is demonstrated.'[15] Elsewhere in *Negative Dialectics*, Adorno defends infinity without considering these problems.[16] He equally tends to understand Kantian critique as the direct anticipation of Hegel's determinate negation, as if the antinomy were already that which Kant himself termed it: 'dialectic' (see Chapter 5).[17] Adorno thereby overlooks Hegel's overall *Aufhebung* of Kant's 'abstract reason' in the name of 'actual reason' – the cue for Rose's Hegelian attack upon *neo*-Kantianism.

Kant's antinomy of reason is 'given to us as a problem' (both '*Problem*' and, more commonly in the *Critique*, '*aufgegeben*', as in *Aufgabe*, task).[18] But since the antinomy is constitutively insoluble, Kant must in the end side with infinity, as the infinite task of reason itself. Crucially, Kant's serial paradigm of conditions looks like what Hegel will term the 'bad infinity'.[19] According to Heidegger, another critic of neo-Kantianism,[20] the second edition of the first *Critique* 'helped to prepare the turn away from an uncomprehended finitude toward a comforting infinitude'.[21]

Rose thus lost patience with Adorno's melancholy science. What was the ground of Adorno's critique of reason, if Adorno's critique was to be without foundations? Which reason, if any, made critical theory possible? Aside from the crucial passage on 'waiting in vain', the 'Meditations on Auschwitz' section at the end of *Negative Dialectics* ultimately relies (it is argued in Chapter 5) on a Kantian philosophy of reflection, and on the conflation of antinomy with dialectic. The disintegration of the philosophical tradition 'after Auschwitz' calls for a new understanding of philosophical reason and of metaphysics. But Adorno's response at this point is seemingly taken from that same tradition. Nonetheless, Adorno's metaphysics is not exclusively Kantian. His writings on music in particular point towards an alternative, ostensibly post-Kantian tradition.

Language, system, music

Adorno's writings on music almost always reflect upon something other than music. Language is a case in point. And it is through the problem of language that Adorno addresses one aspect of the problem of philosophy. This is because Adorno's concept of language is filtered through the early writings of Benjamin, especially after the war (in the context of his co-editing of Benjamin's writings with Gershom Scholem). Like Benjamin, Adorno contends that the problem of philosophy lies immediately in its mode of presentation. For, 'presentation [*Darstellung*] is not a matter of indifference or external to philosophy, but immanent to its idea'.[22] The question of presentation is immanent to the question of the possibility of philosophy to the extent that the philosophical system is the mode of presentation of the whole. The problem of the system and of the whole already impinges upon the problem of infinity, introduced above – either because the whole is said to be inexpressibly infinite or because the system incorporates that infinity within it.

The problem of presentation leads to questions about the signifying status of language, since language is the medium of meaning. The system that represented the whole would have rendered language as transparent to itself. Such a system would be a language beyond language, resulting in a dualism that would paradoxically signal the impossibility of the system and of language. But this impossibility only follows from an exclusively representational paradigm of language. Benjamin refers to this problem in the 'Epistemo-critical Prologue' to his *Origin of the German Trauerspiel* (published in 1928). According to Benjamin's philosophy of language, the whole world may be read as a text, since the world is itself a context of meaning in the broadest sense. Benjamin here invokes Hermann Cohen's work on logic, only to transgress its rationalism (Benjamin and Scholem had followed the Jewish neo-Kantian's work closely during the early 1920s). This is undoubtedly the source of Adorno's remark about *Darstellung*:

> It is characteristic of philosophical writing that it must continually confront the question of presentation [*Darstellung*]. In its finished form philosophy will, it is true, assume the quality of doctrine [*Lehre*], but it does not lie within the power of mere thought to confer such a form. Philosophical doctrine is based on historical codification. It cannot therefore be evoked *more geometrico*.[23]

The attempt to re-present the *logos 'more geometrico'* is a 'renunciation of that area of truth towards which language is directed' because *logos* as language is constitutive of the presentation of philosophy itself. The Latin phrase refers to the rationalist systems that deployed a mathematical criterion of representation – as if philosophy were the measure of an already given whole, not a 'historical' and hence mutable one. In Benjamin, we find a distinction between the rationalism of Descartes and Spinoza on the one hand – who introduced their systems with the epigram on geometric method – and Leibniz on the other, upon whom Benjamin will partly rely for his idea of the monad. This contradictory approach to rationalism, to early modern philosophy, explains the contradictory 'harmony of the spheres' of the 'Prologue' itself, as we shall see (The relationship between Spinoza and Leibniz is in any case complicated by the reception of Spinoza in modern philosophy. Moreover, Benjamin's rationalism critique remains pertinent to the more recent turns to Spinoza in radical thought). Benjamin's critique of Kantianism always risks lapsing into a precritical dogmatism. The 'Epistemo-critical Prologue' contains many dogmatic moments, but Benjamin ultimately maintains the question of presentation. Benjamin does not reject the system as such, but rather responds with a mode of presentation that is systematic yet fragmentary – hence, 'systematicity'. Benjamin attempts to circumvent the formal logic of representation with a mode of presentation called constellation. Adorno will reformulate Benjamin's constellation amidst a renewed questioning of the possibility of philosophy as metaphysics.

Adorno is attracted to the negativity of the antimony as a critique of systematic syncretism. Echoing Benjamin, Adorno attributes the 'systematic need' of rationalism to the bourgeois '*ratio*' itself: 'the systems of the seventeenth century had an especially compensatory purpose'.[24] Adorno questions the appropriateness of mathematical reasoning for philosophical presentation. Mathematical reasoning is 'successful' in that it equates to that which is represented. But philosophical presentation does not equate to the whole: the highest aim of philosophy, the good life, has not been realised. Neither are the two sides incommensurable, however. An understanding of language as non-representational is appropriate to the problem of philosophical presentation insofar as it recognises a corresponding non-correspondence to the whole. The 'model' of the constellation is 'the conduct of language', because the constellation:

> offers no mere sign-system for cognitive functions. Where it appears essentially as language, becoming presentation [*Darstellung*], it does not define its concepts. It procures their objectivity through the relationship into which it posits the concepts, centred about a thing.[25]

Benjamin and Adorno each dismiss the propositional *answer* to the question of the system, but not the *question* of the system itself.

In an essay entitled 'Music, Language and Composition' (1956), Adorno writes the following:

> Music is similar to language in that it is a temporal succession of articulated sounds that are more than just sound. The succession of sounds is related to logic; there is a right and a wrong. But what is said cannot be abstracted from the music; it does not form a system of signs.[26]

The ground of the comparison between music and language is 'temporal succession' and 'articulated sound'. This is more evident in Adorno's German. '*Sprache*' does not readily accommodate itself to the French *langue/parole* distinction. *Sprache* is also speech. Adorno exploits characteristics of both *langue* and *parole* in his *Sprache*. Hence, in *Aesthetic*

Theory, Adorno considers the 'articulation' or 'linguistic quality', *Sprachcharakter*, of the artwork. 'Art's linguistic quality gives rise to reflection over what speaks in art'. Adorno rejects the twofold possibility that the artist or the beholder speaks, subjectively. And yet, the work does speak, as if it were a subject. Lyric poetry and music are obvious cases of *Sprachcharakter*. Although it 'remains undecided whether the latent "I", the speaking "I", is the same in different genres of art', Adorno hints at a preference: 'Here again music gives the most extreme expression to certain characteristics of the artistic, though this by no means bestows any primacy on music.'[27]

Insofar as *Sprachcharakter* refers to speech, Adorno upholds a traditional affinity between music and the voice. But does not this association of language, music and the voice amount to a sustained phonocentricism? Derrida had found in Jean-Jacques Rousseau *both* a privileging of the voice – the self-present 'spirit' as the exclusion of the 'dangerous supplement' to speech, writing – *and* a latent understanding of writing *as* 'différance'.[28] Rousseau belongs and does not belong to the history of the metaphysics of presence. Central to Derrida's deconstruction is Rousseau's *Essay on the origin of languages, in which something is said about melody and musical imitation* (1781). But *modern* music, says Adorno (and Rousseau?) *is* a kind of writing. 'The traditional doctrine of musical forms has its sentence [*Satz*], phrase, period and punctuation.'[29] Music has a grammatical 'right and a wrong'. There is something, perhaps everything, of *écriture* in *Sprachcharakter*.

But given that music has no privilege over what is 'right and wrong', even where art alone is concerned, the question of the specificity of Adorno's question – of the relationship between music and language – comes to the fore. Why is music as *logos* privileged? For Adorno, modern music as art is the other of 'communicative language [*meinende Sprache*]', and '*meinende Sprache*' is the problem of the possibility of contemporary experience, *Erfahrung*. Benjamin and Adorno each conceive of *Erfahrung* as a relation to the whole, hence metaphysically. In his essay 'On the Final Scene of *Faust*' (1959) Adorno makes a distinction between 'communicative language [*der kommunikativen*]' and 'expressive discourse'.[30] Communicative language communicates everything. The subject is not called upon, inter-subjectively, to produce meaning. Sociality would not be possible without communicative language. But the hegemony of the solely communicative paradoxically becomes an index of social alienation. For Hegel, language is 'the existence of spirit';[31] for Marx, 'practical consciousness that also exists for other men'.[32] To say that the human being is the social being and the linguistic being is to say the same thing in different ways. Adorno would have made these connections in the light of Benjamin's 'The Storyteller' (1929). The underlying thesis of 'The Storyteller' is that the transformation of communication presents both a danger and a possibility for the transformation of experience. 'The new form of communication is information.'[33] Information, communicative language, involves the exact transmission of meaning, whereas storytelling involves collective change through innovative interpretation. Benjamin here connects tradition to *Lehre* and experience: *Erfahrung* is nothing other than the mimetic, inter-subjective transmission of itself, the 'chain of tradition'.[34] Mirroring Benjamin's own travails with academic philosophy, the question of the whole must now exceed institutional philosophy, expressing the real whole in practice and not 'mere thought': the system is *Lehre*, and language as collective expression is the privilege of *Lehre*. Benjamin thus pushes towards a metaphysical philosophy of life at this point (and, indeed, what Lukács called 'romantic anti-capitalism'), without yet possessing a Marxian analysis of capitalist society.

Erfahrung is not individual or momentary experience, because it refers to the whole of life. The storyteller:

> joins the ranks of the teachers [*Lehrer*] and sages. He has council – not for a few situations, as the proverb goes, but for many, like the sage. For he is granted the ability to reach back through a whole lifetime (a life, incidentally, that comprises not only his own experience but much of the experience of others; what the storyteller knows from hearsay is added to what is most his own).[35]

As we shall see, Benjamin takes the trope of *the whole* not from Hegel but from a romantic and often mystical tradition – including Hegel's correspondent, Goethe. The 'Epistemo-critical Prologue' begins with a citation from Goethe's work on colour (interestingly, the recurrent topic of Hegel's correspondence with him): 'we must necessarily think of science as art if we are to expect to derive any kind of wholeness from it'.[36] Goethe's pantheism – a key to his revival at the beginning of the twentieth century – is equally apparent from 'The Storyteller'. According to Goethe, 'The happiest man is one who can link the end of his life with its beginning.'[37] The link is not merely the representation of the individual events of life, but rather experience as a whole (*Erfahren* comes from *fahren*, to journey. *Erfahren* is to journey through; also, to learn, which can be related to *Lehre*.). In his 1923 study of Goethe's pantheism, Wilhelm Dilthey observed that it was through a conception of the whole of life that Goethe came closest to expressing a philosophical system. That the infinite, in the whole of nature, must remain 'impenetrable' to human knowledge lead Goethe to doubt the possibility of a 'universally valid metaphysical system'. At the same time, it was due to the 'energy' produced by this very contradiction – of the finitely 'comprehensible' and the infinitely 'impenetrable' – that we 'experience [*erfahren*]' life as a 'journey [*Zug*]' (typical of the Goethe revival, Dilthey conflates Goethe's concept of the whole of life with the whole of the life of Goethe).[38] Contemporaneously with Dilthey's study on pantheism, Benjamin would take Goethe's conceptions of the whole of life and the ur-phenomena, and subject them to a Leibnizian 'harmony of the spheres'. Benjamin thus configured a harmonious conception of the whole – the very conception that Adorno would later attribute to bourgeois rationalism. According to the 'Epistemo-critical Prologue':

> Just as the harmony of the spheres depends on the orbits of stars which do not come into contact with each other, so the existence of the *mundis intelligibilis* depends on the unbridgeable distance between pure essences.[39]

Benjamin was perhaps familiar with Leibniz's belief that music is 'an expression of the universal harmony which God brought into the world'.[40] In appropriating Benjamin's concept of constellation, therefore, Adorno draws upon an apparently precritical metaphysics. Adorno is nevertheless happy to appropriate Benjamin's concept of experience as a speculatively unified whole: the 'unity that artworks...achieve makes them analogous to the logic of experience [*Erfahrung*]'.[41] The unity of the artwork is 'analogous' to the unity of experience because the artwork is but the 'semblance [*Schein*]' of that unity. The artwork is unity 'as' disunity, or harmony 'as' dissonance. Semblance is neither the full experience of truth, nor is it mere deception. This equivocation corresponds not only to art but also to philosophy. For, Adorno does not completely reject Benjamin's 'Leibnizian' metaphysics, but rather disturbs its harmony. Or rather, Adorno seeks to remain true to the spirit of Benjamin's metaphysics, in that Benjamin's metaphysics is already a melancholy science.

In the essay on *Faust*, Adorno states that the 'two antagonistic media', communicative and expressive language, are 'nevertheless still one, never completely separate from one another'. This internal inseparability, semblance, is the political problem and possibility of art. The artwork posits its otherness to communicative language as semblance.

The artwork communicates in spite of, and because of, its otherness. It is in this precise sense incomprehensible. And it is incomprehensibility that provides the final clue to the meaning of Adorno's characterisation of music as *Sprache*. Modern music *is* and *is not* language:

> Music aims at an intention-less language, but it does not separate itself once and for all from signifying language, as if there were two different realms. A dialectic reigns here; everywhere music is shot through with intentions.[42]

'A dialectic reigns here.' Music's 'similarity to language is fulfilled as it distances itself from language'.[43] The meaning of music as art is not intentional, '*meinende Sprache*'. But neither is it meaningless. Its meaning, though the term ought to be qualified, is ambiguous. Is not this movement from the intentional to the ambiguous an abstraction? And if so, why is the abstraction of music privileged over other abstractions? Adorno does single-out the abstraction of music (see Chapter 3). But at issue here is the role of music in Adorno's dialectic of language as it pertains to the problem of the whole. In order to elucidate this, Adorno's 'dialectic' of music and language must be further examined.

Modern music abstracts from intentional meaning to such an extent that the opposite happens: 'intentions flood into it'. This is another way of saying that modern music is *not* absolute because it *is* musically absolute. Even absolute music occupies an already interpreted world of significations. But the intentionless is not merely the occasion for further intentions, a receptacle of signs. That would not be dialectical but reciprocal. The intentionless has a singular character. The musical idea intimates at the intentionless:

> What music says is a proposition at once distinct and concealed. Its idea is the form [*Gestalt*] of the name of God. It is demythologised prayer, freed from the magic of making anything happen, the human attempt, futile, as always, to name the name itself, not to communicate meanings.[44]

It is now possible to begin to understand Adorno's attempt to think the problem of philosophy with an idea of music. The constellation 'offers no mere sign-system for cognitive functions'. Music is Adorno's paradigm for a non-representational mode of presentation. Music 'does not form a system of signs'. But this is only the negative side of Adorno's dialectic. By itself, it would amount to a form of anti-systematic scepticism. Rather, there is a positive, though 'futile' intimation of the absolute. Music is the idea of naming in that the name is non-representational language. In the name, signifier and signified are expressed as one. The expression is itself naming. Intimation is a metaphysical ground for philosophical presentation. But without this possibility of presentation there would be no expression of the intimation: it would remain mute. This understanding of the name and of naming would, once again, have come to Adorno from Benjamin; in particular, from the essays 'On Language as Such and on the Language of Man' (1916) and 'The Task of the Translator' (1921).

Melancholy science in Schelling and Benjamin

Benjamin's first mature philosophical reflection, 'On Language as Such and the Language of Man', started out as a letter to Scholem. Benjamin was now reading widely around a counter-tradition of rational mysticism, of great importance to early German romanticism. These writers included Jacob Böhme and Franz von Baader (a contemporary of the romantics whose collected works Benjamin acquired at this time). In the University of Munich library, Benjamin consulted Franz Joseph Molitor's monumental *Philosophie der Geschichte oder über die Tradition* (1827–1857) on the suggestion of Scholem.[45] Molitor sought to uncover an interfusion of Jewish and Protestant writings (ultimately offering a Protestant interpretation, however), in which the notions of language and tradition were central. Molitor has been claimed as the source of Benjamin's concept of *Lehre*.[46] This background helps us to situate Benjamin's cryptic text by way of the post-Kantian Schelling, the scholar of Böhme and Baader and correspondent of Molitor.[47] Benjamin's readings should also be taken in the context of his involved discussions with Scholem, who was at this time embarking upon his research into the marginalised, Kabbalistic-messianic tradition.

In the essay 'On Language', Benjamin conceives of language as fundamentally non-representational, anticipating the 'Epistemo-critical Prologue'. Hence, 'all language communicates itself *in* itself; it is in the purest sense the "medium" of the communication.'[48] This is contrasted with the 'bourgeois conception of language'.[49] A philosophy of language, rather than a science of language, considers the name, because the name mediates 'spiritual being' and 'thing'.[50] Naming is mediation. However, Benjamin's critique of the bourgeois conception of language cannot succeed on the evidence of the 1916 essay alone. For it relies upon what Adorno will call the bourgeois conception of philosophy itself: nominalism – the school of thought that the thing lies in its name alone, and hence that individuation ideologically precedes the act of naming (critique). Not only are things named (the 'language-lamp'), there are 'thing languages', in which 'we find a translation of the language of things into an infinitely higher language'. Benjamin names some of these languages, languages of art: 'a language of sculpture, of painting, of poetry'. Music is deliberately not listed, however. For, 'We are concerned here with nameless, non-acoustic languages, languages issuing from matter.' Benjamin here combines nominalism with gnostic pantheism: 'we should recall the material community of things in their communication [*Mitteilung*]'[51] – recalling the 'language of nature' of Böhme's *De signatura rerum* (1651), 'whence every thing speaks out of its property, and continually manifests itself'. Benjamin would subsequently read Böhme as a theologian of the *Trauerspiel*. As with Benjamin, Böhme's nature is not silent. However, for Benjamin and the *Trauerspiel* playwrights, nature is *muted* in comparison to Böhme's more joyful celebration. As Benjamin knew, Böhme provides an acoustic description of individuation with respect to the whole: 'as an organ of divers and various sounds or notes is moved with only one air, so that each note, yea every pipe has its peculiar tune'.[52] This theme of music as a trope for mediation re-appears in Benjamin's thesis on romanticism, discussed below.

'On Language' equivocates between being a treatise on names and on naming. The former nominalism (and Platonism) is replicated in the 'Prologue': 'Ideas are displayed, without intention, in the act of naming'. Ideas as names are nothing prior to an act of naming. Essence does not precede existence here. Except that Benjamin's commitment to a notion of anamnesis leads him to conceive of these ideas as of a 'limited number' of 'pure essences'.[53] Although Benjamin's ideas are disclosed historically, they remain immutable singularities. This Platonic immutability comes to be opposed (to some extent) by a Goethean theory of content in the thesis on early German romanticism, and more explicitly by a theory of allegory in the main body of *Origin of the German Trauerspiel*.

There is strong evidence within Benjamin's treatise 'On Language' of an affinity to Schelling's system of freedom, as represented in three texts: *Philosophical Investigations into the Essence of Human Freedom* (1809), the *Stuttgart Seminars* (1810) and *The Ages of the World* (three drafts, 1811–15). Benjamin shared Schelling's aim to overcome transcendental idealism on the one hand and mechanistic pantheism on the other, without either upholding Hegel's absolute in contemporary history or Schelling's former *Naturphilosophie*. Schelling had by this point moved away from his system of absolute identity, including intellectual intuitionism. Is it, asks Schelling, possible to give a systematic account of freedom – in Benjamin's terms, a philosophy of the name *and* of naming? For Schelling, the question of the existence of evil is the question of how human freedom can be dependent upon absolute freedom, since every act of freedom is, qua its freedom, absolutely free or unconditioned. As in Benjamin's text, the absolute is in some way presupposed. But this theological tradition is, as a young Jürgen Habermas observed, a heretical one that traverses Jewish and Protestant mysticisms.[54] This theological viewpoint is filtered through the historical facticity of the nineteenth century's defeat of political romanticism.

For Schelling, the problem of evil dovetails with the Kantian problem of freedom and the *Naturphilosophie* problem of nature. Indeed, the *Freiheitschrift* is best understood against the backdrop of the 'pantheism controversy', that 'thunderbolt' (Hegel) that struck German intellectual life in the 1780s and continued in spite of Kant. Affirming Kant's breakthrough ('the higher light of Idealism shines upon us'), Schelling nevertheless accuses Kantian idealism of relinquishing the whole, leading to the collapse of its system. The rationalist systems of Spinoza and Leibniz did at least posit a single substance – Schelling's complaint being that they did this in an unproblematic manner, reducing the divine to a thing and extinguishing freedom in fatalism. Schelling thus engages in an immanent critique of pantheism. Pantheism means 'one in all', or 'all in one'. If the absolute is everything, or if all things are in the absolute, then human freedom cannot be free. Schelling frames this dilemma in terms of the identity philosophy already familiar to Hegel. What is the identity of identity and difference? This judgement has hitherto been misunderstood. Anticipating Benjamin's and Adorno's understanding of the problem of presentation and language, Schelling writes that:

> The reason for such misinterpretations, which other systems have also experienced in full measure, lies in the general misunderstanding of the law of identity or the meaning of the copula in judgement.[55]

Philosophy as judgement (*Urteil*) is a matter of presenting the opposition absolutely such that it is not absolutely opposed. To this end, Schelling employs language familiar to his earlier, monistic *Naturphilosophie*. But he has now grown dissatisfied with the attempt to define science by way of the natural sciences alone. For Jacobi, the unique insight of Spinoza lay in the consistency with which he employed the principle of sufficient reason. His philosophy concurred with the view of the natural sciences that nature is entirely conditioned. Hence: atheism and fatalism, for God and freedom are each unconditioned. Jacobi stated that the acceptance of the impossibility of the unconditioned for human reason must lead to a necessary act of unreason: faith. Schelling sought to uphold a notion of freedom without the dualism of faith and reason, to produce a system of freedom.[56] The difficulty of this task can be sensed from Schelling's melancholy philosophy.

Schelling attempted to overcome the contradiction of Spinozism, for which nature is immanent, and idealism, for which nature is transcendent, by describing nature in non-mechanistic terms – by attributing freedom to it. Rather than this being solely anthropomorphic, the attribution is the necessary act of freedom itself:

> Man never obtains control of [the] condition [which existence requires in order to be actual], although in evil he strives to do so; it is only loaned to him, is independent of him; thus his personality and selfhood can never rise to full actuality. This is the sadness clinging to all finite life, and if in God, too, there is a condition which is at least relatively independent, then within him there is a well of sadness, which, however, never comes to actuality, but serves only for the eternal joy of overcoming. Hence the veil of despondency spread over all of life, the deep, indestructible melancholy of all life.[57]

'*Schwermut*' and '*Melancholie*' arise from the contradiction between free existence and the condition or ground of existence, which, as conditioned, cannot be free. This is, so it seems, the famous lament to finitude. Except that, since melancholy is the experience of the contradiction of existence and ground, it is the original possibility of real freedom. Real freedom is the concern of nature because it concerns the material act of freedom (on nature as well as in nature). As in Kant, there must be an unconditioned ground of freedom. But this remains formal-transcendental, hence too dualistic for Schelling: 'there is no transition from the unconditioned to the conditioned'.[58] Instead, man and nature are united by melancholy. As Heidegger puts it in his lectures on the *Freiheitschrift*, 'nature also is intrinsically ego-like'.[59] Adorno, who never discusses Schelling's system of freedom, nevertheless acknowledges that the philosophical concept of construction (which, along with 'On Language', lies behind his notion of *écriture*) comes from Schelling. Adorno writes that, in Schelling, 'Nature itself is seen as an aspect of subjectivity'.[60] In comparable terms to Schelling, Benjamin writes of the 'deep sadness [*Trauer*] of nature'. 'Because she is mute, nature mourns.

Yet the inversion of this proposition leads even further into the essence of nature; the sadness of nature makes her mute'.[61] The muteness of nature is at once a lament to its alienation from the language of man and its call to be named by that language, to become *logos*. Nature already possesses 'linguistic being', not as a language of its own, but as a waiting-to-be-named. Since the name constitutes a unity of word and thing, waiting-naming has a redemptive character. According to Schelling, in 'his perfect existence, man must await a ... perfect state of nature'.[62] This initially differentiates Benjamin from Adorno, for whom naming seems to be constitutively in vain:

> In the utopian and at the same time hopeless attempts at naming is located music's relation to philosophy, to which, for this very reason, it is incomparably closer, in its idea, than any other art. But the name appears in music only as pure sound, divorced from its bearer, and hence the opposite of every act of meaning, every intention toward meaning.[63]

To say naming the name is in vain is to propose a transcendent or ideal name beyond all naming. Naming in vain is the impossibility of intimation. Not awaiting, but waiting in vain (nature as thing-in-itself, unconditioned). For Benjamin, the absolute must be constitutive of the naming. For Schelling too, freedom 'can only be thought as what posits and what is posited at the same time'.[64] Melancholy is a positing of unity, the whole, as that which is not yet (*and* not never). Adorno does not say that all naming is in vain but rather that naming the name *in art* is in vain, since it remains *Schein* (or, recalling 'On Language', 'pure sound'). Adorno thus follows Benjamin's subsequent turn against idealism from within language – which, for Adorno, means music.

The melancholy of which Schelling and Benjamin write is no subjective feeling, therefore. Schelling acknowledges that 'many are driven to' the possibility of a pantheism that is not fatalistic 'by the liveliest feeling of freedom'.[65] This romantic feeling is but a clue, since it remains too immediate. It might just as well be the delusion of freedom: ideology. Melancholy is more than feeling because it expresses a relation beyond the immediate to a possible whole. This is what is meant by the attribution of melancholy to nature: 'It is by means of melancholy [*Schwermut*] that man feels a sympathetic relation to nature'.[66] This mode and mood of relating that is more than a feeling can be termed an attunement – *Stimmung* (in German, the word can mean both mood and tuning). Melancholy is an attunement, as both mood and relation. Agamben also highlights a connection between *Stimmung* and *Stimme* [voice], at stake in Benjamin's idea of nature, by way of Böhme. However, Agamben does not consider the possibility of the specifically *non*-harmonious attunement that is proposed by Schelling and Benjamin. For Agamben, '*Stimmung* appears in the German language like a translation of the Latin *concensus*, of the Greek *armonia*.'[67] The attunement of melancholy is, rather, dissonant.

In his 1929–30 lectures on *The Fundamental Concepts of Metaphysics*, Heidegger refers to 'melancholy' as another name for the '*Grundstimmung*' of the 'profound boredom' of 'our contemporary *Dasein*'.[68] Melancholy is a fundamental attunement. *As* fundamental, as the concern of the whole, *this* melancholy is not ostensibly resigned. As Schelling writes, 'Joy must have sorrow, sorrow must be transfigured into joy'. An attunement is an active relation, not a form of contemplation, and can thus act upon that which is attuned. Heidegger's reflections on melancholy and boredom can illuminate Adorno's historical materialism. Indeed, Heidegger explicitly draws upon the musical connotations of attunement: 'in the sense of a melody that does not merely hover over the so-called proper being of man, but that sets the tone for such being'.[69] This 'manner and way of being' is intended to mediate mood and activity (the success of which will be assessed in the last chapter of this book). Schelling speaks of the 'attraction of nature', which simultaneously gives rise to 'longing'.[70] But this brings us to a certain limit of the *Freiheitschrift*. For the indeterminate longing of nature looks like the ideal, not real will. In *The Ages of the World*, this becomes a distinction between an eternal will 'to nothing' and a particular will 'to something'. In the *Freiheitschrift*, Schelling attempted to explain their connection through a notion of existence as productive contradiction. But is not this the existential hypostatisation of Kant's third antinomy (as the birth of existentialism)? The intelligible character is no longer the harmonious 'kingdom of ends', as Kant had it, but conversely 'evil'. It is the darkness against which the light shines. Since evil is similarly foundational (the 'unground'), existence cannot appropriate its ground or condition. Existence never actually gets a foothold on nature, meaning that there is no real freedom. Sorrow and joy are then not dialectical, but infinitely-regressively reciprocal.

Schelling is aware of this problem, as can be sensed from his increasing interest in epochal history, by way of theogony. Rather than separation from the absolute infinitely perpetuating itself, Schelling now speaks of 'periods', 'potencies' and 'ages of the world'. In his essay, 'Dialectical Idealism in Transition to Materialism: Schelling's Idea of a

Contraction of God and its Consequences for the Philosophy of History' (1970), Habermas read *The Ages of the World* and the *Stuttgart Seminars* as foundational works of historical materialism. Schelling upheld the 'Promethean task' of appropriating the divine out of opposition to it, without, like Hegel, upholding the actuality of the appropriation in the status quo. Habermas recalls Schelling's 'baroque worldview', equally applicable to Benjamin's *Trauerspiel* study: 'Does not everything bear witness to a fallen world?'[71] This is Schelling's phenomenological argument from experience, including his experience of the disappointment of the French Revolution. For Benjamin, the political context is the First World War, the failure of the German youth movement and the crisis of capitalism. Not only does the corruption of the world show an absence of unity, the corrupt world now presents itself as a false unity of its own. Schelling comes close to anarchism here, just as the politics of the early Benjamin would be characterised (by Scholem) as 'theocractic anarchism' a hundred years later.[72] For Schelling:

> This natural unity, this second nature superimposed on the first, to which man must necessarily take recourse, is the [modern] *state*; and, to put it bluntly, the [modern] state is thus a consequence of the curse that has been placed on humanity. Because man no longer has God for his unity, he must submit to material unity.[73]

Habermas is drawn to these texts rather than to the *Freiheitschrift* because they open up the possibility of a negation of the negation through historical stages. Melancholy remains a form of alienation: 'man ... must submit to material unity'. But if man is the 'inverted God', an expansion through love into nature as a consequence of God's egoistic contraction into himself, then why, asks Habermas, can this material submission not be overcome materially? Schelling does not grasp the opportunity to pursue this possibility, which is instead half-grasped by Marx. Schelling's system will split, in the late philosophy, into a rationalist materialism on the one hand and a mythological idealism on the other.

Nevertheless, unlike in Hegel's system, Schelling's account of alienation from nature includes nature on the side of the alienated. The negation of this absolute separation, of nature and spirit, is at the same time the hope for their reconciliation: 'the production of the human race offers a prospect for the resurrection of nature'.[74] Habermas reads Schelling in terms of the problematic of identity and difference. The hangover of *Naturphilosophie* in Schelling's system of freedom means that his Böhmean theogony is proto-materialist without being materialist in any naturalistic manner. Schelling's 'second nature' appears as a polemical inversion of Hegel's concept. The modern state leads not to freedom but to submission. Second nature is the time of the fall from first nature. And this is the problem with the interpretation of Schelling in Habermas. For, in following Schelling's self-critique, from freedom to history, Habermas follows and exaggerates its onto-theogonic suppositions. This involves a regression in the concept of nature. The immanent critique of pantheism that is the *Freiheitschrift* becomes an immanent critique of theism in these subsequent texts. In the former treatise, there is a fundamental equivocation over nature's independence. Hence, Schelling can define nature both as the 'dark ground' and as 'the will of love, through which the word is spoken'.[75] Melancholy is already both 'subjective' and 'objective'. Whereas, in the subsequent fragments, nature refers to the initial potencies alone, which precede and ground 'spirit' (hardly mentioned at all in the *Freiheitschrift*, because existence does its work). 'God himself is *above* nature, nature is his throne, subordinate to Him.'[76] This comparison is complicated by the divergence in the employment of 'potencies' and 'stages' between the *Stuttgart Seminars* and *The Ages of the World*. But nature undoubtedly slips back into the ground towards the end of Schelling's system of freedom. In the *Freiheitschrift*, by contrast, nature is as much the end as it is the beginning: 'each successive process comes closer to the essence of nature'.[77]

Specifically, there are two connected problems in Habermas, who was right to connect Schelling's system of freedom to historical materialism, but for the wrong reasons. First: the presupposition of creation, fall and redemption of nature (the potencies: A^1, A^2, A^3). This remained the immanent *problem* of the *Freiheitschrift*. Habermas ultimately understands this teleology according to anthrotheology, along the lines of Ludwig Feuerbach. In which case, why go back to Schelling? The 'transition to materialism' is from Schelling and not Feuerbach, Habermas suggests, because the latter's sensuous humanism marks the abstract negation of 'dialectical idealism', not its sublating transition. The second problem is a consequence of the first. The materialism that Habermas finds in Schelling is a traditional and not historical materialism. Nature as the ground of spirit is read as the material conditions of society. But this involves a split in nature and spirit that Schelling had already confronted in Spinozism. According to Habermas, 'what seems to be called for is…something that precedes reason itself, a ground on which reason denies its own grounding without being able to seize hold of this grounding as such. Matter is such a ground'.[78] The young Marx opposed the materialism of sensuous matter with '*practical,* human-sensuous activity'.[79] It would be unfair to attribute vulgar materialism to Habermas unreservedly, since he seeks to deploy Schelling against that materialism – in a similar way that, he writes in 'Ernst Bloch: A Marxist Schelling' (1960), Marx deployed Böhme's dynamic conception of nature 'against the mechanistic materialism of the English seventeenth and the French eighteenth centuries'.[80] However, Habermas follows Schelling's Aristotelian turn to an opposition of matter and spirit (the unmoved mover *in* the moved), only to reintroduce this idea of nature back into the Aristotelian Marx, partly on the *philological* basis that Marx may have interpreted Hegel's dialectic via Schelling's Berlin lectures.[81] But Habermas has to acknowledge the incongruity: 'Of course Marx confines the material life-process to the reproduction of social life, where Schelling, the natural philosopher, still understood it as universal.'[82] Habermas makes no distinction here between the Spinozist Schelling and the auto-critique of the *Freiheitschrift*, which stated that:

> The error of [Spinoza's] system lies by no means in the positing of things *in God*, but rather that there are *things* in the abstract concept of the world's beings, instead of the infinite substance itself, which in fact is also a thing for him.[83]

Against Spinozism, Schelling introduces a concept of alienation that, against idealism, is immanent to nature and spirit taken as a whole. Habermas remains an idealist to the extent that his alienation pertains to the opposition of inner and outer, spirit and nature. Not only that, matter now refers solely to the pejorative sense of second nature or reification. This concept of matter cannot do the work Habermas wants it to in relation to the '*double* meaning' of objectification in Marx.

But what if the inauguration of historical materialism were read into the system of freedom, as a materialism of historical 'existence' and not 'matter'? The initial affinity between Schelling's 'melancholy science' and concepts of alienation and second nature invites this possibility. In his comprehensive study, *The Concept of Nature in Marx* (1962), Adorno's student Alfred Schmidt sought to avoid the 'neo-existentialist tendency... to reduce Marx's thought to an unhistorical "anthropology" centred on the alienation problematic of the early writings'.[84] Unlike Habermas, Schmidt did not think that metaphysics was to be preserved as well as cancelled in its materialist sublation (Schmidt is quite open about Marx's social Darwinism, for instance).[85] Schmidt and the young Habermas share a philosophy of natural history that diverges significantly from the idea of their teacher (Habermas' essay predates his work with Adorno). Adorno's philosophy of 'natural history', revisited in *Negative Dialectics*, would surely be too metaphysical for Schmidt and not metaphysical enough for the young Habermas.

An intellectual genealogy may therefore be traced back from Adorno and Benjamin to Schelling's system of freedom. This is not the existentialism of Kierkegaard therefore, which, however ironically, 'has nothing to do with the System', *including* Schelling's. According to Adorno's idea of natural history, a philosophical account of alienation does not exclude the philosophy of history, but rather presupposes it, since historical determinacy and nature are inseparable. The result is a notion of historical facticity – but not the subjectivist existentialism that worried Schmidt. In 'The Idea of Natural History' (1932), Adorno complained that, in spite of his critique of historicism, Dilthey 'did not engage facticity with sufficient seriousness'.[86] It remains to be shown *how* the melancholy science is historical, without following Schelling's theogony. The melancholies of Schelling and Adorno diverge as divergent historical facticities: 1810 is not 1965.

The idea of natural history

In his study of the baroque *Trauerspiel*, Benjamin distinguishes between a productive and an unproductive form of melancholy, as if to anticipate Freud's seminal essay. Baroque melancholy is 'sublime melancholy [*erhabene Melancholie*]' as opposed to the 'pernicious kind' of melancholy.[87] This sublation of the earlier, medieval melancholy is signalled in appropriations of non-Christian sources, such as 'Arabian' astrology. Saturn 'rule[s] over the melancholy disposition'.[88] According to Benjamin, the allegorist 'betrays the world for the sake of knowledge'.[89] This formulation captures Benjamin's dialectical science of allegory. The allegorist distances things in order to know things for the first time. Allegorical science must be temporal, or rather temporalising (hence the *Origin*), since the same thing cannot be simultaneously distant and near. There is, in effect, a temporal-historical splitting of 'world', just as there must be a splitting of 'nature' in Schelling. The 'world' that is betrayed is the 'fallen world'. But this world is all-too-near (Adorno calls it 'second nature', recalling Schelling). The distancing of this all-too-near world, in allegory, yields to a world of 'knowledge'. Distancing on its own would constitute world denial. Of course, such 'knowledge' might be understood as completely theoretical and not practical at all – hence the figure of contemplation in Dürer's engraving, *Melancholia*. But read in relation to Benjamin's essay 'On Language' and Schelling's system of freedom, this melancholy dialectic implies human-sensuous activity in a situation of its possibly finite delay, not an impossibly deferred task. This temporalised idea of nature means that the attunement is of itself temporal. The 'despondency' of this attunement is the dissonance between dominant facticity and its marginalised, redemptive possibilities.

In 1932, Adorno was curious about, if not positively motivated by Heidegger's failed attempt to produce a philosophy of history after Hegel. Like Heidegger, in many ways a more obvious heir to Schelling, Adorno was interested in 'the concrete unity of history and nature'.[90] Adorno's response at this early yet formative juncture involved the synthesis of Lukácsian reification with Benjaminian allegory (Adorno had been teaching Benjamin's recently published *Trauerspiel* book). The idea of natural history is, as a consequence, deeply ironic. History tends towards nature through reification (second nature). But nature becomes historical through allegory. As Benjamin writes, '"History" is writ across the countenance of nature in the sign language of transience'. For Adorno, the 'deepest point where history and nature converge lies precisely in this element of transience'.[91] Reification, transience as decay, here becomes *also* the possibility for interpretation, transience as construction. Reification is the all-too-near world, interpretation is the allegorical distancing, and new construction is knowledge.

As in the *Freiheitschrift*, nature and spirit are dialectical, *as* existence – or rather, for the young Adorno, historical facticity. The difference is that, whereas Schelling can define nature philosophically as well as philologically, Adorno's early concept tends to rely upon the philological alone: the art and literary historical elements of Benjamin and Lukács. These traditions are conferred with a truth content that is not accounted for. By contrast, Schelling *philosophically* argues that nature cannot be the absolute other of history if we are to have history and subjectivity at all. This philosophical deficit of 'The Idea of Natural History' leads Adorno to repeat the neo-Kantianism (what he terms in the lecture 'critical idealism') that he outwardly opposes in both historicism and *Being and Time*. Is not the irony of 'The Idea' its problem? If history tends towards nature and nature towards history then another infinite regress ensues, siding with nature and not history. This problem is surely repeated in *Dialectic of Enlightenment*, which in many respects comprises the development of 'The Idea' under horrifically transformed conditions.[92] In the lecture at least, Adorno is latently aware of this issue of infinity, since it is internal to the 'nature versus history' problem. The problems of historicism and value-judgement in the human sciences, to which Adorno was in part responding, are forms of the problem of the regressive infinity – suggesting that Adorno was well aware of Rose's concerns. Like Schelling, Adorno worries that, conceptually, history either dominates nature (Hegel) or simply leaves nature to its own law (historicism, positivism, ideology). There are, of course, varying and contradictory notions of nature at stake in Adorno's idea: fate, myth, death – even Being. Adorno takes over a messianic idea of nature from Benjamin, but this in turn seems to rely upon a later Kantian determination of nature as the harmonious 'kingdom of ends'.

Benjamin's Schellingian *Trauer* should thus be emphasised within Adorno's melancholy science. As was suggested, there is a limit to this response. The younger Adorno is aware, and perhaps wary, of his proximity to Schelling: 'if philosophy wanted to be nothing more than the shock that the historical presents itself at the same time as nature, then such a philosophy would be subject to Hegel's criticism of Schelling's philosophy as the night of indifference in which all cats are grey. How does one avoid this night?'[93] Hegel's critique concerned the followers of Schelling's absolute identity more than Schelling himself.[94] Yet the notion of an 'absolute indifference' remains fundamental to the *Freiheitschrift*. And, insofar as the treatise did not succeed in breaking out of the immutability of the existential aporia, Hegel's criticism stands. Habermas ultimately knows that *The Ages of the World* cannot do the historical work that he wants it to. Towards the end of 'Schelling's Idea of a Contraction of God', Habermas thus reads the dialectic of contraction and expansion through Hegel's dialectic of externalisation.[95] In Adorno's later version of natural history, by contrast, Hegel's 'world spirit is the ideology of natural history'. In fact, Habermas attempted to find a metaphysical ground for the negation of this second nature, which required an alternative account of sublation. Hence, Habermas pursued an immanent critique of the Hegelian dialectic. Is it possible to produce a strong concept of history without either the assumption of progress or the presumption of catastrophe? In order to answer this question, Hegel's articulation of history must be briefly reconstructed. This is found in the *Phenomenology of Spirit* (1807), the book that hastened the parting of ways between the friends Hegel and Schelling.

Hegel sought to overcome the subjective idealism of Kant and Fichte by showing that cognition is constitutively recognition.[96] The subject, always already inter-subjective, is the production of an object – crucially, *without remainder*, in-itself. If the 'not-I' is not to remain perpetually 'in itself' (as 'negation') then it must be cognised without becoming 'all reality' once over. Only another self-consciousness, or the otherness of self-consciousness, can negate the negativity of the in-itself. The '*in itself* turns out to be a mode in which the object is only for an other'. This is the 'Notion of *Spirit*', played out in the structurally and historically successive shapes of consciousness. Since recognition requires an interaction with nature, the *Phenomenology* has been a formative text of historical materialism (as Lukács knew, Hegel had crucially transformed Fichte's 'fact of consciousness' into the 'act of consciousness').

The success or otherwise of Hegel's overcoming of transcendental idealism depends upon whether his speculative whole is *in fact* historically constitutable. According to the dialectic of recognition, the in-itself is *expected* to be cognised by others to come – there is no waiting in vain in Hegel. Knowledge (*Wissen*) is as finite as humanity, humanity as finite as knowledge, because science (*Wissenschaft*) will prevail. Hegel will later acknowledge the circularity of this 'speculative' gesture (in the *Science of Logic*: 'With What Must Science Begin?'). If Hegel cannot get to the end then he cannot begin at the beginning. The fact that a quasi-naturalistic foundation is *also* pursued ('Force and the Understanding') alongside the historical one raises the suspicion that Hegel only secures his historical absolute by way of a lapse into the very *Naturphilosophie* that Schelling would go on to critique.[97] What is more, Schelling confronts this problem of beginning more severely than does Hegel. Knowledge of the absolute is not a presupposition – not even speculatively. This is the irony of Hegel's remark about Schelling's earlier 'shot from the pistol'. The absolute is *constantly* presupposed in Hegel, even though this positing is only confirmed retrospectively from the phenomenologically uncertain standpoint of the end. For Schelling, by contrast, the problem of knowledge of the absolute is phenomenologically constitutive of the problem of existence. For this reason, the speculative unity of humanity and nature must be borne out of an experience of the speculative from the standpoint of a historical facticity that is not yet this unity (the not yet *of* this unity). There is accordingly an active hesitation over the identity of dialectic and history in the middle Schelling. Hegel, Schelling complains, does not hesitate to identify the two:

> From time to time the opinion is ventured that the most complete dialectic is to be regarded as science itself; but this reveals a restricted outlook, inasmuch as the very existence [*Daseyn*] and necessity of the dialectic proves that the true science (ἱστορία) has not yet been found.[98]

As Benjamin and Adorno are equally aware, this 'not yet' is the fundamental problem of philosophy. The system must strive towards the presentation of a whole that is not yet – it cannot present '*more geometrico*'. Schelling's speculation is phenomenologically internal to the problem of contemporary existence – as the melancholy attunement. Rather than being the 'potency' of something positive, this distancing imposes its sheer negativity in the name of nearness: positive, collective freedom.

Hegel tends to deploy a traditional concept of existence, especially in the *Science of Logic*. Nevertheless, well-known passages from the Preface to the *Phenomenology* come close to an idea of existence as at once alienation and negation of alienation. The 'science of the experience of consciousness' is 'the path of despair'.[99] It is this concept of '*Erfahrung*' that Adorno interprets in Hegel, alongside Benjamin's equally post-Kantian concept. And it is the experience of the speculative that Hegel stands accused of neglecting, not the speculative possibility of the whole as such. The actual (contemporary) divergence of the rational from the actual calls for an experience of the speculative, not its relinquishment. Rose consistently distinguishes Hegel's speculative from Kant's regulative, only to treat the speculative as a logical problem of the copula in speculative judgement. This differs from Schelling's problematisation of the copula because Rose's predicates are already posited (politics and religion). The copula is equally unproblematic, against the stated intentions of the speculative judgement itself. This can equally be directed against Rose's earlier attack on Adorno, who, she wrote, failed to produce 'a speculative sociology of the proletariat'.[100] For, rather than positing a universal subject *abstractly*, only to apply the speculative framework after the fact, the speculative must also be a positing, the positing also speculative. This leads to a non-representing positing (see Chapter 2).

'Philosophy', Adorno writes, 'is neither science nor the thought-poetry to which positivism, with a ludicrous oxymoron, would degrade it, but is rather a form just as mediated by what is divergent from it as by what it sublates. That which is suspended is nothing but the expression of the inexpressible in itself. In this way philosophy is truly the sibling of music.'[101] The suspended is not merely a decision for indecision. This would be the negative moment alone. According to Adorno, and if we follow Benjamin, the inexpressible, which music attempts to name in vain, makes expression possible for the first time. Strictly speaking, therefore, the inexpressible is not inexpressible. The speculative whole, as the name, is constitutive of naming, of the melancholy science. Adorno's 'intimation' is too negative (too romantic) because it has already decided to be in vain – whereas, an *expression* of waiting in vain remains open to the possibility that it is not in vain after all.

Adorno comes close to this conclusion in his later reflections on metaphysics, which distinguish him from Schelling the absolute idealist. In Schelling, the pure indeterminacy of absolute indifference takes on a positive character, anticipating Schopenhauer's will that wills nothing. Hence, it could be said that Schopenhauer misunderstands the indeterminacy of music by absolutising it – or rather, he understands music only harmoniously. Longing is both too abstract and, for that reason, too determinate (the will *to* nothing remains a will *to* some-thing represented). Adorno's ban on an image of utopia, the *Bilderverbot,* extends to representation *both* in the sense of the image *and* in the sense of a structure of willing that posits the whole before it. For these reasons, the 'messianism' of Benjamin and Adorno diverges from that of Ernst Bloch's *Principle of Hope,* full as it is of 'wishful images'. The determinacy of these images distinguishes Bloch's speculative materialism from the idealist will that wills nothing. But this will to something is, like the will to nothing, close to a representional willing: '*Antizipation*'. An expression of waiting in vain does not posit the object of longing. Neither does it proscribe all such positing. An expression of waiting in vain is anticipation without expectation. This is the nature of its positing. A reconciled Adorno and Bloch could agree in the 1960s that the problem of utopia should appear under the heading of a line from Brecht's *The Rise and Fall of the City of Mahogany* (1928–9): 'Something's Missing'.[102] This expression comes closer to an expression of waiting in vain than to *Sehnsucht.* Adorno's waiting-expression names the temporality (and spatiality) of his 'anti-system'. His account of the constellation and of the modern artwork, each a 'monad', is an elaboration of the melancholy science.

Heidegger's melancholy history?

The 'Ontological Need' section of *Negative Dialectics* confirms Adorno's initial curiosity about Heidegger's attempt to produce a philosophy that engaged historical facticity. The 'ontological need' arose at the beginning of the twentieth century, Adorno suggests – philosophically, from dissatisfaction with positivism and idealism, and culturally, from dissatisfaction with the conditions of a burgeoning, late capitalist society. Adorno acknowledges Heidegger's 'protest against reification' only to conclude that Heidegger is complicit with it: 'With duplicity alone is reification pushed back into Being and the history of Being, thereby mourning and consecrating as fate that which self-reflection, and the praxis it can kindle, might change.'[103] The later Heidegger's tendency to treat Being autonomously had become easy pickings by the time of Adorno's 1960s Heidegger-critique. As a resurrected absolute (hence for Adorno, 'nothing'), this concept of Being secured Heidegger's ultimate regression into idealism, showing his failure to realise his early promise to contest it. The 'history of Being' and the 'forgetting of Being' became entirely fatalistic, beyond the futile powers of Dasein.

At the same time as bearing this fundamental critique in mind, by neglecting to follow *Being and Time*'s arguments concerning the interrelationship between Dasein and Being (Dasein as '*fragwürdig*'; worthy of the questioning of Being), Adorno thereby tends to focus upon the Heidegger of the *Kehre* alone, precluding the possibility of reading the later Heidegger in relation to the earlier one – that is to say, the history of (the forgetting) of Being as the history of (the forgetting of) Dasein's questioning of Being. The re-emphasis of Dasein might soften the fatalism of Heidegger's fate [*Geschick*] of Being, and restore history [*Geschichte*]. Indeed, if the history of Being is the destiny of Being *as* a *destining* [*Schickung*] of Being – or better, a destining of Being out of its having-been fatefully forgotten – then the structure of Heidegger's philosophy of history becomes at least superficially comparable to Adorno's idea of natural-history. Is not 'reification' equally 'pushed back' into Adorno's natural history? And is not the absolute (for Heidegger, 'Being') tied up with, not transcendent of, that history? In Heidegger, Adorno writes that the 'absolute becomes what it would least like to be, and what critical truth in fact said it was: natural-historical'.[104] It is, moreover, notable that Adorno describes Heidegger's subsumption of reification to fate as an act of 'mourning' – Adorno even uses the word '*trauert*' here. As with Adorno's melancholy science, the negation of reification needs to be articulated within and beyond Heidegger's philosophy, given Heidegger's own sense of the melancholy attunement. Heidegger's thought nevertheless remains antithetical to Adorno's natural-history, in that Adorno's concept of reification is informed by Marx's account of the commodity form – by, that is, the specific form of capital. This is despite the fact that Adorno *also* tends to understand this form as an almost inevitable – fatalistic? – outcome of bourgeois rationality, and hence of the longer-standing modernity that concerned Heidegger.

Adorno's dismissal of the relationship between Dasein and the question of Being equally leads to the accusation that Heidegger upholds an archaic dualism: 'Fundamental ontology eludes itself not least because it upholds an ideal of "purity" [...] as the contrast of Being to being.'[105] But for Heidegger, a being [*Seiendes*] 'is' only insofar as Dasein is capable of questioning (it), a questioning that in turn derives from the ontological question (Adorno's 'childish question'): why is there Being and not nothing? In Heidegger's terminology, the relationship between being and Being is more 'primordial' than Adorno will allow it, though Heidegger does not help himself by frequently lapsing into a scholastic nominalism of beings as pre-questioned things (see Chapter 5). In one sense at least, the relationship between being and Being in Heidegger amounts to a seeming reiteration of the relationship between condition and unconditioned in Kant. Just as the question of Being stirs Dasein into questioning beings, and thereby determines them, so the unconditioned is 'given as a problem' for rational human beings to pursue knowledge conditions. In *Hegel Contra Sociology*, Rose even lumps the 'new ontology' of Heidegger in with neo-Kantianism.[106] For Adorno, 'ontology' was 'a second reprise of the old philosophies of the absolute, their first reprise having been post-Kantian idealism'.[107] Adorno thus forgets that Kant himself termed the unconditioned the 'absolutely unconditioned' and the 'absolute totality of conditions' – something that concerns Adorno directly, given the spectre of the infinite task in the Kantian *Unbedingt*, and the degree to which Adorno relies upon an updated Kantian metaphysics in *Negative Dialectics*.[108] Adorno is not always up front about his metaphysics – a metaphysics that, when read in relation to the counter-tradition of melancholy science, he has little reason to be ashamed of. This metaphysics includes his philosophy of language, presentation and music, as it comes to him from Benjamin. But this did not originate in Benjamin. A philosophical tradition of the musical idea needs to be reconstructed in order to show how Adorno interrupts its consonant harmony.

Ideas of music and the musical idea

In his early project, Benjamin reiterates the belief, shared by Herder, Hamann and Rousseau, that music is a language *sui generis*: 'the last remaining universal language since Babel'.[109] This tradition includes early German romanticism, with which Benjamin was preoccupied even before his thesis on 'The Concept of Criticism in Early German Romanticism' (1918). It is therefore surprising that, in *The Literary Absolute* (1978), Philippe Lacoue-Labarthe and Jean-Luc Nancy take their study of the Jena romantics to concern 'exclusively the *question of literature*.' They 'eliminate ... music in particular', only to entitle their first chapter, 'Overture: The System Subject'. The anonymous 'Earliest System-Programme' (in fact penned by either Schelling or Hölderlin) provides them, quoting Novalis, with 'the musical theme' of the early romantic project: 'An overture, then, in more than one sense'.[110] But what is this multiple sense, if the question of music has already been eliminated? Lacoue-Labarthe would later come to recognise the problem of this elimination, referring to Agamben's translation of Benjamin's '*das Musische*' – in the context of an essay on Wagner – as the '"concurrence" of all the arts'.[111] Benjamin's concept of 'the muse-ical', introduced in the additional section of his thesis on early romanticism, reflects his on-going fascination with Goethe and Leibniz as correctives to the regressive infinity – both in terms of reflection in Fichte and poetry in Schlegel. The *muse-ical* does not name the totality of (the names of) the muses, but rather their individuation with respect to the whole – the 'ideal of art'. Goethe's ideal of art:

> can be grasped only in a limited plurality of pure contents, into which it decomposes. Thus, the ideal manifests itself in a limited, harmonic discontinuum of pure contents. In this conception, Goethe makes contact with the Greeks, The idea of the Muses under the sovereignty of Apollo, interpreted by the philosophy of art, is the idea of the pure contents of all art. The Greeks counted nine such subject areas, and certainly neither their kind nor their number was arbitrarily determined. The quintessence of pure contents, the ideal of art, can therefore be characterised as the muse-ical [*das Musische*].[112]

Assuming that Benjamin's philosophy of art can be read as a theory of knowledge (since the thesis begins with Fichte's science of knowledge), the concept of the muse-ical stands as an attempt to mediate the one and the many, as a means of determining content and avoiding the bad infinity of solipsistic formalism. Benjamin appears to borrow the metaphor of colour from Goethe when writing that 'the connection of this ideal with art is not given in a medium but is designated by a refraction [*durch eine Brechung bezeichnet*]'.[113] Perhaps the Muses are refracted in their different 'colours' through the prism of the muse-ical? But one could just as well take the metaphor in a musical direction, given the 'harmonic discontinuum of pure contents', and given the trope of the musical idea in early romanticism. The connection to language renders this direction highly plausible: *Bezeichnung* is naming (of *something*). Benjamin thus attempts to respond to the problem of nominalism in 'On Language'. He does so by shifting from the 'harmony of the spheres' (actually in the slightly later 'Epistemo-critical Prologue') to the 'harmonic discontinuum of pure contents' in the thesis. This discontinuum hints at the shift towards dissonance taken up by Adorno – but it does not by itself constitute a highly sophisticated concept of mediation.

Benjamin did not then *fully* exploit the early romantic, musical connotations of the muse-ical. The *Musische* would in fact re-appear in 'The Storyteller', where it refers to collective memory – leading us back to Benjamin's philosophy of language, experience and *Lehre*.[114] The interest of the early German romantics in an idea of music, about which Benjamin must have known, should be understood according to a broader romantic aesthetics. Karl Dahlhaus showed that evaluations of instrumental music followed the rising importance of aesthetic autonomy. For most eighteenth-century aestheticians, moral sentiment was represented in historical and allegorical themes – hence, the dominance of history painting, sculpture and literature. But what if art could be morally sentimental without the distractions of such narrative or representation? What if art could intimate at representation *as such*? That which was banal was now considered profound: absolute music as autonomous art. According to E. T. A. Hoffmann, critic of Beethoven, instrumental music was 'the independent art'.[115] But sentiment and autonomy are not the same things. The early romantics rejected 'the eighteenth century culture of sentiment and social life, a culture they found narrow-minded.'[116] They were instead drawn to the *ambiguity* and *rhythm* of music. In one of his 13 *Athenaeum* fragments to mention music (but no actual music), Friedrich Schlegel writes:

> Many people find it strange and ridiculous when musicians talk about the ideas in their compositions; and often happens that one perceives they have more ideas in their music than they do about it. But those who have a feeling for the wonderful affinity of all arts and sciences will at least not consider the matter from the dull viewpoint of a so-called naturalness that maintains music is supposed to be only the language of the senses. Rather, he will consider a certain tendency of pure instrumental music toward philosophy as something not impossible in itself. Doesn't pure instrumental music have to create its own text? And aren't the themes in it not as developed, reaffirmed, varied, and contrasted in the same way as the subject of meditation in a philosophical succession of ideas?[117]

Schlegel's musical idea is not merely one idea among others. It approximates that which Schlegel (as opposed to Goethe) will elsewhere disavow: an idea of ideas, the Idea itself. Where the 116th *Athenaeum* fragment sets-out the programmatic 'aim…to reunite all the separate species of poetry...with philosophy', the above fragment describes 'the wonderful affinities of all arts and sciences' in relation to an idea of music and a musical idea. Which idea of music informs this idea? Which works – ultimately, which work – informs it (if in-forming is the correct and revealing term)? The near-absence of music criticism in the Jena circle would suggest that this idea of music is in fact traditional and classicist. Music, or rather that which is musical, denotes a concurrence, as flow and as bringing together (*Bund*). This meaning is also given in Benjamin's 'harmonic discontinuum of pure contents'. Moreover, Benjamin takes over the early romantic penchant for using ideas of music in the absence of music. Or, perhaps Benjamin worried that music's formalism would threaten to exacerbate, not address his problem: 'what is missing in Schlegel... is the *content of art*'.[118] Absolute music is supposed to be what Eduard Hanslick later termed 'tonally moving form', with 'no nameable content'.[119] In this sense, Schlegel's infinitely becoming literature is a symptom of the formalism that he inherits from Fichte.

Several interpretations of the early romantics, Agamben's included, draw upon this sense of harmonious flow. Manfred Frank and Andrew Bowie have, in different ways, reconfigured the early romantic experiment as a model for interpretation, according to which musicality and rhythm are central (see Chapter 3). Paul de Man attempted to show the constitutive blindness and insight of all criticism by way of a critique of Derrida's deconstruction of Rousseau. Music is the secret to Rousseau's modern break with Platonic mimesis. Rousseau already knows what Derrida is trying to make him say, but Derrida is necessarily blind (or deaf) to him. De Man's reading nevertheless turns on a preconception of music. In Rousseau's *Essay*, 'Diachronic structures such as music, melody, or allegory are favoured over pseudo-synchronic structures such as painting, harmony, or mimesis because the latter mislead one into believing in a stability of meaning that does not exist'.[120] But what does it mean to speak of music *as such* as 'diachronic structure'? As with Schlegel and Novalis: *which* music are we talking about? It should be noted that de Man opposes music to Neoplatonic harmony. Nevertheless, the early romantic problem is unproblematically repeated. For de Man, 'movement', 'narrative' and 'succession' are the musical attributes of rhetoric – musical, because they are fundamental attributes of music. But there is no *music* to which these attributes could be attributed, given that they are attributable to any and all music – to traditional, not modern music, that is. There are two connected problems here: firstly, generalisation; and secondly, the determination of this generalisation as harmony – drawing, no doubt, upon the 'harmony of the spheres' of the early romantics themselves.

Bowie gives an account of the historical convergence between philosophical romanticism and romantic music. Against Dahlhaus, he stresses the significance of practice for theory.[121] Dahlhaus has good reason not to stress this however. As one commentator on the relationship between Jena romanticism and music has noted:

> It was amongst the dying wishes of Friedrich von Hardenberg (Novalis) in March 1801 to hear his brother play a piece by Mozart on the harpsichord. Mention of any great knowledge or appreciation of music, of specific composers and musical works, and evidence of any practical musical skill are, nevertheless, absent from the corpus of his writing.[122]

The closest instance of music criticism in the early romantic circle occurs with Schelling's lectures on art, given at the University of Jena between 1802 and 1803 (the *Athenaeum* journal had already ended). They provide the first elevation of music within a philosophical system: 'The art form in which the real unity [with the ideal] purely as such becomes potency and symbol is music'.[123] But Schelling's sole example, Haydn's *Creation*, is faulted for its programmatic content. Hence, this is not early romantic *criticism*.

A certain non-convergence thus reigns between early romantic ideas of music and contemporaneous music, specifically Beethoven, pointing to a larger issue. While Novalis was asking for Mozart on his deathbed, Beethoven was composing some of his mature works: the opus 30 piano sonatas, opus 31 violin sonatas, and the *Eroica* Symphony all date from 1801–2. This moment of Beethoven's oeuvre marks a sublation – completion and negation – of musical classicism (Haydn included). Modern music is, after Beethoven, dissonant in the expanded sense of being paradoxically autonomous in, and thus against, bourgeois society. The staccato chords that announce the *Eroica* are ruptures in the classicist orthodoxy of a music of the spheres (the Copernican revolution in music). This reversal of harmony was already Friedrich Schlegel's programme, albeit for literature alone.

Early romantic wit concerns the unity of ideas and the *Bund* of its members. But there is an opposing, dissonant moment – this *Bund* is 'without any exaggeration...the first "avant-garde" group in history'.[124] Wit tends to become ironic, not affirming the actuality of a concurrent polis, but negating it. The 'musicality' of the early romantics is not affirmative (according to the ideology that music brings people together). Commodity music has no doubt contributed to a dystopian social synthesis (see Chapter 4). But what if the musical idea were informed by a dissonant, not harmonious music? Dissonance could in that case be understood *against* the pre-established harmony of the bourgeois *ratio* and its system.

Dissonant nominalism

The tension within Adorno's reception of Benjamin's early writings – his critique of nominalism and harmony – can, in fact, be understood by way of Schelling's immanent critique of pantheism. The introduction of alienation into pantheism raises the possibility of a mutable metaphysics, whereas in the early Benjamin we often find a precritical, immutable metaphysics. The Platonic idea becomes the Leibnizian monad, the ur-phenomenon and the name. This might be understood as a critical re-appropriation of Leibniz, in the manner of Schelling. For Benjamin too, of all the rationalists only Leibniz remains attentive to the individual and the whole in an *active* manner. But in the 'Epistemo-critical Prologue', Benjamin tends to leapfrog the critical debate back into a static ontology:

> The idea is a monad. The being that enters into it, with its past and subsequent history, brings – concealed in its own form – an indistinct abbreviation of the rest of the world of ideas [*Ideenwelt*], just as, according to Leibniz's *Discourse on Metaphysics* (1686), every single monad contains, in an indistinct way, all the others.

Leibniz is initially appropriated analogously here ('just as'). Yet the terminology shifts from '*Ideenwelt*' to '*Welt*'. The monadology becomes a binding account of 'world', not a restricted epistemology or logic. 'The idea is a monad – that means briefly: every idea contains the image of the world'.[125] For Kant, Hegel and Schelling, Leibniz's metaphysics remained incoherent because he gave no account of individuation with respect to the whole from the standpoint of the experience of such individuation. In Schelling's terms: how is the individual to be free *of* the whole but not *from* it? How is there to be positive and not solely negative freedom? In the words of Leibniz himself, the monads in 'a confused way all strive after the infinite, the whole'.[126] The absolute of Leibniz is infinite *and* whole, a 'simple' *and* 'infinite Substance'. Creationism is invoked in order to resolve an absolute contradiction, and to avoid fatalism. Ours must be the 'best of all possible worlds', chosen from an infinity of possible worlds. 'God is sure always to choose the best'.[127] God saves Leibniz from the regressive infinity but he pays the price of relinquishing pantheism in the name of theism once over. God, not man, establishes the 'pre-established harmony'. Benjamin writes of 'the unbridgeable distance' between monads. But this distance is itself harmonised 'between pure essences'. Adorno's melancholy science negates this harmony of the spheres, but takes over something of its form of mediation. Translated from rationalism to the bourgeois *ratio*, harmony serves to conceal an absence of harmony (capitalism as the best of all possible worlds). A science that upheld this nominalism would be powerless against it, since the archetypal names, of a second nature, thereby preclude the possibility of naming (mediation) and hence science. In *Negative Dialectics*, Adorno thus extirpates Benjamin's constellation of its metaphysical – including Marburg neo-Kantian – content:

> We need by no means start out from [the object's] own content, in line with such metaphysical investigations as Benjamin's *Ursprung des deutschen Trauerspiels*, which grasp the concept of truth itself as a constellation. We could go back to a scholar of so positivistic a bent as Max Weber. He understood the 'ideal types', quite in keeping with subjectivistic epistemology, as an aid in approaching the object, devoid of any inherent substantiality – to be reliquefied in any which way. But just as in all nominalism, however insignificant it may consider its concepts, something of the composition of the thing penetrates and reaches beyond the thought-practical interest – not the only motive for the critique of unreflected nominalism – so are Weber's material works far more object-oriented than the southwestern German [Baden neo-Kantian] methodology would lead us to expect.[128]

Adorno finds in Weber a post-metaphysical interpreter of Goethe's ur-phenomena, to counterpoise against Benjamin's metaphysical reading of Goethe. It is rare to find Adorno uphold a thinker from the recent tradition so openly. Weber's constellation 'proves his thinking to be a third possibility beyond the alternative of positivism and idealism.'[129] The philosophical orientation of Weber remains unclear here, however. In spite of the 'ideal types', Weber did not attempt to ground a speculative philosophical whole. Which 'totality' does Adorno thus take from Weber? Such a determination of philosophy as guided by 'important scientific investigations' appears to lead to the problem of methodology flagged up in *Hegel Contra Sociology*.

Adorno's post-metaphysical constellation can nevertheless be said to avoid methodologism if it is understood according to his overall melancholy science. For Adorno does not refute Benjamin's nominalist metaphysics. Instead, he radicalises it in light of Weber's 'value free' philosophy (see Chapter 4). This is a consequence of the historically dialectical nature of the monad, which refers both to the principle of private property and to positive freedom. Leibniz thus presents the danger and the possibility of modernity. Adorno refers to this danger in his 'Meditations on Metaphysics'. The Lisbon earthquake prompted Voltaire to deride Leibniz's 'best of all possible worlds'. Where this natural catastrophe challenged the unity of reason in the age of rationalism, the contemporary historical catastrophe challenges the unity of Western metaphysics and its (economic) systems. This is why Adorno attempts to ground his 'micrology', another name for dissonant nominalism, in the 'fall' of metaphysics.[130]

Adorno's nominalism is a reflected nominalism in that the monad refers negatively to a speculative whole, just as the melancholy attunement is the attestation of 'Something's Missing'. The monad – as a real expression, not an essence – is the positing of a speculative whole against the existing whole, characterised in a market society as unreflected nominalism, just as allegory is directed against second nature from within it. The speculative whole does not mean a depiction of utopia, therefore, but rather the semblance of wholeness in the 'coherence' and 'unity' of the monad as semblance (see Chapter 4). 'Unreflected nominalism' means nominalism that is not self-conscious of its nominalism, and thereby considers itself the only possible, and to that extent *true* whole. The system – both economic and philosophical – presents itself ideologically as existing utopia (or, least worst dystopia), thereby precluding the thinking of a different totality. The question of utopia today, Adorno remarks to Bloch, is one of thinking 'the totality as something that could be completely different', in a situation where 'people [are] sworn to this world'.[131]

Adorno's philosophy of dissonance is, uniquely among the philosophers of the musical, informed by an experience of real music. As in Schoenberg's music dating from around 1910, dissonance is atonal rather than non-tonal. Dissonance, though antithetical to harmony, must act upon harmony. Hence, Adorno writes in *Minima Moralia*, the 'task of art today is to bring chaos into order.'[132] This does not imply an ordered chaos, a harmony of the Dionysian and Apollonian forces (*The Birth of Tragedy from the Spirit of Music*). Neither does Adorno's remark signify a call to replace order with chaos, acosmism. For, the determination of dissonance as 'complimentary harmony' in fully 'twelve-tone' music threatened to negate the specificity of dissonance altogether.[133] Instead, chaos is brought into an existing order in the name of a different 'order'. The anti-system of the negative dialectic is not anti-*systems* (he *anti-* corresponds to the *negative*). In response to the charge of resignation introduced at the beginning of this chapter, this is the speculative character of the melancholy science. The whole is neither awaited in vain nor expected. The specifically temporal, historical and spatial character of this waiting-expression remains to be examined.

2
Twisting Free With/Of Wagner

> Through Wagner modernity speaks most intimately, concealing neither its good nor its evil – having forgotten all sense of shame.[1]
>
> Nihilism. It is ambiguous.[2]
>
> – Friedrich Nietzsche

The 'actuality' of Wagner

In spite of the manifold divergence between Adorno and Heidegger, each converged upon the figure of Richard Wagner in the second half of the 1930s. Adorno's book-length essay *In Search of Wagner* comprises an explicit treatment of the composer. But Wagner is no less fundamental to Heidegger's lecture course on Nietzsche, 'The Will to Power as Art' (1936). This coincidence might initially be explained away as a continuation of the divergence, between the one who fled Nazism and the one who supported it. *In Search of Wagner* comprises, Adorno will later state, a search for the 'source of Hitler's ideology'. Heidegger's assessment of Wagner is mediated through his reading of Nietzsche. As the English-language editor of these lectures puts matters, 'Take the thinker of the "blond beast". Add another who is a card-carrying member of the Nazi Party. The result bodes ill for the matter of *thinking* that is Heidegger's *Nietzsche*.'[3] Add an anti-Semitic composer, and the matter does not seem to bode any better.

Several factors contradict this thesis of continued divergence between Adorno and Heidegger, however. Most obviously, Heidegger opposes Wagner and Wagnerism in his lectures. The phenomenon of Wagnerism was in decline during the 1930s, even though the composer had become sanctified by Hitler with the approval of Wagner's descendants. In his posthumously published interview with *Die Spiegel* (given in 1966 but published in 1976), Heidegger retrospectively situated his break with Nazism within these lectures: 'Anyone who had ears to hear heard in these lectures a confrontation with National Socialism.'[4] As ever, we must be extremely careful not to take Heidegger at his word where political statements are concerned. For Richard Wolin, this 'confrontation with National Socialism' was a confrontation with Heidegger's own National Socialism – without taking responsibility for it.[5] Nevertheless, the lectures do confront the biological-vitalist interpretation of Nietzsche that had attempted to legitimate racism. By the time of the last *Nietzsche* lectures, 'European Nihilism' (1940), and apparently prompted by Germany's occupation of France, Heidegger would implicate both Nietzsche and Nazism within the catastrophe of European nihilism itself. The grounds for this implication do not concern politics as such, but rather military technology:

> It is not enough that one possess tanks, airplanes, and communication apparatus; nor is it enough that one has at one's disposal men who can service such things... What is needed is a form of mankind that is from top to bottom equal to the unique fundamental essence of modern technology and its metaphysical truth; that is to say, one that lets itself be entirely dominated by the essence of technology precisely in order to steer and deploy individual technological processes and possibilities.[6]

By 1940, therefore, it is possible to say that Adorno remains closer to Nietzsche than does Heidegger. Indeed, Nietzsche is crucial to Adorno's reading of Wagner, by way of Horkheimer. Where Heidegger opposed Wagner, Adorno's position is self-characterised as 'ambivalent', in the sense of 'attraction and repulsion'. The critical Adorno is more sympathetic to (the reactionary) Wagner than was (the reactionary) Heidegger. Even this statement is complicated by the history and reception of Wagner – the left Hegelian turned student of Schopenhauer. Given the tensions between Adorno and Heidegger, this intellectual triangle remains intriguing – but what are the philosophical stakes of this old debate today? What is the 'actuality' (to use a false friend) of Wagner? Specifically, the problem of the relationship between capitalist modernity and the will lies at the heart of each Wagner study. But generally, at stake is nothing less than a rethinking of subjectivity itself. This chapter will claim that Adorno and Heidegger each address this issue through an understanding of modernity as being, in crucial respects, musical. There can be no waiting (for a better society) without willing it – the German *wollen* means both 'to wish for' and 'to intend'. At the same time, willing as intending turns utopianism into a bad science. From a historical materialist perspective, this question concerns a critique of dialectic. What, then, is the relationship between willing and waiting?

From the late 1930s, Adorno and Horkheimer found in Nietzsche a resource for responding to problems arising within historical materialism – namely, the possibility of change amidst a perceived crisis within the Marxist tradition. The philosophical turn within Marxism was already underway by the 1920s, in the work of Lukács and Karl Korsch. This was subsequently fuelled by the discovery of Marx's 'Paris Manuscripts'. The *Institut für Sozialforschung* nevertheless remained distinctive in its identification of the question of humanism.[7] Rose thus notes that, 'Adorno and many other German writers of the inter-war period were attracted to an anti-humanist stance'. In the tradition of enlightenment philosophy, Marx was not unique in partially misidentifying the subject of history. What was required was not a rejection of enlightenment philosophy, however, but rather a critique of the partial misidentification. As a prospective historical materialism, this rethinking of the subject retained the enlightenment project of cosmopolitan universalism in Adorno and Horkheimer – hence, beyond the 'province' of Heidegger (see Chapter 4). Yet Heidegger's deepened account of the will is itself concerned with the metaphysical, humanist problems addressed by Adorno. Reading Heidegger against Heidegger, a rethinking of the willing subject can provide insights into a speculative historical materialism.

Adorno on Wagner

Ego(t)ism and love

In Search of Wagner was written between 1937 and 1938. In an introductory note to its eventual 1952 publication, Adorno explained his intentions to contribute to an understanding of Nazism:

> The aim was to shake off the notion of a mere historical accident and to uncover the origin of fascist totalitarianism within the social processes that supported it. The source of Hitler's ideology was to be researched without regard for its relation with appropriated cultural values. The work of Richard Wagner forced itself to the forefront of this task.[8]

The source of Hitler's ideology precedes and circumscribes both Wagner and Hitler. Adorno goes in search of a psychological type. The first two chapters of the Wagner monograph address the authoritarianism and anti-Semitism of this character-type. Adorno draws upon Wagner's output as a whole – the theoretical tracts, the letters and the libretti. In the music too we hear the convulsive movements of the reactionary. But this bombastic Wagner is not the only Wagner. The composer would remain a profoundly 'ambivalent' figure for Adorno – the term he uses in his 1963 talk, 'Wagner's Relevance for Today [*Wagners Aktualität*]'.[9] This later text does not mark a conciliatory turn towards the composer, but partly a return to Adorno's experience of an other, progressive Wagner from the later 1920s. A young Adorno had reviewed Otto Klemperer's performance of *The Flying Dutchman* in a minimalist production at Berlin's Kroll Opera. In their negation of 'metaphorical dust, hollow symbolism, theatrical piety and romantic costuming', the Kroll had 'mobilised a reserve of actuality [*Aktualität*] in Wagner... which will explode today or tomorrow.'[10] Adorno thus suggests that the other Wagner is opposed to the traditional, Bayreuth Wagner. At the same time, this untapped actuality was only ever a possibility; hence, 'today or tomorrow'. The Kroll production was presented at the 1938 exhibition of 'degenerate music'.

As ambivalent, Wagner encompasses the regressive and the progressive. The two moments are neither antinomical nor ironic. Rather, a progressive movement is possible out of – in the sense of the emancipation from – the regressive. The resources of progress are not transcendent of a corrupted history. This is the lesson of Adorno's idea of natural history, as well as of Horkheimer's essay, 'Egoism and Freedom Movements' (1936) – with which the composition of *In Search of Wagner* was, confesses Adorno, 'intimately bound up'.[11] On account of this ambivalence, it is no exaggeration to say that Wagner stands at the centre of Adorno's key intellectual concerns. In Wagner, not only do we find the source of German fascism, we find the source of the culture industry and the source of modern art. Adorno takes Nietzsche completely seriously: 'the philosopher is not free to do without Wagner'.[12] As in Nietzsche, Wagner stands for modernity itself. The importance of Wagner for Adorno can be understood in relation to the 'musical' metaphysics examined in the previous chapter. For the dissonant, melancholy science is already a philosophy of modernity, or a modernist philosophy.

In Search of Wagner is a collection of essays. There is no single 'main thesis', as Slavoj Žižek has put it, seamlessly uniting the problems of fascism, commodification and art – though these are indeed its chief concerns.[13] Is *In Search of Wagner* then a constellation? That would depend upon whether the whole is greater than the sum of its parts. And it is with this question that a revealing asymmetry emerges. The progressive Wagner corresponds to his anticipation of modern art, to 'the artwork of the future'. The form of the autonomous artwork is paradoxically bound to the form of the commodity. Adorno had already begun to conceive of this relationship in his contemporaneous essay 'On the Fetish-Character in Music and the Regression of Listening' (see Chapter 3). The problems of art and commodity are thus indirectly related to the problems of fascism and anti-Semitism. Adorno and Horkheimer conceive of this mediation in terms of the problem of egoism amidst the emergence of an authoritarian ego – whether the ego of the real dictator or of the spectral dictator, the market.

Adorno tends to find the progressive Wagner in the music alone, thus dismissing Wagner's dramatic myth. This is a consequence of Adorno's absolutist conception of music – though this is not to say that Adorno opposes programme music.[14] But Adorno's evaluation equally arises from his Nietzschean critique of Wagner's early humanism. *Der Ring des Nibelungen* (conceived in the 1840s but only performed in the 1870s) is steeped in ideas taken from Ludwig Feuerbach, whom Wagner had studied in exile after his contribution, alongside Mikhail Bakunin, to the Dresden uprising of 1849. Wagner's manifesto *The Artwork of the Future* (1849) is dedicated to Feuerbach. Adorno's problem with Feuerbach can be sensed from his attribution of the *Ring*'s mythic narrative to Hegel and Schopenhauer alone:

> In its form, the *Ring* is a metaphor of the totality of world history that perfects itself by achieving consciousness of what it had been in itself from time immemorial. If this reminds us as much of Hegel as of Schopenhauer, from whom Wagner borrowed the content of the allegory, then it remains true that beyond all this there is one particular aspect in which the *Ring* is in agreement with Hegel's philosophy of history. And this is the ruse of reason. Whatever opposition there is to the totality, to Wotan's universal will, is also in accord with it, because Wotan's absolute spirit has nothing in mind but its own annihilation.[15]

Wagner produces a dramatisation of world history, a history that has already passed ('from time immemorial'). More generally, Adorno disregards the central problematic of the *drama* of the *Ring*: the relationship between love and the law – both the law of the state and of private property. Wagner, like many of the young Hegelians, conceived of this relationship in terms of the modern problem of the political itself. Adorno's suspicion of kitsch dilettantism in Wagner – the *representation* of a system in art-myth – threatens to spill over into a scepticism towards these genuine concerns that extend beyond Wagner and Schopenhauer into the historical materialist problematic that Adorno himself is seeking to address.

According to Adorno, Wagner's high romantic valorisation of bourgeois love serves to conceal its ideological character. In *Minima Moralia*, Adorno writes:

> The very involuntariness of love, even where it has not found itself a practical accommodation beforehand, contributes to the whole as soon as it is established as a principle. If love in society is to represent a better one, it cannot do so as a peaceful enclave, but only by conscious opposition. This, however, demands precisely the element of voluntariness that the bourgeois, for whom love can never be natural enough, forbid it.[16]

Love as conscious opposition to bourgeois love means the transformation of bourgeois love. Adorno does find 'love' in Wagner, but only in certain moments of the music. For, Adorno can be said to conceive of the structure of the autonomous artwork itself, which is analogous to the autonomous subject, in a similar way to how both the younger Hegel and the young Hegelians had conceived of love.[17] Adorno's critique of bourgeois love is equally filtered through the insights of Nietzsche, whereby the question of the ego becomes a question of the will, the question of egoism a question of willing.

The drama of the *Ring* centres on an opposition between self-interest and love. This opposition can be mapped onto further, Promethean oppositions: the gods and humanity, fate and history. The *Ring* is politically inconclusive (*contra* Adorno) because these oppositions are not presented dualistically. The gods are capable of human love, as in Wotan's partial mercy towards Brünnhilde. The human representatives of love, Siegfried and Brünnhilde (who becomes human for the love of human love) are, like the gods, flawed. The ring symbolises both love, in the union of the hero and Brünnhilde, and self-interest, when it is revealed that a drugged Siegfried has tricked Brünnhilde into being released into Gunther's bondage. All are tainted in the *Ring*, by the ring. Wagner had studied Feuerbach's *Thoughts on Death and Immortality* (1830) in 1849.

He almost certainly read the mature works, including *The Essence of Christianity* (1841), in the following years.[18] Feuerbach's conception of love finds its way into Wagner's theoretical writings, as well as the *Ring* itself. In Feuerbach's *Thoughts*, Wagner would have read that:

> In order to be capable of love, the person must be able to surrender his harsh, excluding, being-for-self. But the person cannot accomplish this surrender if there does not exist in him an abode, so to speak, where he is not-person, where he is not divisive separator and expelling distinction, but in which all is one and one is all ... love is being-together, being-in-common.[19]

By the time of *The Essence of Christianity*, Feuerbach's pre-Marxian communism is in place. Love is now understood quasi-dialectically: self-relinquishment is found in another ego, as a moment, in the mutual negation of another ego. Equally Hegelian – but only initially – egoism is not founded in the love of two beautiful souls, but is universally constituted and universality constituting. However, this non-individual other remains universal humanity itself – which, being an externalisation of God's abstract perfection, can only be determined abstractly.

In Wagner's fragment *Der Künstlertum der Zukunft* (1849), Feuerbach's love becomes the following: 'It is in communism that egoism achieves its greatest satisfaction, in other words, through the total denial and supersession of egoism.'[20] In comparison to Feuerbach's anthrotheology, Wagner finds his universal humanity in androgyny.[21] The Volsungs, of whom Siegfried is the first, are born of the incestuous love between Siegmund and Sieglinde: 'Bride and Sister you are to your brother – thus let the Volsung's blood bloom.'[22] Adorno takes exception to this biological and naturalistic conception of humanity – which, in a rare reference to the philosopher, Adorno relates to Feuerbach.[23] Wagner's proto-communism is enslaved to an archaic model of community. Alberich's theft of the gold, which sets the curse of the ring in motion, signals the despoiling of an original state of nature through self-interest – the extraction of capital, in the exchange of its curse, from pure gold (nature). Wotan repeats the curse by not paying the giants for Valhalla. But the hero, Siegfried, is exempt from the law, having been kept in isolation from it. Neither does he understand fear, meaning that he is not alienated from his labour (forging the sword with no expertise). Siegfried is the prototypical reactionary anti-capitalist: 'The Romanticized concept of the proletariat ... is complemented here by the no less Romantic notion that society would be able to regenerate itself if only it could find its way back to its unsullied origins.'[24] In Wagner, we find 'the chimera of the pure, unhistorical, immediate human being'. This is Adorno's critique of naturalistic humanism in Wagner – and by extension in Feuerbach, who is notable by his absence from *In Search of Wagner*.

Adorno tends to read the *Ring* through the character of Siegfried alone, who only appears in the third music drama. But in the so-called 'Feuerbach Ending' – an early draft of *Götterdämmerung* – Brünnhilde speaks of redemption through love, not death, as happens in the final 'Schopenhauer Ending'. The ring is not the despoiling of nature alone therefore. The ring is the origin of self-interest *and* love. Against Adorno's reading, this contradiction is historical in his own sense of natural history. The contradiction of the ring must be sublated if the cyclical repetition of fate is to be broken and love is to become the law. The problem of the ending is not Brünnhilde's death, for she remains, just about, one of the gods, but rather the need to return the ring to the Rhine – to nature, and not to history.

Adorno substantiates his critique of the *Ring*'s naturalism by arguing that Wagner's *Gesamtkunstwerk* rests upon a misapprehension of art and the arts – of poetry and music in particular: 'Music is called upon to do nothing less than retract the historical tendency in language, which is based upon signification, and to substitute expressiveness for it'.[25] As we have seen, Adorno himself indulges in the romantic unity of music and language, albeit as a dissonant unity. It is nevertheless a lost unity. Adorno conceptualises music as (anti-) language. All art is a question of 'logicity' and '*Sprachcharakter*'. Where Wagner is concerned, Adorno equates an absence of logical development with the pre-linguistic.[26] The pre-linguistic is the language of ineloquent gestures (an anecdote recalling a tempestuous encounter between Wagner and Nietzsche, in which Nietzsche remained silent, recalls the tumult of Wagner's character type). In the absence of logical development, Wagner dramatises the individual gesture – pre-eminently, as the *Leitmotiv*. Wagner is thus contrasted with the 'Hegelian' Beethoven. In Beethoven, themes are developed through variations. These are in turn overcome in new contrasting themes and variations: 'the history of a theme' (Adorno's much loved quote from Schoenberg). There is no such history in Wagner's music-drama, complains Adorno. But Wagner is doing something altogether different to Beethoven. Indeed, beneath the surface of Adorno's critique of Wagner lies a thesis on decadence as the possible transformation of egoism.

Dialectic of decadence

Wagner's later music – including parts of the *Ring* – now expresses a dialectical relation to language, Adorno will acknowledge. Citing the prelude to *Tristan und Isolde,* Adorno suggests that the complaint of logical inconsistency – its 'unending melody' (Nietzsche) – only arises from a classicist or baroque music aesthetics.[27] Wagner not only marks the de-cadence from these styles, but equally anticipates the music of the next century. Nietzsche 'still heard' Wagner 'with the ears of the Biedermeier listener'.[28] At the same time, the regressive Wagner anticipates the culture industry. Adorno compares the *Leitmotiv* to advertising: 'the music is designed to be remembered, it is intended for the forgetful'.[29] In 'On the Fetish Character', the *Leitmotiv* is described in terms of unreflected nominalism: listening 'atomistically' and 'less attentively' is distinctive of all 'commodity music'. Music as art 'can only be bodied forth' in 'the most intense effort of memory and anticipation'.[30] Lack of attention is symptomatic of a weakened ego amidst a flawed society:

> the weaker the social and hence, too, the aesthetic determination the ego became, the less it was able to exteriorise itself as an objective expression of a totality, the greater the arrogance with which an unfettered individuality asserted itself.

On Adorno's more ambiguous reading of Wagner, however – if we stress the *dialectical* character of ambiguity – the later music *is* a music of 'memory and anticipation', but only *as* a music of forgetting and distraction. Far from displacing concentration with distraction, or anticipation with presence, Wagner redefines concentration *within* distraction, anticipation *within* presence. Chromatism is supposed to oppose concentration because it is tonally decentred. But Adorno observes that, in works such as *Tristan,* Wagner developed chromatic harmony within smaller-scale tonal structures. The three-part 'bar' form that governs this structure is itself quasi-dialectical:

> Wagner draws his productive force from an irreducible contradiction, and wrests a progressive constructiveness from the regressive moment of gesture. This goes as far beyond mere subjective expression, as it cancels as it preserves it in the double Hegelian sense.[31]

What is this 'irreducible contradiction' from which Wagner draws his 'productive force'? An answer can be proposed in light of both the essay on music and language, and *Aesthetic Theory*. The logic of tonality disintegrates, but modern music integrates another logicity out of this disintegration. Far from seeking an unhistorical union of music and language, Adorno suggests that Wagner emphasises their mythic affinity in a newly exaggerated manner:

> In fact, Wagner, with his radical demand for a declamation that would do justice to language, not only drew vocal music much closer to music than it had ever been before, and did so in a specifically mimetic way, but also assimilated musical construction itself to the gesture of language to the point of exaggerated clarity.[32]

Wagner turns the disintegration of music – and language – against itself, as an integrating gesture. He 'wrests a progressive constructiveness from the regressive moment of gesture'. The individual gesture is pushed to an extreme, and is exploded beyond its isolated individuality. It *becomes* eloquent gesture, speaking beyond itself to another, and from another: the 'latent "I"'. The eloquent gesture is expressive language, the language of naming. Wagner's nominalism is in this sense a dissonant nominalism. Nietzsche's definition of decadence in 'The Case of Wagner' (1888) was indebted to the French novelist and critic Paul Bourget. Nietzsche thus defined Wagner's decadence in literary, not musical terms:

> What is the sign of *literary decadence*? That life no longer dwells in the whole. The word becomes sovereign and leaps out of the sentence, the sentence reaches out and obscures the meaning of the page, the page gains life at the expense of the whole – the whole is no longer a whole.[33]

For Nietzsche, Wagnerian atomisation signals an unreflected nominalism. Decadence is a symptom of the sickness that is passive nihilism. But the definition of this sickness in the *Genealogy of Morality* should be recalled in order to indicate *its* ambivalence. 'Bad conscience is a sickness, there's no point in denying it, but a sickness rather like pregnancy'.[34] Decadence as pregnancy is the nominalism that promises to give birth to its other.

Following his return to Europe, Adorno adjusted his position on Wagner: 'I am not distancing myself from the book [*In Search of Wagner*] nor am I abandoning the conception.'[35] Taken together, *In Search of Wagner* and 'Wagner's Relevance for Today' express Adorno's continued ambivalence towards the composer, not a sudden turn towards him:

> The position of consciousness toward Wagner that I experience as my own whenever I encounter him, and which is not only mine, is even more deserving of the appellation ambivalent [*ambivalent*] than the earlier position – an oscillation between attraction and repulsion.[36]

Wagner continues to provide lessons for modern music. The tendency to compose spatially, in 'blocks', is anticipated in Wagner's explosion of logical development, as is the allied prioritisation of colour in orchestration. Colour is no longer 'phantasmagoria', as it was in the monograph.

The two poles of Adorno's ambivalence can be said to correspond to Acts I and II of *Siegfried* respectively. In Act I, Siegfried dominates the music, just as he dominates Mime. The music recapitulates Siegfried's authoritarian character (Bloch spoke of 'Siegfried's brutal forging songs').[37] In Act II, the music masters Siegfried. Through his experience of the song of the wood-bird, Siegfried masters himself and frees Brünnhilde into her mastery (as love). Siegfried finds himself outside of himself – that is, outside of his mythic representation, outside of bourgeois humanism as such – in the music, which stands here for a speculative human language. The wood-bird is not original nature. The proto-modern music of the 'forest murmurs' – which Adorno suggested should be performed on its own – proposes a language of a peculiar nature.

The 'adjustment' in Adorno's stance towards Wagner was surely prompted not only by the incomplete fall of Nazism in post-war Europe, but also by his perception of a divergence between the culture industry that Wagner anticipated and the one that transpired: 'With regard to Wagner the situation has changed generally.' The parallel development of Hollywood – upon which Wagner had no small influence – and the musical avant-garde, leads to a resituating of Wagner. Hence, Pierre Boulez, acquainted with Adorno, would conduct the centennial *Ring* of 1976 in Patrice Chéreau's 'left Hegelian' production. Adorno's ambivalence 'only points back to the Janus-like character of the work itself. Undoubtedly, every art of significance exhibits something like this, Wagner's especially.'[38] Art 'of significance' is modern, autonomous art. Autonomous art is 'Janus-like' because it is also a commodity. 'Wagner's especially' – meaning, it seems, that Wagner is structurally prototypical of modern art. Adorno thus writes in *Aesthetic Theory* that dissonant art is art 'since Baudelaire and *Tristan*'[39] (and did not Baudelaire want to *be* Wagner?).[40]

Given Adorno's 'oscillation', 'Wagner's Relevance for Today' can be read back into *In Search of Wagner* in order to extend the foregoing thesis on decadence and ambivalence. Wagner's nominalism in music is a nominalism of egoism. This gives new meaning to an important passage from the monograph: 'By reflecting and displaying its own weakness, the ego differentiates itself infinitely [*das Ich differenziert sich unendlich*], but by the same token that weakness causes it to regress to a pre-ego stage.'[41] It was suggested in the previous chapter that Adorno conceives of bourgeois society as a false whole, in that it mistakes its nominalist whole for the true one. The artwork negates the false whole with a false singularity of its own. False singularity is the self-consciousness of the false whole (hence, reflected nominalism). The necessary ambivalence of 'every art of significance... Wagner's especially' is the possibility of this self-consciousness. The ambivalence of 'Wagner', as art, is the dialectical ambivalence of ego*tism* (self interest, ego weakness) and ego*ism* (free inter-subjectivity). But what, precisely, is meant by egoism? The concept of egoism in Horkheimer's 'Egoism and Freedom Movements' – with which *In Search of Wagner* was 'intimately bound up' – is taken from Freud and Nietzsche. The latter's *Genealogy of Morality* (1887) underpinned this 'Anthropology of the Bourgeois Ego', an ego that misrepresents Nietzsche:

> The *Übermensch*, the most problematic concept with which the psychologist left the analytical realm Nietzsche had mastered, has been interpreted along the lines of the philistine bourgeois's wildest dreams, and has been confused with Nietzsche himself. The adventurous element seemed so appealing. Greatness, blood, and danger have always been cherished in paintings and monuments. But Nietzsche is the opposite of this inflated sense of power. His error lay in his lack of historical understanding of the present, which led him to bizarre hypotheses where clear theoretical knowledge was possible.[42]

As in the *Genealogy*, Horkheimer's egoism is not interchangeable with, but rather contradicts egotism: 'The bourgeois revolution did not lead the masses to the lasting state of joyful existence and the universal equality they longed for, but to the hard reality of an individualistic social order instead.'[43] For Nietzsche, the ego as essence is a 'pure, will-less, painless, timeless subject of knowledge... an eye which cannot be thought at all, an eye turned in no direction at all'. Whereas, egoism is '*only* a perspective seeing, *only* a perspective "knowing".'[44] The self-valorisation of the ego is reactive in that it proceeds from a hatred of the other. This 'eye', 'turned in no particular direction', is '*nothing*' of itself. Conversely, egoism proceeds from the original production of a perspective – a perspective that belongs to the production, not the ego. Horkheimer calls this spontaneous production 'play'.

Horkheimer's Nietzschean and Freudian conception of egoism finds its way into Adorno. For, in the Wagner monograph, Adorno prefers the terminology of 'ego', 'the I', and 'egoism' over that of 'subject' or 'subjectivity'. But Adorno would nevertheless give his 'ego' a Kantian twist. Egoism names the original power of judgement, *Ürteilskraft*. Ideology interrupts the power of judgement by passing judgement on behalf of and in place of the judging subject. The authoritarian ego wills subject-object identity – domination. For Adorno, the will to identity is concomitant with (not merely determined by) the commodity form: 'The exchange-principle, the reduction of human labour to the abstract, general concept of average labour-time, is primordially related to the identification-principle.'[45] Modern art places a demand on the power of judgement. Adorno's Kantianism is philosophical and historical. The weakening of egoism is measured against gains made for it during the enlightenment. Narratives of decadence must posit a height from which the decline set in – hence, the danger of nostalgia. Adorno knows that this height was always a *promise* of maturity, not maturity itself. 'Philosophy, which once seemed obsolete, lives on because the moment to realise it was missed'.[46] By contrast, and as the category of 'play' might suggest, Horkheimer's egoism remains nostalgic. Spontaneous egoism is supposed to have existed prior to the 'bourgeois epoch'. Not since Kant, but Hobbes, the intellectual bridge between the pre-bourgeois and bourgeois ego.[47] Horkheimer presupposes a pre-bourgeois 'pleasure' in social relations – much like the community 'sentiment [*Gemüt*]' of Ferdinand Tönnies' *Community and Society* (1887). And unlike in Georg Simmel's contrasting, metropolitan 'blasé-type', Horkheimer's modern ego does not, at this point, promise any new form of freedom (see Chapter 4). In this respect, Horkheimer formally repeats the initial archaism of the *Genealogy*. The aristocratic masters valued egoism, where the slaves devalued it through their hatred of their masters. Modernity is thereafter an experience of decadence. Morality itself is decadent because the distinction between good and evil proceeds from a reactive evaluation of the good: 'it is only with a *decline* of aristocratic value-judgments that this whole antithesis between "egoistic" and "unegoistic" forces itself more and more on man's conscience'.[48] The reversal in values means that the slave morality parades as the master morality. Today – this is Nietzsche's turn *against* archaism – '*ressentiment*' defines the rulers, and the slavish need of rulers. According to Horkheimer, 'As much as the whole world must tremble before [the leaders] in fear, they themselves display the image of fear of still higher and supreme beings' (does this statement lie behind Adorno's interpretation of Siegfried as *Führer*?).[49]

Horkheimer's 'play' blends Hobbes' instinctual desires and Nietzsche's concept of life. Having accepted the terms of Hobbes, Horkheimer rejects their suppression under Hobbes' own scientific rationality. This vitalist egoism remains unproductive within Horkheimer's overall historical narrative. Horkheimer does not act upon the fundamental insight of the *Genealogy*: the sickness of nihilism does not call for a return to the healthy life of the Greeks, or whoever, but rather for a 'self-overcoming [*Selbstaufhebung*]'.[50] Horkheimer accepts Nietzsche's diagnosis without accepting his 'bizarre' cure (but is evaluation possible without revaluation?). Adorno's reliance upon Horkheimer's essay would suggest that he too seeks to re-value the ego in terms of egoism. But Adorno's post-Kantianism paradoxically brings him closer to the 'free spirit' of the *Genealogy* than does the 'Nietzschean' Horkheimer. In this sense, the terminology of 'egoism' should be interpreted rather than rejected.

In the earlier Wagner monograph, Adorno writes that:

> the fault-line discernible in Wagner's work – his impotence in the face of the technical contradictions and the social conflicts underlying them, in short all the qualities that prompted his contemporaries to speak of 'decadence' – *is also the path of artistic progress.*[51]

'Decadence' is '*also*' the path of artistic progress. In differentiating *itself* infinitely, the ego acts, as egoism. Egoism is here the power of differentiation. This is not thereby solely the 'regress to a pre-ego stage'. On the contrary, the act of infinite self-differentiation means the relinquishing of the existing ego in a new egoism – and not, therefore, the relinquishment of egoism as such, characteristic of Feuerbach's love and Schopenhauer's nirvana.

In what sense is this differentiation 'infinite'? Adorno writes in *Aesthetic Theory* that the experience of 'shudder' in art is not merely *an* 'experience [*Erlebnis*]'. 'This experience [*Erfahrung*] is contrary to the weakening of the I that the culture industry manipulates.'[52] There is a continuity with and a divergence from the Wagner studies here. First, the continuity: modern art mimics the weakening of the ego, 'manipulated by the culture industry'. Art 'is modern art through its mimesis of the hardened and alienated.'[53] In Wagner, 'the ego differentiates itself infinitely'. In the 'shudder', the 'I perceives its own limitedness and finitude'. If the infinite is read as the non-finite then the two statements become compatible. This non-finitude nevertheless looks formal-transcendental: the exceptional shudder always, infinitely, falls back into the status quo. In contrast to Kant's sublime, Adorno's shudder is historically mediated. Yet its structure is not historical. Shudder, like mimesis, then resembles Horkheimer's naturalistic play. By contrast, the modern, post-Wagnerian shudder – here is the divergence from the naturally sublime shudder – is of a historically singular character. The relationship between the 'I that the culture industry manipulates' and the 'I that perceives its own limitedness and finitude' is more dialectical in the Wagner monograph than in *Aesthetic Theory*, where the poles tend to remain antinomical. This means that the possible, new egoism – occasioned by the emergence of the culture industry, the cultural form of capitalism – is unique to that capitalism. This is to say that, to characterise Wagner in terms of distraction and boredom – experiential descriptions of the social form of capital – is then to characterise specifically modern forms of distraction and boredom. The infinity to which Adorno refers names an originary historical negation. The negation corresponds to the 'non-' of the 'non-finitude'.

Horkheimer has Aristotle's *Poetics* in mind when he concludes his essay on egoism: 'Catharsis through dramatic plays, through play in general, presupposes a changed humanity.'[54] Horkheimer belatedly concurs with the *Genealogy* that existing modernity is the sole precondition of its self-overcoming. The inversion of values turns life against itself. But a necessary consequence of the ascetic ideal, the self-discipline of this inversion, is the emergence of the modern will itself. For, 'In spite of ... suffering' the ascetic ideals:

> man was *saved*, he had a *meaning*, from now on he was no longer like a leaf in the breeze, the plaything of the absurd, of 'non-sense'; from now on he could *will* something, – no matter what, why and how he did it at first, the *will itself was saved*... a *will to nothingness*... is and remains a *will*! ... And, to conclude by saying what I said at the beginning: man still prefers to *will nothingness*, than *not* will [Nichts *wollen*, *als* nicht *wollen*].[55]

The will must, says Nietzsche, be re-oriented *out of* nothing *to* power – not 'passive', but 'active nihilism'.

Though he finds Nietzsche's *Übermensch* 'problematic', Horkheimer proposes a historical materialist interpretation in his 'changed humanity'. A changed humanity means a new egoism, not the old ego following new imperatives, as attributes to its essence. This constitutes the challenge of Adorno and Horkheimer to traditional historical materialism – both humanist and structuralist, given the controversy over the early Marx's structural reliance upon Feuerbachian metaphysics.[56] This equally constitutes their ongoing challenge to any vitalism without a cosmopolitan intent. Nietzsche confronts the paradox proposed in the opposition of an old and new humanity. How can the overcoming of the old proceed from the old? Nietzsche's mediation is not, observes Horkheimer, sufficiently historical. But Horkheimer and Adorno take from both Nietzsche and Marx the thesis that a changed humanity means a changed comportment of humanity.

Though not unique in this respect, modern art should demand the new comportment. Art distracts perspective seeing from the old comportment, an eye turned in no particular direction, in the attention of a new perspective – or rather, the 'perspectival'. The 'I' is 'liquidated'. In spite of Adorno's cool reception of 'The Work of Art in the Age of its Mechanical Reproducibility', something like Benjamin's thesis on 'distraction [*Zerstreuung*]' can be sensed in Adorno's contemporaneous 'theory of decadence'.[57] For Benjamin, the 'contemplation' of traditional art (its 'aura') is displaced by the 'distraction' of mass art – specifically cinema. The cinema promises to politically 'mobilise' the masses. In correspondence with his friend, Adorno contended that, 'in a communist society, work would be organised in such a way that human beings would no longer be so exhausted or so stupefied as to require such distraction.'[58] However, according to the second, latent moment of Adorno's analysis of Wagner, the 'weakening' of the ego, its distraction, is equally the possibility of its transformation. Concentration and distraction are in that case mediated in, and as, the modern artwork – coming closer to Benjamin than Adorno would like to have admitted. For, in 'The Work of Art' essay, we read that 'Distraction and concentration form an antithesis'.[59]

For Benjamin, 'Just as the entire mode of existence of human collectives changes over long historical periods, so too does their mode of perception [*Sinneswahrnehmung*].'[60] The 'Just as' is equivocal here. What is its determining function? On the one hand, humanity's mode of existence determines its perception, as material conditions determine life. But Benjamin suggests that the change in perception also determines the change in the mode of existence. Adorno says a similar thing about autonomous art, where 'experience' is at stake – albeit as 'semblance'. The transformation of egotism into egoism in that case constitutes Adorno's social alternative to Benjamin's mass art. Benjamin's mediation of art and politics remained one-sided from a

Hegelian perspective: the 'I' becomes 'We' without the 'We' becoming 'I' – or, vice versa.[61]

Willing and waiting (I)

Adorno bemoans 'the chimera of the pure, unhistorical, immediate human being' in Wagner's myth. He thus rejects both Wagner's attempt to realise sociality in his art-religion and Schopenhauer's aesthetics of redemption, which does not in any case contradict Feuerbach's sensuous humanism (Love, says the author of *Death and Immortality*, 'is a consuming fire'.[62] According to Feuerbach's erotic humanism, the fire threatens to consume love itself – anticipating the fate of Brünnhilde.). But given Adorno's problems with Hegelian metaphysics also, can Adorno uphold a universalist form of inter-subjectivity in art (when he writes of art's 'latent subject')? That is to say, what is Adorno's conception of spirit? Adorno's avoidance of Feuerbach renders the question more pressing, to the extent that the early Marx's '*Gattungswesen*' constituted a radical materialist revision of the Feuerbachian inversion of Hegelian spirit – an attempt to ground the universal subject in practical activity. Feuerbach's deduction of the universality of thought neglected '*practical*, human-sensuous activity', stated Marx. But the problem of formalism was inherited insofar as the content remained as abstract in the case of practical activity as in the case of thought. We saw that Adorno dismissed 'unhistorical' humanism in his Wagner book. But Adorno there added a Kantian adjective to the 'unhistorical': '*geschichtslos-**reinen**, unmittelbaren Menschenwesens*'. Hence, in parallel to the problem of naturalism, Adorno identifies the problem of formalism – of, that is, an abstract universal that is not critically posited from experience. In Kant, pure (*rein*), signifies the formal-transcendental ('pure reason', 'pure concept'). Following Hegel's critique of Kant, this purity remains without mediated content: the historical experience of consciousness.

What, in that case, constitutes a philosophical positing of subjectivity? As was explained in the previous chapter, Hegel attempted to determine spirit by way of an historical dialectic of mutual recognition. This marks Hegel's universality out from both the anthropological universality of Feuerbach and the transcendental universality of Kant. Adorno does not lurch from the problem of positing to non-positing, however – to a sceptical anti-humanism. Adorno conceives of spirit as internally divided, between what society is and what it is not yet. The hope for virtuous universality, for social content, is the question of what Adorno will call 'metaphysical experience'. Hope for reconciliation of the 'is' and the 'ought' is precarious amidst the crisis of metaphysics – its humanism included. Reflecting upon this, Adorno conceives of an expression of waiting in vain (see Chapter 5). The meaning of this expression can partly be understood in relation to the foregoing account of music, egoism and distraction. Distraction and waiting in vain are connected via boredom. Adorno thus writes of the 'Wagnerian *longueurs*'.[63]

Hegelianism of all colours dictates that history progresses according to a ruse of reason. Adorno's critique of humanism includes a critique of this assumption or positing of this ruse (Wotan), at a historical moment when the promise of progress has been broken. Indeed, Adorno locates the problem of positing metaphysical concepts in the context of the metaphysics of willing. The comportment of positivistic dialectics is structurally identical with the principle of identity-thinking that dominates contemporary capitalism. Adorno knows that this will to identity culminates in nihilism: 'Auschwitz confirms the philosopheme of pure identity in death.'[64] Again, Adorno does not seek to negate the will. Rather, we may speak of a different willing: a willing as waiting, in terms of a 'musical' auto-differentiation of subjectivity that dialectically posits its collective subjectivity.

A significant problem remains concerning the qualitative meaning of this waiting-expression. As with the third *Critique*, everything appears to rest upon an experience of modern art ('Wagner'). And even if the waiting-comportment exceeds art in the narrow sense – as it must – why should there be any promise to such waiting? Why should the expression of waiting in vain not be an all-too-human vanity? There remains a problem of joining the waiting to the a-waited here, such that the waiting should be constitutive of the awaited *without* becoming expectation. Though far from a tradition of historical materialism, Heidegger, a student of Nietzsche, addresses this problem. Not coincidentally, he can be shown to do this by way of Wagner and waiting. In contrast to Adorno's intra-metaphysical response to metaphysical willing, Heidegger attempts to look beyond the metaphysics of willing itself, towards a post-metaphysical situation.

Heidegger on Wagner

Turning Heidegger against Heidegger

In the mid-1930s, hence following his resignation of the Freiburg rectorship, Heidegger underwent the 'turn [*Kehre*]' that would mark out his later thought. Heidegger himself would subsequently locate the beginning of his *Kehre* in 'On the Essence of Truth' (1930), but the later position arguably receives its first clear expression in the four lecture-courses on Nietzsche (1936–40).[65] Though riddled with difficulties and inconsistencies, Heidegger's turn can be summarised in a threefold manner: from Dasein to Being [*Sein*], from 'Being and Time' to 'Time and Being' (Heidegger's own characterisation), and from fundamental ontology to the history of the forgetting of Being, or the history of metaphysics. According to Richard Wolin, 'So extreme is the philosopher's reconceptualization of the relationship between between Being and Dasein that one could plausibly interpret the *Kehre* as a "Reversal" rather than a "Turn" in Heidegger's thinking.'[66] Following Löwith's criticism of his ex-teacher's later thought, Wolin argues that the *Kehre* is fatalistic, negating the possibilities for human agency that were prioritised in the earlier, existential analysis of Dasein, in the name of a newly transcendent (and even vengeful) Being. In the face of Being's fatefulness, all that remains is a contemplative philosophy of inaction: hence, 'the quietistic concepts of "releasement," "letting be," and "openness to the mystery."'[67] Wolin thus equally follows Adorno's critique of the 'incapacitation of the subject' in Heidegger: 'a mythically impervious history of Being, to which hope may cling, denies reconcilement. Its fateful character [*Fatalität*] should be dispelled as a context of illusion.'[68] Unlike Adorno, Wolin addresses the nature of the *Kehre*, concluding that its psychological motivation was Heidegger's avoidance of responsibility for his self-confessed 'blunder'. The *Kehre* constituted an attempt to explain away the failure of the German national revolution (and hence the Second World War and its genocide) as an inevitable consequence of the 'forgetting of Being [*Seinsvergessenheit*]'. Heidegger's tendency to suggest a form of autonomy with respect to Being, beyond Dasein, remains a fundamental and damning flaw in the later Heidegger. Dismissing the question of Being as a 'childish question', Adorno focuses upon Heidegger's 'ontology' as a preoccupation with Being, a vulgar idealist resurrection of the absolute – as 'the cosmos' – but without following the necessary inter-relationship between Dasein and Sein that is set up in *Being and Time* (once again, Adorno's approach is polemical rather than exegetical). The later Heidegger invites this critique, but it is surprising that Adorno remains so adamant about the dualism of being/entity [*Seiend*] and Being [*Sein*] given that this is precisely what Heidegger seeks to overcome (Being as the 'cosmos' would be an entirely metaphysical concept of Being, insofar as the question of Being would have been answered), and given that, as was said in the previous chapter, Heidegger continues in an eminently post-Kantian tradition of mediating the conditioned with the unconditioned (absolute).

Wolin excludes the possibility of reading the earlier and later Heidegger dialectically – taking what is promising from each side to criticise what is less promising from the other. Such a reading (attempted in this chapter and in Chapter 5) would attempt to hold Heidegger's concept of *Seinsvergessenheit* to his earlier prioritisation of the *question* of Being, and hence of *questioning* Dasein. Wolin is more sympathetic than Adorno to the philosophical merit of *Being and Time,* and thus to the possibility (which he does not pursue) of reading the earlier Heidegger into the later, that which represents the 'conception of Being as that which "essences" [*west*] independently of all human will and endeavour'. The dialectical reading also offers to put Heidegger back on the hook with respect to his own 'will and endeavour' during the years 1933–4.[69] Neither do Adorno or Wolin analyse the manner by which Heidegger's turn to the history of metaphysics was a necessary consequence of both the limitations in his earlier concept of 'historizing', and of the more generally ahistorical and solipsistic character of his fundamental ontology. Heidegger is moved towards the philosophy of history by an incoherence of ontology and history in the development of his thought. Moreover, by aligning the philosophy of history with the history of philosophy, Heidegger comes structurally closer than he could have expected to the philosophy of Hegel – as Adorno in fact knew.

Aesthetics of willing

In the lectures on 'The Will to Power as Art', Heidegger sets out his 'history of metaphysics'. Prior to the *Kehre,* Heidegger had attempted to radically redefine metaphysics as that which concerns both 'beings as a whole' and 'Being as a whole' – hence, opposed to the Platonic scission between the sensuous and the supersensuous. This can be glanced at from Heidegger's earlier titles, such as *The Fundamental Concepts of Metaphysics* and *Kant and the Problem of Metaphysics*. As with Adorno and Benjamin, metaphysics *proper* refers to the whole – even though these thinkers understand the whole in very different ways. By the time of *Nietzsche,* however, metaphysics comes to be beyond redefinition or redemption, and must rather be 'overcome'. The 'history of metaphysics' constitutes an attempt – shared in many respects with historical materialism – to periodise a problem in order to raise the prospect of its future overcoming. In spite of the concept of 'historizing' in the second part of *Being and Time,* that work remained primarily concerned with the 'existential structure' of Dasein. The later Heidegger effectively accepts Adorno's critique of formalism in his earlier philosophy of history.

second concern marks him out from Nietzsche, whose valorisation of 'feeling' must now be to the detriment of 'being as a whole':[77]

> Feeling, as feeling oneself to be, is precisely the way we are corporeally. Bodily being does not mean that the soul is burdened by a hulk we call the body. In feeling oneself to be, the body is already contained in advance in that self, in such a way that the body in its bodily states permeates the self... We do not 'have' a body; rather, we 'are' bodily.[78]

Narratives of embodied Dasein often react to the mind-body dualism with a naturalistic monism. The *Stimmung* of Dasein, its being-bodily, nevertheless concerns a historical dissonance – not an unhistorical harmony. What marks the *Nietzsche* lectures out from *Being and Time* is their account of the historical idealisation of the sensuous that comes to determine the historical self-understanding of contemporary Dasein. In *Being and Time*, historicity belonged to Dasein, but, as Adorno complained from 'The Idea of Natural History' onwards, Dasein was not of itself subjected to historicity.

In the third essay of the *Genealogy*, we recall that Nietzsche introduced Wagner as exemplar of the 'ascetic ideal'. The ascetic ideal embraces affectivity, either as consolation or as narcotic. With typical humour, Nietzsche refers to the marriage scene of *Die Meistersinger von Nürnberg*:

> What does it mean if an artist like Richard Wagner pays homage to chastity in his old age? I accept that he has always done this in a certain sense; but only in the very end in an ascetic sense. What does this change of 'sense' mean, this radical alteration of 'sense'? – because it was such a change, Wagner made a complete turnabout and became his exact opposite... For there is not, necessarily, an antithesis between chastity and sensuality; every good marriage, every real affair of the heart transcends this antithesis.[79]

Nietzsche locates the 'turnabout' of Wagner in his last music-drama, *Parsifal* (completed in 1882) – though their parting of ways was already in the making from the 1870s. And the attack is not confined to Wagner's libretti, even though Nietzsche's attack preceded his having listened to *Parsifal*. Rather, the later Nietzsche hears in Wagner's hypnotic 'tone' the will to redemption through sensational 'effects'. Wagner is now the 'actor'. The 'unending melodies', 'sick' and 'feminine', opposed art in the 'grand style'. Nietzsche compares *Carmen* favourably to the German's compositions. At least Bizet was honest about sensuousness. Wagner's sensuousness is, by contrast, in bad faith, reactively compensating for self-denial. 'So what do ascetic ideals mean?', Nietzsche asks. 'In the case of an artist, we have concluded: *nothing at all*! ... or so many things that it is tantamount to nothing!'[80] Nietzsche attributed Wagner's aesthetic of redemption to Schopenhauer's aesthetics of music, which Wagner had studied from the 1860s onwards:

> All at once [Wagner] grasped that with Schopenhauer's theory and innovation *more* could be done *in majorem musicae gloriam*, – in fact, with the *sovereignty* of music as Schopenhauer understood it: music set apart from all the other arts, the inherently independent art, *not* providing reflections of the phenomenal world like the other arts, but instead, speaking the language *of the* will itself straight out of the 'abyss', as the latter's most unique, original, direct revelation.[81]

Nietzsche's assessment of his old 'educator' is based upon book three of *The World as Will and Representation* (1818/1844):

> Music is thus in no sense, like the other arts, the image of ideas, but the image of the *will itself*, which also takes objective shape in ideas; and for this very reason the effect of music is far more powerful and penetrates far more deeply than the other arts; for they communicate only shadows, whereas it communicates the essence.[82]

As an image of no image, music is an image of the will itself – the thing-in-itself beyond all things as the ground of all things (see Chapter 3). Schopenhauer is for Nietzsche and Heidegger a passive nihilist because the highest aim of the will, from the standpoint of a life that is meaningless, is nothing. Nietzsche attempts to overcome his former Schopenhauerian pessimism (the '*amor fati*') with the 'will to power', the 'countermovement to nihilism'.

Revealingly, Heidegger looks for a confirmation of Nietzsche's polemic in the theoretical writings of Wagner. Heidegger is sufficiently interested in the case of Wagner, and by extension the case of music, to go beyond Nietzsche's own research. We may doubt Heidegger's knowledge of Wagner's music. But Heidegger does not need to listen to Wagner because his music-dramas are the mere instantiations of crass theoretical intentions:

> the nineteenth century once more dares to attempt the '*Gesamtkunskwerk*'. That effort is associated with the name of Richard

> Wagner. It is no accident that his effort does not limit itself to the creation of works that might serve such an end. His is accompanied and undergirded by reflections on the principles of such works, and by corresponding treatises.[83]

Wagner's 'reflections' exemplify the attempt to objectify art. Heidegger accuses Wagner of willing his art into existence, too intentionally. Heidegger speaks of 'a will as a going after', in which 'we are directed towards a thing by way of representation'.[84] Because the music-drama is willed representationally, Wagner's art is no will to power. Against affective willing and against representing willing, Heidegger interprets the will to power as art as a 'resolute openness to oneself... always a willing out beyond oneself'. Heidegger here distinguishes 'passion' from 'mere feeling' in Nietzsche's concept of 'rapture [*Rausch*]'.[85] At this point, apparently refuting a clean break with the earlier work, Heidegger re-interprets a concept from *Being and Time*, 'resoluteness [*Entschlossenheit*]' (the 'authentic' response to Dasein's 'thrownness'). *Entschlossenheit*, which had much to do with the charge of heroic stoicism, now evolves into *Erschlossenheit*, an openness to the question of Being. Each comportment is motivated by the ontological question, but only the latter designation can lose the exclusive 'mine-ness' of Da-sein, in favour of a *Sein* that is, in fact, ours. As we shall see, it is through this concept of openness, which he will later call *Gelassenheit*, that Heidegger attempts to overcome metaphysical willing.

The willing-representing subject will become, in Heidegger's post-war utterances, the comportment of 'modern technology' (a comportment, as opposed to a totality of technology). Modern technology, the fulfilment of metaphysical willing, becomes the 'danger' of 'enframing [*Gestell*]'. Enframing is the 'destining' of metaphysical willing, and of 'man's ordering attitude', in the sense that the will to domination (of the object, of others, of nature) finds its ultimate mastery.[86] But this all seems very far from the music of Richard Wagner. How does Wagner stand for the 'height' of metaphysics for Heidegger? The answer to this question must proceed by way of an understanding of Heidegger's philosophy of language.

Music or poetry?

According to Heidegger, what is intended in the total work of art is a stimulation of the senses in their totality – a 'pure affective state'. Wagner's drama:

> possesses its importance and essential character, not in poetic originality, i.e., not in the well-wrought truth of the linguistic work, but to things pertaining to the stage, theatrical arrangements and gala productions. Architecture serves merely for theatre construction, painting provides the backdrops, sculpture portrays the gestures of actors. Literary creation and language remain without the essential and decisive shaping force of genuine knowledge. What is wanted is the domination of art as music, and thereby the domination of the pure state of feeling – the tumult and delirium of the senses, tremendous contraction, the felicitous distress that swoons in enjoyment, absorption in the 'bottomless sea of harmonies,' the plunge into frenzy and disintegration into sheer feeling as redemptive.[87]

Wagner's dilettantism lies not in his attempt to unify the arts as such but rather in his subjugation of this unity to music and not poetry. For Adorno, of course, matters stand the other way around. For Wagner, music remained too absolute by itself. Music must incorporate the other arts, non-music, in order to fulfil its essence as music. Heidegger's conjunction 'the domination of art as music, and *thereby* the domination of the pure state of feeling' denotes a series of equivalences: 'Wagner', 'music' and 'pure state of feeling'. Music is 'thereby', in its essence, affective. Music is the valorisation of the sensuous, according to the supersensuous. Music is thus the art of nihilism *par excellence*:

> Whenever Nietzsche deals with art in the essential and definitive sense, he always refers to art in the grand style. Against this backdrop, his innermost antipathy to Wagner comes to light most sharply, above all because his conception of the grand style includes at the same time a fundamental decision, *not only about Wagner's music, but about the essence of music as such*.[88]

For Heidegger, music as such, not only the music of Wagner, occupies the height of subjectivist metaphysics. As in Adorno, there is a coinciding of passive and dominating willing. But is Heidegger right to say that Nietzsche made a 'fundamental decision' about 'the essence of music as such'? Perhaps not: we read that 'The Case of Wagner' was 'inspired...by gratitude'. Indeed, the two postscripts and epilogue are symptomatic of Nietzsche's 'difficulty' over his divorce from the musician.[89] It is true that Wagner has '*made music sick*'. But Nietzsche does not equate Wagner with the sole possibility of music.[90] Nietzsche thus makes no such 'fundamental decision' about music as such, and this has important consequences for the meaning of Heidegger's lectures.

Heidegger cites some *Will to Power* fragments in order to substantiate his claim about Nietzsche's renunciation of music: 'The poet allows the drive for knowledge *to play*; the musician lets it take a rest.' But once again, it is by no means clear that the later Nietzsche treats this 'rest' pejoratively. Indeed, in the contemporaneous *The Gay Science* (1882), Nietzsche writes warmly of the 'slow periods' of artists:

> This is not the expression of weariness – rather that of a certain autumnal sunniness and mildness that the work itself, the fact the work has become ripe, always leaves behind in its creator. Then the pace of life slows down and becomes thick and flows like honey – to the point of a long *fermata*, of the faith in *the* long *fermata*.[91]

The 'long *fermata*', the musical pause, is 'not an expression of weariness'. It is the time of waiting for further possibilities of creation – not only waiting *for* creation but *of* creation. The later Nietzsche held Goethe's least appreciated work, the *Venetian Epigrams*, in the highest regard.[92] Here, Goethe names the mother of the muses as, not Mnemosyne, but 'Boredom'.[93]

Like many a thinker before and after him, Heidegger at this point employs an idea of music that is not informed by an experience of music. In the 1930s, Heidegger is either unable or unwilling to recognise the experimental music that had been under way for well over two decades (and which had been forced into exile). Heidegger recognised several German expressionist poets, but no musical settings of this poetry. In an essay on Stephan George ('The Word', 1958), Heidegger writes that, 'If we fail to understand the lofty meaning of song as Saying, it becomes the retroactive setting to music of what is spoken and written.'[94] The Second Viennese School, Eisler, Bartók, Ravel and Stravinsky were all drawn to the 'retroactive setting of music' during the first third of the twentieth century. The rejection of Wagnerian bombast led to a foregrounding of the poem (for example, Anton Webern's opus 14 Georg Trakl settings). Schoenberg would thus write in *The Blue Rider Almanac* (1912) that the text is a vehicle for the voice and not vice versa. Equally, as a continuation from Wagner, the text now provided music with a durational structure amidst the disintegration of musical logics. Schoenberg and his students effectively took up Wagner's example of non-strophic, through-composed 'song' (in works such as *Erwartung*), though stripped of its phantasmagoria.

For Heidegger, by contrast, music exemplifies everything that poetry is not. The limitation of Wagner's music-drama does not primarily concern the poverty of Wagner's poetry. Rather, it concerns the reduction of *poesis* to *mousike* (though Heidegger would have done well to consult his beloved Presocratics on this point). Music marks the impossibility of 'literary creation', which Heidegger tellingly refers to in the contemporaneous 'Origin of the Work of Art' (1936) as '*Gestell*'. Variations on *stellen* are to be found throughout the *Nietzsche* lectures, prompted by Nietzsche's 'grand *style*' (for instance, '*der* ***gestalteten*** *Wahrheit des Sprachwerkes*'). 'The Origin of the Work of Art' corroborates with the verdict on the relative standing of poetry and music given in *Nietzsche*: 'If the essence of art is poetry, then architecture, the visual arts and music must all be referred back to poesy.'[95] As Lacoue-Labarthe pointed out, Heidegger proposes an affinity between style and the figure(s) of poetic language in an avowedly phallocentric manner.[96] Music, it seems, cannot 'style' in the manner Heidegger would like art to.

Like Adorno, Heidegger conceives of music and language as opposing terms. It is their evaluation of this opposition that is – on the surface, at least – divergent. For the Heidegger of the 1930s, music is not so much 'discourse [*Rede*]', as 'idle talk [*Gerede*]'. These are concepts taken from *Being and Time*, and Heidegger's earlier philosophy of language provides an insight into his subsequent evaluation of music. The 'public understanding' and 'average intelligibility' of 'the They [*das Mann*]' is the 'They-self' of everyday, inauthentic Dasein. The 'They-self' is the 'most everyday and most stubborn "Reality" of *Dasein*', a reality that is articulated in idle talk.[97] Heidegger claimed that idle talk 'is not… a "disparaging" signification'. But he could not conceal the implicit evaluation, given that discourse discloses the world of Dasein itself. 'They' are the crowd – *Being and Time* having been composed in a time of socio-economic transformation in urban Germany. The anxiety about crowds in the 1920s is not unique to Heidegger, who had been impressed by Georg Simmel's writings. Heidegger addresses the authoritarianism of the crowd: 'the dictatorship of the They'. But there is no recognition of the possibilities of the collective – not until 1933. In spite of its claim to neutrality, 'the They' is both a critique of authoritarianism and an anti-modern reaction to a burgeoning capitalist culture industry. Heidegger learns from Nietzsche that Wagner is the decadent manipulator of the urban masses: 'Let anyone walk through a city: everywhere he will hear how instruments are ravished in a solemn rage – interspersed with a savage howling. What is going on? – The youths are worshipping Wagner.'[98] Wagner, '*the actor should not seduce those who are authentic*.'[99]

Heidegger's portrait of Wagner resonates with his earlier account of everydayness. The following excerpts are taken from *Being and Time* and *Nietzsche* respectively – each side of the *Kehre* – but they share a nautical metaphor:

> While the particular [everyday] *Dasein* drifts along towards an ever-increasing groundlessness as it floats, the uncanniness of this floating remains hidden from it under the protecting shelter.[100]
>
> the... absorption in the 'bottomless sea of harmonies,' the plunge into frenzy and disintegration into sheer feeling as redemptive.[101]

In *Being and Time,* idle talk is connected to 'curiosity' and 'concern'. 'Care becomes concern with the possibilities of seeing the "world" merely as it *looks* while one tarries and takes a rest... curiosity is concerned with the constant possibility of *distraction* [Zerstreuung]' and 'ambiguity [*Zwiedeutigkeit*].'[102] Given these parallels between *Being and Time* and *Nietzsche,* 'musical' Dasein cannot be authentic. As with Adorno, the distraction and ambiguity of Wagner is initially assessed pejoratively. But can Heidegger's verdict similarly follow Adorno's revised – ambivalent – position on Wagner and distraction?

Twisting free as *Aufhebung*

According to Heidegger, Nietzsche finally attempted to 'twist free' of Platonic metaphysics by way of an historical-philosophical analysis. In *Twilight of The Idols* (1888), Nietzsche recounts 'How the True World Finally Became a Fable: the History of an Error'. 'Nietzsche divides the history into six parts, which can be readily recognised as the most important epochs of Western thought, and which lead directly to the doorstop of Nietzsche's philosophy proper.'[103] The 'six parts' name the history of metaphysics itself (Plato, Platonism, Kant, German idealism, Schopenhauer and positivism). They are six comportments towards the 'True World', as evaluations of the sensuous and supersensuous. Each part shares the 'above and below' structure, but in the sixth and last part, Nietzsche suggests that (his) positivism has abolished the supersensuous only to deny the consequences of its nihilism: 'The true world we abolished: which world was left? the apparent one perhaps?... But no! *along with the true world we have also abolished the apparent one!*'[104] Heidegger understands Nietzsche's attempt to overcome passive nihilism as the will to power of the *Übermensch*: 'the overturning of Platonism and the ultimate twist out of it imply a metamorphosis of man.'[105] And it is here that Heidegger reintroduces his interpretation of the will to power as art. Art in the grand style is a metamorphosis of sense, *Sinn*. With art, the sensuous and the supersensuous, the real world and the apparent one, do not perpetually oppose one another, in the 'above and below' manner. Heidegger states that Nietzsche's perspectivism should be understood ontologically and not pantheistically. Being 'is in itself perspectival-perceptual, and that means, in the sense now delineated, "sensuous".'[106] This allows for a new interpretation of the sensuous, which is not simply opposed to the supersensuous, and hence need not be 'abolished' along with it. Instead of appearance, or the apparent: 'semblance [*Schein*]'. As with Adorno's understanding of the concept, *Schein* evades the opposition of appearance and true reality by way of a self-temporalisation (since its unity is structurally speculative with respect to the whole). When 'Nietzsche uses the word semblance [*Schein*] it is usually ambiguous. He knows it too.'[107] *Schein* is *merely* appearance *only* 'when what becomes manifest in one perspective petrifies and is taken to be the sole definitive appearance'. If Being is perspectival then Being is becoming.

For Heidegger, art is not one perspective among others. It presents the perspectival as such, in the midst of which, according to 'The Origin of the Work of Art', a new perspective or world becomes possible. Hence, the artwork neither transcends world-perspectives, as it does in Schopenhauer's aesthetics, nor does it show the real world as it is. Instead: 'Art induces reality.' Reality, truth, is the fixed. Art, the 'shining of the perspectival', must then be in 'discordance [*Zweispalt*]' with the truth. The 'unity of their belonging together is granted by the *one* reality, perspectival shining.'[108] This discordance has not yet been understood or experienced, suggests Heidegger. The 'twisting free' of Platonism would comprise this experience, though Heidegger, unlike Adorno, situates this twisting free in art alone (and this is the difference between their respective concepts of *Schein*). For Heidegger, '"*Übermensch*" is the man who grounds Being anew – in the rigor of knowledge and in the grand style of creation.'[109] Heidegger thus brings out the historical dimension in Nietzsche. 'The greater a revolution is to be, the more profoundly must it plunge into its history.'[110] Heidegger refers to 'essential stages [*wesentlichen Schritte*]' here, appearing to combine his reference to Hegel's *Aesthetics* with Nietzsche's six-part history of Platonism. Of course, 'stage' is not to be understood in a strictly Hegelian sense, as the one-sided manifestation of spirit or the Idea. 'Western thought', *including* that of Hegel, has perpetuated the error of Platonism. The affinity to Hegel does not however concern the concept of stage but rather height. Twisting free of Platonic metaphysics is a singular event at its height rather than a series of sublations though historical epochs.[111] For, twisting free is a twisting free of the 'above and below' logic of, so it would seem, *Aufhebung* itself:

> At the end of Platonism stands a decision concerning the transformation of man. That is how the phrase 'highpoint of humanity [*Höhepunkt der Menschheit*]' is to be understood, as the peak of decision, namely, decision as to whether with the end of Platonism man as he has been hitherto is to come to an end, whether he is to become that kind of man Nietzsche characterised as the 'last man', or whether that type of man can be overcome and the 'overman' can begin... By the word '*Übermensch*' Nietzsche does not mean some miraculous, fantastic being, but the man who surpasses [*hinauskommt*] former man.[112]

The highpoint of humanity is the last 'essential stage' and is also the occasion for the possibility of the 'overman'. Michel Haar has recognised the structural resemblance between Heidegger's history of metaphysics and Hegel's philosophy of history, 'insofar as each epoch finally finds its sense with respect to the totality of the process' (the absolute or Being). Such a concept of the totality is not to be found in Nietzsche. Haar concludes, however, that this similarity also marks:

> the point of greatest remove [from Hegel] inasmuch as the Heideggerian totality rests on the abyss of the ungrounded, and inasmuch as the Greek dawn is not the only commencement possible. Besides the Greek dawn there is indeed a 'new dawn' that offers the possibility of an end of history that is radically different from that of Hegel insofar as for Heidegger it is not a recommencement but a totally different, unprecedented, absolutely new commencement.[113]

Hegel's history of spirit and Heidegger's history of metaphysics must therefore be sharply differentiated according to the issues of totality and teleology. Hegel presents us with a progressive series of epochs, whereas in Heidegger we find a catastrophic perpetuation of Platonic metaphysics, combined with the Hölderlinian possibility of a new beginning. Heidegger's history of metaphysics is in this sense structurally more akin to Marx's *prehistory* than to Hegel's *history*. For Marx, 'the productive forces developing in the womb of bourgeois society create the material conditions for the solution of [its] antagonism. This social formation constitutes, therefore, the closing chapter of the prehistoric stage of human society.'[114] Turning Hegel against Hegel, the younger Marx conceived of the commencement of history proper in terms of an *Aufhebung*: 'Philosophy cannot realise itself without the transcendence [*Aufhebung*] of the proletariat, and the proletariat cannot transcend itself without the realisation [*Verwirklichung*] of philosophy.'[115] The crucial point of differentiation between Marx on the one side and Heidegger and Adorno on the other is that the latter thinkers are less expectant about the new commencement. *Structurally* modelled upon Hegelian logic, there remains an impeccability to Marx's 'history' (in spite of the fact that it must of course be put into *practice*) – whereas, according to Adorno's and Heidegger's deepening of the problem of metaphysical logic itself, if the commencement is to be genuinely new then it cannot proceed out of the old metaphysics. This messianic trope – of a radically new and unprecedented future – connects the thought of Benjamin, Adorno and Heidegger – each, not coincidentally, students of Hölderlin. But, just as the radically different future cannot be divined from the past, neither can it come from out of nowhere. The advantage of a Hegelian-Marxist concept of *Aufhebung* lies in its multiple signification, of rising up, preserving and cancelling. It offers a means, as mediation, to the new. Insofar as the old is risen up to its height (*hebt auf*) the new is in some sense borne out of the old. As we have seen, both Nietzsche and Marx use the metaphor of birth to express a relation to the new.

In his 'Letter on Humanism', a response to questions posed by Jean Beaufret in 1946, Heidegger attempted to distinguish his 'history of Being' from Hegel's attempt to 'subsume history into a system'. For, 'Thought in a more primordial way, there is the history of Being to which thinking belongs as recollection of this history, propriated by it. Such recollective thought differs essentially from the subsequent presentation of history in the sense of an evanescent past.'[116] But Hegel's history of spirit (which Heidegger states 'is not untrue') is *equally* a recollection, as *Erinnerung* – Heidegger would thus appear to have historicism in mind here. Once again, the shared factor is rather that of the *ruse*. Wolin highlights the role of a ruse of Being in the later Heidegger. He criticises Heidegger's conflation of this history with destiny, leading to the problem of fatalism (transcendent Being as the 'subject' of the destining of history). Hegel's appeal to a ruse of reason thus bears the advantage over the ruse of Being of including the *use* of reason itself. But if reason is to be understood from a pragmatic perspective, this argument becomes circular, insofar as the use of reason cannot make a claim on how it will be used for the better in the future. Pragmatism opposes speculation. Seen in this way, the two ruses are equally problematic – and promising. Where Hegel's reason is speculative, Heidegger's history of Being is formed from an experience of its expropriation, combined with an intellectual-historical analysis. It is no coincidence therefore that, in 'The Letter on Humanism', Heidegger turns to the question of alienation:

> What Marx recognized in an essential and significant sense, though derived from Hegel, as the estrangement of man has its roots in the homelessness of modern man. This homelessness is specifically evoked from the destiny of Being in the form of metaphysics, and through metaphysics is simultaneously entrenched and covered up as such. Because Marx by experiencing estrangement attains an essential dimension of history, the Marxist view of history is superior to that of other historical accounts.[117]

This excerpt reveals Heidegger's search for a non-fatalistic concept of destiny. For, just as in Marx and Hegel, destiny has both a fatalistic and emancipatory dimension – if that destiny includes the prospect of emancipation, as positive freedom. The problem then concerns the 'logic' of the 'twisting free' – which, for Heidegger, relies upon a blend of Hegelian reason (since the *question* of Being *is also* the question of beings) and Hölderlinian messianism. This messianism corresponds to a form of the active nihilism that Heidegger had already attempted to twist free of, insofar as nothingness and catastrophe are the (un)ground of 'healing'. In the face of nothingness, we experience Being for the first time.

Heidegger's sense of overcoming thus prioritises the moment of *Aufhebung* in its triple-movement. The 'penultimate' and 'last' stages run into each other in Nietzsche's 'history of an error', to the extent that Nietzsche himself turns from the brink of positivism. In Heidegger's account, Nietzsche broke with Wagner – the 'penultimate' stage – in order to become Nietzsche 'proper'. Nietzsche turned to an affirmation of life by way of a negation of its negation. Hence, as Adorno knew (without explicitly saying it), the decadent is not only the last but, reflected in an expression, is the occasion for the first. Wagner – the name that stands for the 'highpoint' of metaphysical 'humanity' – is to be 'surpassed' in this sense.

Nietzsche's ambiguous decadence is initially lost on Heidegger, only for Heidegger to take it over more emphatically in his sensitivity towards Nietzsche's overall understanding of the ambiguities of metaphysics. For, to say that the 'highpoint of humanity' must be surpassed is to imply some notion of 'fulfilment' – the term that Heidegger uses in 'European

Nihilism'. Perhaps unwittingly, Heidegger acknowledges the role of music, of musical subjectivity – to the extent that it must be experienced in its fulfilment in order to be twisted free of. Indeed, Heidegger must incorporate both sides of Nietzsche's 'ambiguous' nihilism in order for his own interpretation, his original contribution, to remain coherent. If the height of metaphysics is musical then its being surpassed, its being twisting free of, is also musical – recalling Adorno's understanding of modern music as a form of non-representational willing. Heidegger will subsequently conceive of the fulfilment of metaphysics in terms of modern technology – that which, Heidegger reveals in his *Spiegel* interview, is to be '*aufgehoben* in the Hegelian sense'.[118] This belated – and posthumous – gesture towards Hegel, whom Heidegger had once held responsible for disastrously identifying logic with metaphysics, is revealing in the context of the preceding discussion. Relating this 'Hegelian sense' back to *Nietzsche*, musical metaphysics must similarly be risen up to its height and cancelled. As Löwith and Wolin each make clear, Heidegger's interest in the fulfilment of modern technology is apocalyptic and even 'chiliastic' – in the sense of his much loved line from Hegel's friend, Hölderlin: 'But where danger threatens / That which saves from it also grows'.[119] Read in a violently Hegelian manner – on Heidegger's invitation – this *Aufhebung* contains a necessary moment of musical distraction in the twisting free itself. The manner of the twisting free is, with Heidegger against Heidegger, 'musical' – authentically inauthentic (the 'I' what is 'We').

This more dialectical evaluation of music is anecdotally supported by a letter in which Heidegger praises a performance of two works by Stravinsky. 'They are music in the highest sense of the word: works sent from the muses.'[120] Heidegger's letter evidences, at the very least, a recognition that modern music is not Wagner alone. From the art of passive nihilism to art in 'the highest sense' – the trope of height is unmistakable – Heidegger's re-evaluation of modern music seems complete. Or at least, these two moments correspond to an *ambivalent* evaluation of music – even to the 'repulsion and attraction' that characterised Adorno's relation to Wagner. This sense of ambiguity is fundamental because the same cannot be said of Heidegger's relation to (modern) technology. The fulfilment of musical subjectivity does not therefore necessitate a fulfilment of modern technology – which, for Heidegger, means global catastrophe. In any case, if modern technology is to be *aufgehoben* in the Hegelian sense then something of that technology must be preserved and utilised. Heidegger shares with Marx an understanding of Dasein as the being gifted with *technē*.[121]

Willing and waiting (II)

What are the consequences of the foregoing interpretation of 'twisting free' for Heidegger's understanding of the problem of willing? Heidegger's contribution to this problem is to be found beyond the *Nietzsche* lectures. 'The Will to Power as Art' lectures were intended to be devoted to the problem of the will as well as to the problem of art. But in their delivery and constant revision, the latter was disproportionately developed over the former. Twisting free of metaphysics is not the privilege of art alone. It is a question about willing as such – including practical and political willing (it is quite tempting to understand 'twisting free' in its literal, physiological movement – as, to use Adorno's term, a 'gesture'). The twisting free that is to bring about a changed humanity would require a moment of representing willing. At the same time, representing willing is part of the problem of the existing bourgeois humanism. Twisting free must overcome the 'above and below' oppositions of willing and non-willing, active and passive (nihilism), expectation and waiting in vain. The later Heidegger does indeed develop a *structure* of willing, as also waiting, that attempts to overcome these dualisms.

The turn away from the will to power in 'European Nihilism' paved the way for texts such as the 'Letter on Humanism' and the imagined conversation between the teacher, scientist and scholar (1944–5), published in *Discourse on Thinking* (1959). In this latter text, '*Gelassenheit*' (usually translated as 'releasement') became the name for a non-willing willing. The reader of these later texts may be forgiven for thinking that Heidegger has lapsed into the very Schopenhauerian metaphysics that he opposed in *Nietzsche* – and that this explains a possible musical turn. But *Gelassenheit* might be open to interpretations that contradict Heidegger's intentions – indeed, this contradiction already lies within Heidegger's corpus of writings. In the conversation, 'non-willing' is taken to mean 'willingly to renounce willing'.[122] An obvious difference to Schopenhauer opens up when we consider that it *is also* a kind of finite willing: Heidegger's Being is not Schopenhauer's Will (again, so long as we hold Heidegger to his question-worthy, ec-static, not static Being). Hence, as Heidegger states, *Gelassenheit* is no releasement from Being but is conversely intended as a 'releasement toward things', and as the 'openness to the mystery' of Being.[123] Equally against vitalism and positivism, *Gelassenheit* is no representational willing. Heidegger's teacher must distinguish waiting from awaiting, 'for awaiting already links itself with re-presenting and what is re-presented.' Indeed, agrees the scholar, waiting is the opposite of awaiting: 'as soon as we re-present to ourselves and fix upon that for which we wait, we really wait no longer.'[124] 'Open' waiting is not an open waiting for nothing. In order to argue this, Heidegger must paradoxically 'spatialise' waiting ('...into the expanse of distance...', and 'Then thinking would be coming-into-the-nearness of distance'). Heidegger distinguishes between an expecting a-waiting, waiting for, and waiting upon. That upon which the comportment of *Gelassenheit* waits is the appropriating event of Being, as intimacy with its mystery/question. The waiting of *Gelassenheit* is not, it would seem, the quietistic waiting in vain of the infinite task – whereby the horizon of waiting is always infinitely distant. It is an expression, as twisting free. *Gelassenheit* is a kind of willing that does not perpetuate the representing willing of a subject that seeks to 'enframe' the world. Heidegger's *Gelassenheit* and Adorno's expression of waiting in vain each constitute responses to the problem of the metaphysical will – a will that comes to characterise a dystopian modernity. Heidegger's concept remains *philosophically* 'more' radical in the sense that it seeks an ontological twisting free of metaphysics itself. The spectre of quietism remains, however, in the absence of a *means* (beyond poetry) – in the later Heidegger we find 'meditative thinking' rather than mediating practice. In response to Wolin's critique, it remains to be shown – in the final chapter of this book – how Heidegger's later conception of waiting as *Gelassenheit* can be read in terms of his earlier accounts of waiting, boredom and anticipation, so as to necessitate practical activity. In his 'Letter on Humanism', Heidegger complains that existing humanism does not 'realize the proper dignity of man'. It 'does not set the *humanitas* of man high enough'.[125] But Heidegger does not propose any determinate way towards this highpoint. We are not ready for such an orientation, not yet on the right way, such is our forgetfulness of Being – 'we can at most awaken the readiness of expectation'.[126] Adorno's waiting-expression remains more practical because he knows that the historical materialist task remains, in spite of its problems, the only one worth waiting upon, and therefore worthy of being practiced today. Could these two 'waitings' be combined – as a combination of the philosophically and politically radical moments?

3
The Dialectical Image of Music

Two spheres of musical experience

Adorno's essay of 1938, 'On the Fetish-Character in Music and the Regression of Listening', has been received in the Anglophone context (since its appearance in English in 1991) by discourses of both cultural studies and new musicology.[1] The essay can, however, be read as an eminently philosophical reflection upon the temporal experience of modernity. In this chapter, 'On the Fetish-Character' will serve to introduce a hitherto neglected philosophy of time in Adorno's thought – one that can further elucidate the meaning of 'waiting in vain', as 'music alone' can express. It will be argued that Adorno's evaluations of both 'modern music' and 'commodity music' can be understood according to music's relation to time and to the image. And it is in this latter respect that Adorno's dialectical understanding of music can be read in terms of Benjamin's 'dialectical image', a concept largely formulated in his *Arcades Project*. As we have seen, Adorno is more critical of the later than then earlier Benjamin, even though Adorno appears to have appropriated several of the later concepts. Without claiming a direct appropriation of the dialectical image, a structural affinity will nevertheless be proposed between the dialectical image and Adorno's philosophy of music – or rather, of musical experience. Moreover, it will be shown how Adorno came to appreciate the complex relationships between music, image and space through the 'new music' that he himself experienced in Darmstadt during the 1950s and 60s. Though largely unacknowledged by Adorno, the music of Luigi Nono can be shown to illustrate an expression of waiting in vain.

The 'Fetish-Character' essay in part comprises an interpretation of 'The Fetishism of the Commodity and its Secret', from the first volume of *Capital* (1867). For Marx, the 'fetish' refers to the 'strange' form of the commodity. The commodity does not consist in its immediate materials or properties. Neither does the commodity directly manifest the labour of its producers. For, the abstraction of exchange value from use value is at the same time an abstraction of the commodity from the conditions of its production – hence, 'abstract labour'. The commodity is the bearer of 'congealed labour'. Marx identifies the contradiction between the appearance of the commodity and its social reality. The commodity is 'nothing but the definite social relation between men themselves which assumes here, for them, the phantasmagorical form of a relation between things'.[2] 'Fetish' and 'phantasmagoria' connote magic: the 'relation between things' implies a world in which commodities have taken on a form of subjectivity at the same time as subjects themselves ('relations between men') have lost theirs. However, Adorno re-interprets Marx by emphasising that the fetish character not only names the estrangement of social labour in the commodity but equally the compulsion, as a consumer, to enter into its promise. What is more, the commodity promises an escape from the estrangement that it in fact reproduces.[3] This 'fixation' with the commodity recalls Freud's essay on fetishism – though Adorno is reluctant to acknowledge this model ('the concept of fetish character cannot be psychologically derived').[4] Adorno's understanding of the fetish character is more likely informed by the identity philosophies of Marx's German idealist forebears – Hegel in particular, whom Adorno was reading extensively at this time.

Adorno conceives of identification in terms of identity and non-identity. This might appear to conflate a process with a result. But identification is regarded here not as identity itself but as the will to identity – recalling the above Wagner-critique. The commodity fetish structures and manipulates the will through an illusory subject-object identity – 'just in this way [the fetish] becomes "property".'[5] The 'fetish character of music produces its own camouflage through the identification of the listener with the fetish.'[6] The fetish is identification. But this identification is subjected to a second identification that conceals the fetish *character* of the fetish. The commodity fetish is in this sense viciously circular. Identity falsely appears, each and every time, as non-identity, and thus as enchantment. At the end of the essay, Adorno speaks of his hope for musical listening to 'leave the road of the always-identical' and to align itself with Hegel's idea of 'progress in the consciousness of freedom'.[7] Adorno's account of musical experience is nevertheless informed more by the preface to the *Phenomenology of Spirit* than by Hegel's lectures on history (from which Adorno's quotation derives). The fetish aims at the identity of consciousness and its object. But the contradiction that this identity must yield to difference, that which the identity is not (because that identity is not all reality) is pre-empted in commodity music. This form of musical experience thus closes off experience as understood by Hegel: '*Inasmuch as the new true object issues from it*, this *dialectical* movement which consciousness exercises on itself and which affects both its knowledge and its object, is precisely what is called *experience* [*Erfahrung*].'[8] The subsequent importance of this passage to Adorno's understanding of Hegel is clear from the later essay on 'The Experiential Content of Hegel's Philosophy' (1958).[9] Adorno takes from Hegel's concept of experience its dialectic of becoming, combined with its speculative relation to the whole (which, as we saw in Chapter 1, remains negative. Adorno will privilege the moment of non-identity over identity). Various oppositions, between stasis and becoming, reification and freedom, and the old and the new, stand behind Adorno's philosophy of time.

Not uniquely among German intellectuals of the first third of the twentieth century, both Heidegger and Adorno were concerned with these oppositions. As Rose points out in *The Melancholy Science*, the worry about stasis amidst the tumult of capitalism came to be known under the rubric of 'reification' – a term that Marx himself did not use. Equally, for Heidegger and Adorno, reification manifests itself not only in cultural forms but also in academic philosophy (*as* a cultural form). For example, one attempt to counteract reification was to be found in the philosophy of life (*Lebensphilosophie*), represented by thinkers such as Dilthey and Simmel. But as we saw from Adorno's distinction between the two concepts of aesthetic experience in *Aesthetic Theory*, the lived experience (*Erlebnis*, a central concept of *Lebensphilosophie*) provided no antidote to reification, and was in many respects symptomatic of it. Unlike *Erfahrung*, the *Erlebnis* is neither inter-subjectively nor historically constituted. Hence, Adorno will dismiss Benjamin's appropriation of Simmel, ironically on the grounds of Benamin's former, Goethean concept of *Erfahrung*.[10] However, rather than proposing a merely individual and exceptional *Erlebnis* in the dialectical image, Benjamin had sought to transform the *Erlebnis* into a messianic-political 'shock experience [*Chockerlebnis*]' in the name of *Erfahrung* – not a vitalistic end in itself.[11] The *Chockerlebnis*, a description of the experience of surrealism, is to break the law of traditional experience. But the law, *Erfahrung*, is already in a state of exception. It has 'fallen in value'.[12] Hence, the *Chockerlebnis* takes exception to the exception. This account of experience from 'The Storyteller' can be compared to Benjamin's later thesis on historical exceptionality: 'the tradition of the oppressed teaches us that the "state of emergency" in which we live is not the exception but the rule.'[13] Although Benjamin's *Erlebnis* differs fundamentally from the concept as it is found in *Lebensphilosophie*, the point of differentiation from Adorno thus concerns the issues of exception and mediation, in that Adorno is happier with the latter than with the former. It is in this sense that Agamben is right to suggest that Adorno is no thinker of the messianic.

In light of his preference for the Hegelian terminology of mediation and identity, Adorno draws a contrast between stasis and becoming in the 'Fetish Character' through a pairing of forgetting and memory:

> Just as every advertisement is composed of the inconspicuous familiar and the unfamiliar conspicuous, so the song remains salutarily forgotten in the half-dusk of its familiarity, suddenly to become painfully over-clear through recollection, as if in the beam of a spotlight.[14]

The reciprocal can be contrasted with the dialectical here: forgetting and sudden recall substitute, in terms of Hegel's concept of experience, for 'remembrance'.[15] Exchange value appears as use value, as if new. But because of its determination in the exchange process, this is not new socially. The relations of production reproduced in the commodity remain the same old ones. *Adorno takes the commodity of music to be privileged in this process*:

> If the commodity in general combines exchange-value and use-value, then pure use-value, whose illusion the cultural goods must preserve in completely capitalist society, must be replaced by pure exchange-value, which precisely in its capacity as exchange-value deceptively takes over the function of use-value. The specific fetish character of music lies in [this] quid pro quo.

Commodity music thus exemplifies the substitution of exchange value for use value – Marx's 'quid pro quo' denoting an exact substitution. How does Adorno make this claim for (or rather against) commodity music? The 'feelings [*die Affekte*] which go to the exchange value create the appearance of immediacy at the same time as the absence of a relation to the object.'[16] The affectivity of music is simultaneously the production of its novelty. Novelty is immediate. Or, immediacy is novel. The feeling is prior to mediation. Adorno seems to propose a dualistic account of experience here, in his suggestion that feeling is not understood and the understanding is not felt. Yet Adorno's point is surely that the commodity form imposes this dualism upon experience from within it. Commodity music is contrasted with what Adorno will call 'serious music', and elsewhere, 'modern music'. But here is the peculiarity of Adorno's construction: 'the diverse spheres of music must be thought of together... The unity of the two spheres of music is that of an unresolved contradiction.'[17] This statement stands out amidst Adorno's valorisation of modern music, the 'pure' art.[18] How can music be pure commodity and pure art? The paradoxical autonomy of the artwork leads to an exaggerated formula in *Aesthetic Theory*: 'The absolute artwork converges with the absolute commodity.'[19] But Adorno's thinking of these absolutes *in music* hints at a particular account of capitalism from the standpoint of the problematic of time.

Adorno notes that the notion of music as the art of feeling appears as early as Plato's *Republic*. However, as with Heidegger's (initial) assessment of music, there is something unsatisfactory about the equating of music with feeling. Rather, music's affectivity should be understood according to its imagistic and spatial characteristics, both intrinsically and extrinsically. And it is through these associations that Adorno's philosophy of time may be articulated, often beyond his own articulation. The privileging of music as affective corresponds to a temporal privileging. Specifically, both 'spheres' of music involve the image in ways that bring Adorno's concept of experience into a relationship with Benjamin and Heidegger.

Music as image(less)

Adorno's most explicit consideration of the relationship between music and the image was prompted by an actual work of music. Schoenberg's unfinished *Moses und Aron* was composed in the 1930s but only premiered (albeit in part: the *Dance of the Golden Calf*) at the 1951 summer course for new music in Darmstadt – which Adorno attended.[20] Schoenberg's fragment addresses the meaning of the image in the biblical story. For Adorno:

> The Jewish prohibition on making images which forms the centre of the text also defines the approach of the music. Another chorus from Opus 27 begins, 'Thou shalt make no graven image'. Music is the imageless art and was excluded from that prohibition. That is no doubt the key to the relationship between Judaism and music.

> But at the historical stage of *musica ficta, stile rappresentativo* and of expressive music which makes sensuous something other than itself, music had become interwoven with the pictorial arts throughout Europe ... Music learned to imitate.

The *stile rappresentativo* to which Adorno refers emerged out of debates within the Florentine Camerata over how the ancient chorus should be imitated in the 'new music' – the problem being that no ancient models (scores) existed in any parallel manner to the visual or literary arts. Modern music was accordingly a *musica ficta*.[21] A response to this quandary emerged in the guise of Monteverdi's *seconda prattica*, a new musical language of monody and dissonance that sought to represent feelings in music. Tragic pathos was reconfigured as baroque affectivity. Adorno aligns the attempt of music to represent with the word and not the image. Indeed, much of the compositional theory (of the *seconda prattica* and Caccini's *nuove musiche*) was motivated by an interest in lyrical articulation – the mimesis of antique declamation. The proliferation of songs during this period is symptomatic.[22] But the *stile rappresentativo* was a representation of *drama* as a whole, and hence the concern of word *and* image. It is remembered not so much for its madrigals as for the inauguration of opera: *Orfeo* (1607). Adorno recognises this attempt to 'imitate'. But music is not fully 'interwoven' into the 'pictorial arts'. Music 'itself ... is' (not was) the 'imageless art'.

What, then, is the relationship between Adorno's evaluation of modern music on the one side and his thinking of the image on the other? In which ways does he thereby valorise the imageless? Adorno takes the ideal of the image to signify synthesis. The ideal image equates to the expropriation of *Erfahrung*, understood as becoming. Clearly, Adorno has in mind a certain Platonic heritage. The prototypical ideas are, after all, eternal. This image-critique marks another point of convergence between Adorno and Heidegger. In his *Nietzsche* lectures, Heidegger recalls the etymological affinity between *idea* and *eidos*. Platonism, in its variety of manifestations, wills identity. Heidegger will subsequently go on to claim that the whole 'world' itself has come to be grasped in an image: 'Understood in an essential way, "world picture" does not mean "picture of the world" but rather "the world grasped as picture".'[23] The determination of 'world' as 'totality of beings' collapses the ontological difference.[24] By comparison, in one of his two essays on music and painting (discussed below), Adorno writes that, 'in an image everything is simultaneous [*Gleichzeitig*]'. Adorno's claim invites the question as to whether and how a real image can be simultaneous. Adorno acknowledges Kant's attempt to disentangle his critical philosophy from the Platonic image (and from empiricism):

> In the context of his chapter on schematism, Kant observes that even the pure act of thinking involves traversing the temporal series as a necessary condition of its possibility, and not only of its empirical realisation. The more emphatically a painting presents itself, the more time is stored up in it.[25]

Adorno's initial claim about the image resists this attempted readjustment. Simultaneity is emphatically simultaneous. But Adorno makes a similar move to the one made in the 'Fetish-Character' essay. As with identity, the simultaneous image has a 'regulative' significance. Hence, for Adorno, art that is worthy of its name must negate its image character: 'Those pictures seem the most successful in which what is absolutely simultaneous seems like a passage of time that is holding its breath.'

In *Negative Dialectics*, Adorno's critique of the image is more explicit: 'imagelessness [*Bilderlosigkeit*] converges with the theological ban on the graven image. Materialism secularised it by not allowing utopia to be positively depicted – this is the content of its negativity.'[26] But Adorno's image critique not only concerns the critique of utopia as an image. It also concerns a critique of images in capitalist society. In his collaborative study with Hanns Eisler, *Composing for the Films* (1947), Adorno contends that the image is in some way more conducive to commodification than is music. In the 'bourgeois rational and, ultimately, highly industrialised order', write the authors, 'the eye...has become accustomed to conceiving reality as made up of separate things, commodities, objects that can be modified by practical activity.' By contrast, 'listening, as compared to seeing is "archaic"; it has not kept pace with technological progress.'[27] The concepts of simultaneity and stasis are once again invoked. A 'reality as made up of separate things' is a reality of things side-by-side one another in idealised space. Adorno draws a parallel between the immediacy of the fetish character – the absence of genuine reflection – and the immediacy of the (near-)simultaneous image. However, judging from *Minima Moralia*, Adorno has in mind the image-character of commodity production and consumption. Again following Kant's deconstruction of the image, the dominance of the real image is said to short-circuit the conceptual work of schematism. In the 'real abstraction' of 'people to each other and to things', abstraction becomes a mere product, not a production (abstract, not abstraction). The image is the already schematised, already subsumed concept, thus excluding the mediation of the 'schema-image' (more about which, below). Adorno conceives of a mythic iconography: 'advertisements, newspaper stereotypes [and] toys'. This is an anti-Eden of already named things, devoid of the human freedom to name. Adorno concludes that the image is paradigmatic of the dialectic of enlightenment, including its philosophy. For, the enlightenment critique of ideas inaugurated by Kant (and, in a sense, Aristotle) 'is now becoming a second figurativeness [*Bildlichkeit*]'.[28] Adorno comes close to conceiving of society itself in terms this *Bildlichkeit* – not only a plurality of images, since this describes the pre-modern world, but also society itself as image-like. Adorno thus anticipates *The Society of the Spectacle* (1967), in which Guy Debord states that, 'Consumable pseudo-cyclical time is the time of the spectacle: in the narrow sense, as the time appropriate to the consumption of images, and, in the broadest sense, as the image of the consumption of time.'[29] The time of capitalism itself, it would seem, takes on an image character – something that Benjamin was well aware of when thinking about the dialectical images of nineteenth-century Paris.

Schematism, rhythm, temporalisation

The schematism chapter of the *Critique of Pure Reason* addresses the fundamental issue of how the *contents* of intuition – 'representations' – are mediated with the *formal* concepts of the understanding (via the 'pure concepts' or categories). An account of how objects are logically subsumed under concepts, in judgement, is required in order to substantiate the transcendental deduction of apperception. This is because the synthetic unity of apperception (subject) requires the synthetic unity of representations (object). The schematism chapter attempts to elaborate the workings of the 'productive imagination', that which – Heidegger is at pains to point out – occupies the *middle* synthesis in the threefold synthesis of the first edition.[30]

Kant initially proceeds according to the Platonic paradigm of the image: 'For the imagination [*Einbildungskraft*] is to bring the manifold of intuition into an image [*Bild*].'[31] This is consistent with the eidetic paradigm of the *Critique* as a whole (*Erscheinung, Anschauung*). Kant's original move – his twofold critique of empiricism and rationalism – is to ask how the image is produced and not simply received. There must be a 'third thing' that mediates intuition and conceptual image: 'This mediating representation must be pure (without anything empirical) and yet intellectual on the one hand and sensible on the other. Such a representation is the transcendental schema.'[32] Adorno's 1959 lecture on the chapter reproduces Kant's conclusions in an unproblematic manner: 'time is the factor that is both common to thought and intuition'. Adorno thus repeats the problems associated with Kant's mediation. Time, along with space, is a 'pure form' of intuition, 'in which nothing is to be encountered that belongs to sensation'.[33] But how can 'pure' time *mediate*? Neither does Adorno discuss the problem of the image. The chapter is instead read as an example of confronting contradictions.[34] But as Heidegger sees matters, in his *Kant and the Problem of Metaphysics* (1929), it is precisely the meaning of time that is at stake in this chapter, which comprises 'the central core of the whole voluminous' *Critique*.[35] For Kant, the schema presents the definiteness of an image for a concept. It is image-like. At the same time, 'the schema is clearly distinguishable from the image'. The schema is a product of the schematism. Schematism is nothing without the schema. Equally, the schema is nothing without the image. A problem with Kant's mediation thus concerns the hierarchical dependency upon the image, which the schema was intended to avoid. Whence comes the image? Kant reveals the gravity of this problem in his textual contortions:

> This schematism of our understanding with regard to appearances and their mere form is a hidden art in the depths of the human soul, whose true operations we can divine from nature and lay unveiled before our eyes only with difficulty. We can say only this much: the image is a product of the empirical faculty of imagination, the schema of sensible concepts (such as figures in space) is a product and as it were a monogram of pure *a priori* imagination, through which and in accordance with which the images first become possible, but which must be connected with the concept, to which they are in themselves never fully congruent, always only by means of the schema that they designate.[36]

Heidegger cites this passage in the introduction to *Being and Time*. Kant is 'the first and only person who has gone any stretch of the way towards investigating the dimension of Temporality'.[37]

The interest of the early romantics in an idea of music can be understood as a response to the problem of schematism. Following the romantics, Andrew Bowie considers the schematism to be musical. He has two characteristics in mind. Firstly: its ambiguous meaning-production. The schema is neither chaotic nor finally subsumed, as *an* image. This corresponds to the discursive nature of schematism. Hence, for Schelling, 'the whole mechanism of language will rest upon' it.[38] Secondly: the synthetic role of time in schematism. Schematism is 'musical rhythm'.[39] Adorno similarly defines schematism as 'traversing the temporal series.' But these definitions touch upon the fraught meaning of time in Kant's chapter. It is no more evident, Heidegger observes, than in Kant's remark that, 'the pure image of all magnitudes (*quantorum*) for outer sense is space; for all objects of the senses in general, it is time.'[40] Time itself is a 'pure image'. This statement can be understood in radically different ways.

Kant defines the schemata as 'nothing but *a priori* time-determinations in accordance with rules'.[41] Time is immanent to the schema because time is *both* the 'formal condition of the manifold of inner sense' *and* is 'contained in every empirical representation of the manifold'.[42] But time-determination could signify either determination *in* time or determination *of* time. This fundamental ambiguity is reflected in Kant's elucidation of the role of time with respect to four of the categories, the last of which, magnitude, concerns 'the sum total of time in regard to all possible objects.'[43] The 'pure image' of time is, it seems, the subsumption of 'all possible objects' under one overarching concept – as one object and one subject. But this positive, absolute synthesis is antithetical to Kant's negative-critical project as a whole, even if such a concept were to be understood as regulative (and yet: Kant's 'ideal' of reason). As we saw in Chapter 1, reason seeks a totality of conditions in vain because the task of discovering the totality adds another condition to the totality. The unconditioned cannot be made apparent: 'this unconditioned is always contained in the absolute totality of the series if one represents it in imagination. Yet this absolute complete synthesis is once again only an idea.'[44] If Kant's 'pure image' of time *is* then an image of the unconditioned then it must be an inconceivable image – apropos of *Moses und Aron*:

> *Einziger, ewiger, allgegenwärtiger*
> *unsichbarer und unvorstellbarer Gott!*
>
> [The one, infinite, omnipresent
> unperceived and inconceivable God!][45]

Hölderlin, aware of Kant's example of the Jewish prohibition in the 'Analytic of the Sublime', named Kant as 'the Moses of our nation' – a Protestant identification of Jewish identity, of course.[46] Hence, Kant's 'pure image' of time might be understood in this monotheistic sense.[47]

However, Kant refers to a pure image for 'all objects of the senses *in general*', and hence to the *transcendental* conditions for the possibility of objects *as such*, not some purported totality. But how, in that case, can there be *one* time-image of objects *in general*? In what sense can the transcendental structure be an image *of itself*? Another possible interpretation of the 'pure image' arises from Kant's definition of time in the Transcendental Aesthetic:

> time cannot be a determination of outer appearances; it belongs neither to a shape or a position, etc., but on the contrary determines the relation of representations in our inner state. And just because this inner intuition yields no shape we attempt to remedy this lack through analogies, and represent the temporal sequence through a line progressing to infinity, in which the manifold constitutes a series that is of only one dimension, and infer from the properties of this line to all the properties of time, with the sole difference that the parts of the former are simultaneous but those of the latter always exist successively.[48]

Could the 'line' constitute a pure image of time, the form of all possible forms *on which* (its) determinations are, in a sense, 'punctuated'? This would tally with Kant's serialism – following a traditional, Aristotelian understanding of causation. Or rather, Kant renders metaphysical Aristotle's physics, just as he renders Aristotle's categories transcendental. This tradition is already seen in Leibniz's 'order of successions'. Kant's time series, the 'repeated addition of units to each other', faces the same criticisms made of the rationalist paradigm. Indeed, Kant himself acknowledges in his thesis to the first antinomy that the infinite time line leads into its opposite: simultaneity. All points of the infinite line are equally infinitely distant from the beginning as from the end.[49] This is destructive for Kant, if it is true that the antinomy ultimately sides with infinity. For Heidegger, the understanding of time as a series of points on a line ('within-time-ness') is the determination of time as space and not time at all. It is the 'ordinary [*vulgär*] conception of time'. Kant's 'pure image' of time is nevertheless fundamental to Heidegger's alternative (or, as Heidegger puts it, 'violent') reading of the schematism chapter.

Heidegger focuses upon the role of the schema in the above-mentioned category of magnitude, to which Kant attributes 'the generation of time itself.'[50] Having interpreted intuition [*Anschauung*] as the 'pure look [*Anblick*]' of the 'horizon' – the horizon of possibility – Heidegger now states that intuition refers to the 'schema-image' with respect to the 'pure image' of time.[51] The varied but interrelated terminology of 'image' in the *Critique* acknowledges a unifying ground (the ground that unifies but is not united) of the 'sources of knowledge': intuition and the understanding.[52] Heidegger's 'pure image' is finitely disclosing, the 'look' and not the Platonic *eidos*. As the horizon of possibility of the productive imagination, time is finite in a *disclosing* manner. Hence, its limitation (the horizon is 'finite') is not to be understood pejoratively. In the terms of *Being and Time*, which the *Kantbuch* was intended to 'clarify', the schematism of the productive imagination corresponds to the temporalising of possibility (see Chapter 5).[53] The subsequent, post-*Kehre* Heidegger will situate temporalisation in the origination of the work of art: 'To be a work [of art] means: to set up a world'.[54] The 'resoluteness' of *Being and Time*, the ground for the authentic temporalisation of possibility, is exemplified in the work of art – which, as enigmatic, is best placed to bring the 'enigma of Being' into nearness. The work of art gives historical, 'thingly' substance to Heidegger's earlier, solipsistic existentialism. But at the same time, this valorisation of the work of art leaves Heidegger open to the charge of blocking concrete possibilities outside of art. Or, the concrete possibility that Heidegger takes art to temporalise is – given his proposition about 'the Greeks and the Germans' – an already temporalised possibility: national chauvinism.

It has been claimed across a variety of traditions of philosophical aesthetics that the time of the artwork is an unfamiliar time – where familiar time is variously termed vulgar temporality, chronometric time, *temps espace*, and so on. The autonomous artwork is, either in actuality or as semblance, supposed to point towards authentically lived time, *chairos*, *temps durée* or *Erfahrung*. The peculiarity of modern music, however, is that it remains irredeemably chronometric, and to that extent always inauthentic – hence Heidegger's initial evaluation of the medium. Of course, every artwork endures *in* time – including, as even Adorno remarked, the visual arts. Perhaps then we may speak of a certain 'musical' tendency. This tendency is paradigmatic in music, which, according to Adorno 'has time as its problem'.[55] If we are to follow Adorno's account of autonomous art, and Heidegger's account of originary art (effectively, the two post-Kantian, modernist theories of art) then the case of modern music is particular in that it occupies each side of the temporal categorisation at the same time. This contradictory structure offers a clue to Adorno's comment about the 'unity of the two spheres of music'.

Schelling's philosophy of music resonated with the schematism chapter of his *System of Transcendental Idealism* (1801), itself a reworking of Kant's chapter.[56] As with Hegel, spirit – of which art is a unique manifestation – is the finite determination of the infinite. 'The necessary form of music is succession, for time is the universal form of the informing of the infinite into the finite and to that extent is intuited as form, abstracted from the real.'[57] Schelling was familiar with August Schlegel's definition of music in his lectures, *Schöne Literatur und Kunst* (1801–04) and *Vorlesungen über Philosophische Kunstlehre* (1798). Schlegel defined music as 'rhythm, modulation and harmony'.[58] The historical lag of actual music behind its idea, discussed in Chapter 1, is evident from Schelling's Schlegelian consideration of rhythm. Musical rhythm is said to incorporate two 'levels'. The first is measure: 'An image of this might be equally large, equally separated points'. The second is '*tact*' (a category that gained currency with Beethoven), which Schelling defines (unaware of Beethoven) as the alternation between strong and weak beats.[59] But with Beethoven, the two levels cannot be conflated. Indeed, the emancipation of rhythm from measure comes to *define* modern and autonomous music. Neoplatonic *rhythmos* migrates from the number to the name, but it retains the memory of its number, which it cannot forget so long as it is music. The revolution in rhythm is not to be found in the classicism of Haydn (Schelling's sole example) but in Beethoven, already into his middle period by 1800. Rhythm was no longer the mere elaboration of baroque and classical dance forms (the minuet, for instance). Adorno notes the following in his unfinished project, *Beethoven*: 'By work, time is killed *in earnest*... Extremely important: to be taken further – Beethoven's *rhythm* and tonality.'[60] This is also the period of the invention of the metronome, a rationalisation of the chronometric in music. Beethoven's enthusiasm for metronome tempo markings should be understood as his attempted *definition* of rhythm, articulated though the unfolding musical material as a whole, rather than as the valorisation of tempo for its own sake. Schelling tends to posit measure and rhythm dualistically, as nature and spirit. Music is, for Schelling, the harmonious unity of the ideal and real 'series' – in Kantian terms, the unity of the transcendental and the empirical.

In his *Rhythm and Tempo* (1953) musicologist Curt Sachs asks, 'What is rhythm?' and replies in the following manner: 'The answer, I am afraid, is, so far, just – a word: a word without generally accepted meaning...The confusion is terrifying indeed.'[61] The concept of rhythm remains confused. And much of the confusion concerns the question of the relative autonomy of rhythm from measure. In this respect, the confusion is symptomatic of the contradiction that is modern music itself. Rhythm can be defined as musical time, but musical time is positively interrupted by chronometric time. It is the vulgar temporality of music that has drawn philosophers of time to its *clear* example. Adorno cites the concept of rhythm sparsely, perhaps because it connotes an archaic reaction into the mythic-rationalist *rhythmos* (in Stravinsky). He nevertheless alludes to a *productive* rhythm in his work on Beethoven: 'On the theory of Beethoven and the symphony, Schelling's concept of rhythm in the *Philosophy of Art*'.[62] Adorno characterises the peculiarity of musical time in his own way, but it follows the general notion of a contradiction of times in Schelling and beyond: 'The self-evident fact, that music is a temporal art, that it unfolds in time, means, in the dual sense, that time is not self-evident for it, that it has time as its problem. It must create temporal relationships among its constituent parts, justify their temporal relationship, synthesise them through time.' Modern music is 'in time' and (yet) is a synthesis 'through time':

> *Zeitkunst*, the temporal art, is equivalent to the objectification of time. This applies to the individual elements, or musical content, to the extent that they come together in a context by means of the organisation of their sequence, rather than dissolving as they pass away; and to the temporal dimension itself, which aims, potentially, at its own sublation [*Aufgehoben*], based on the strength of the unity of what occurs within it, following the example of certain movements of the truly symphonic Beethoven.[63]

Typically, Adorno renders music's relationship to time dialectically. And yet, even dialectics struggles to grasp this extra-musical problem.

As art, modern music calls for aesthetic judgement. Such judgement is, according to Kant, without a concept. This means: conceptual (logical) without being subsumed under *one* concept.[64] Adorno coins the term 'logicity'.[65] In the third *Critique*, Kant cites the schematism chapter of the first *Critique* as an account of the subsumption of *determinate* and not *reflective* judgements.[66] But if, given Heidegger's reading, the schematism is productively indeterminate *in* its determining judgement, then modern music, as art, temporalises. The work of modern music aims at a 'sublation' of time according to Adorno. Which time does musical time sublate (include and cancel)? Music 'must act upon time, not lose itself to it; must stem itself against the *empty flood*'. Is not the empty flood another time-series, another representation of time as accumulation of points *in* time? Adorno's formulation is indeed Bergsonian, to the extent that the sublating time of music must negate a 'quasi-spatial time'. Thus, Adorno complains that, in the 1960s Darmstadt debates about musical time, 'the concept of time is used equivocally. It covers both *temps espace* and *temps durée*, physically measurable, quasi-spatial time and experiential time. Bergson's insight into their incompatibility cannot be erased.'[67] In *Time and Free Will* (1889), Bergson took 'notes of the tune...rhythm' to exemplify 'true duration'. By contrast, spatial time was the representation of a 'series' of 'states of consciousness' before (that) consciousness, in an 'image'. Representation thus distinguished spatial time from experienced duration, time's presentation (tellingly, Adorno calls the latter '*experiential* time').[68] Bergson takes music to subvert the re-presentation of time on account of its proximity to time's self-presentation – Kant's 'inner sense'. And yet, as has been suggested, the genesis of modern music is entwined with chronometric time. Bergson unwittingly reminds us that, as much as music opposes intra-temporality, modern music must also contain it. Hence, Heidegger concurs with Bergson that spatial time is the problem, but claims, against Bergson, that *temps durée* is in the final instance another *temps espace*.[69] Heidegger's criticism is recognisable: for Bergson, the notes of the tune are analogous to the series of 'states of consciousness', points in the consciousness time-series. The same observation can be made of Husserl's musical analogy in his lectures *On the Phenomenology of the Consciousness of Internal Time* (of course, Heidegger did not object, having co-edited the lectures himself in 1928).[70] Bergson's 'vulgar' conception of time is more than a mere conception however. In Heidegger's own terms, everyday temporality is a temporalisation, albeit one already temporalised by 'the They'. Heidegger confronts, but also reacts against this time of modernity, a time that is, moreover, represented in a figure of Bergson. But the advantage of Heidegger over Bergson is twofold, here at least. Firstly, Heidegger opens up an understanding of possible temporalisations according to, and within, a systematic and not ostensibly dualistic philosophy of time (nor a monistic one, as is found in the later work of Bergson). The possibility of temporalisation is once again a possibility of Dasein *as* facticity. Dasein is already thrown into its historical time. Hence, temporality is not subjectively produced. Heidegger instead makes a claim for fundamental ontology, according to which the question of Being is the only possibility of possibility itself: Dasein's self-temporalisation. Secondly, the conjunction of temporalisation with the horizon of possibility promises to overcome the spatial representation of time, which, being representational, threatens to collapse ec-static Dasein into stasis. Heidegger calls this inauthentic because to be Dasein *is* to be '*Fragwürdig*': worthy of the question of ec-static Being. The example of music in Bergson nevertheless provides the basis for a critique of Heidegger. Bergson returns the charge of dualism, for he problematises the *decisive* structure in Heidegger: authenticity or inauthenticity; resoluteness or everydayness; poetry or music. This criticism is not to relativise decision into an ahistorical, invariant category – to decide, that is, for indecision. Rather, the possibility of authenticity and of temporalisation is the possibility of all futural temporalisation. If the time of capitalism is regulated by the cyclical time of the image then temporalisation is the possibility – *as* the seeming impossibility – of a break-out from the mythic cycle into history.

Music is modern by virtue of its vulgarity. Is music's 'own sublation', as Adorno puts it, thereby possible? Can music cancel *and* preserve its time, the time that it already is? Adorno suggests that the late work of Beethoven anticipates this problem. The 'intensive type' of Beethoven's classical period marks the expression of musical time through symphonic unfolding. This is the rhythm of the French Revolution – of the *Eroica*. 'By work, time is killed *in earnest*'. Time is, as it were, prematurely, hastily fulfilled. In Beethoven's late-middle period, however (following the disappointment of the revolution) the 'extensive type' emerges. This time is characterised as the sublation of the former types, eventually culminating in the late style. 'The actual organising principle of the extensive form is', admits Adorno, 'still very obscure to me':

> The extensive form contains a certain moment of renunciation, an abandonment of the balance of opposites to be found in paradox, so that the fractures already emerge, although they do not yet become, as in the late style, ciphers; rather, they contribute to contingency in the sense that greater weight is given to the moment of abstract time than to the construction of the constitution of form. But this temporal moment is itself thematic, perhaps as in the novel, and is the main subject: not an 'idea' which fills time…Abdication before time, and the *shaping* of this abdication, make up the substance of the extensive type.[71]

The later work of Beethoven shapes 'abstract time', the shapeless time of the 'empty flood'. This is the extensive type. Can Adorno's conception of 'empty time' be clarified?

In *Negative Dialectics*, Adorno suggests that, by conceiving of schematism as logical time determination, Kant paved the way for Hegel's identification of time, history and logic: 'Hegel, Kant's critic, was Kant's executor.' Adorno could have cited the *Philosophy of Nature*, in which Hegel places time solely on the side of spirit: 'it is not *in* time that everything comes to be and passes away, rather time itself is the *becoming*, this coming-to-be and passing away'.[72] Hegel negates Kant's mechanistic antinomies only to expose a new contradiction between absolute idealist time and the time of natural science. Hegel radicalises Kant's 'objects in general' into a unitary Idea, whose task and essence is the inwardisation of the object from the standpoint of an absolute subject. The *Bilderverbot* thus extends to Hegel. Hegel's 'attempt to deduce time' amounts to the 'detemporalisation of time [*Entzeitlichung der Zeit*]'.[73] Adorno here reiterates Feuerbach's verdict, also found in Schelling, that 'Hegelian philosophy must necessarily result in the immobility of time.'[74] Adorno cites Bergson as the strongest intellectual protest to date – alongside Proust – against bourgeois detemporalisation. Bergson, not Husserl and certainly not Heidegger, provides Adorno's philosophical alternative to Kant and Hegel. Adorno entertains and even relies upon what he calls Bergson's 'crass dichotomy'. In re-presenting *both* times (in both spatial and imagistic terms, including movement, the movement of some-thing in space) Adorno faces the objection that multiple spaces cannot occupy the same space at the same time. It is thus a spatial and not a temporal contradiction that now confronts Adorno. Adorno's earlier notion of the 'two spheres' of music (the spatial metaphor is not accidental) can nevertheless offer, along with Heidegger's critique of metaphysical time, a more promising response to this contradiction.

Fantasy and spectacle

Adorno's claim that modern music is imageless contains an assumption that music takes place in an imageless environment. He tends to conflate musical form with the abstract (the 'pure' and 'imageless' art). But the abstract is the opposite of abstraction. As imageless, without *one* image, modern music *is* concerned with the image, negatively – and has been so since at least the *stile rappresentativo*. The possibility of representation in music is surely premised upon its ambiguously imagistic character. This is attested to by the prominence of fantasy in music and its discourse. Wackenroder's musical aesthetics, for instance, followed Ludwig Tieck's aesthetics of painting (but once again, the absence of music when addressing music is notable within early German romanticism):

> Sometimes music appears to me like a phoenix, which lightly and boldly raises itself for its own pleasure, floats upwards triumphantly for its own gratification, and pleases gods and men for the flapping of its wings ... what a magnificent fullness of images![75]

In his 'Beethoven's Instrumental Music', E. T. A. Hoffmann similarly saw 'Burning flashes of light shoot through the deep night... we become aware of giant shadows that surge back and forth, driving us into narrower and narrower confines until they destroy us.'[76] This musical romanticism reveals a constitutive, not accidental role of the imagistic in music. By contrast, Adorno's essay 'On the Contemporary Relationship of Philosophy and Music' (1953) refers to an 'enigmatic character' that is 'specific to music' and is 'emphasised by its distancing from the visually or conceptually determined world of objects'. Furthermore 'this character is almost urged upon us by music itself'.[77] In the visual arts, by contrast, the 'relationship to objects is merged with the content, even in the case of the associations of abstract painting'.[78] What does it mean to suggest that musical abstraction is *more* profound than painterly abstraction, or other abstractions? Does not music's 'distancing' of the image imply the possibility of another moment of nearness to the image – as in the 'dialectical' case of music and language? Matters are more nuanced in Adorno's 1965 essay on music and painting: 'The old aim of secular music, that of the *divertissement* that distracts from boredom, testifies to [music acting upon time], a fact that lives on in the relationship to time of autonomous music.'[79] Adorno's remark can be radicalised here, so as to indicate that distraction makes possible music's claim to autonomy *for the first time* – both historically and structurally – and that, insofar as distraction involves fantasy, music remains 'imagistic'.[80] Music is modern by virtue of its propensity for the image, not in spite of it. This was, for Wagner, the *privilege* of music.

Following tradition, Adorno takes music to be both the 'imageless art' and the 'art of time'. But what if modern music were imageless *insofar as* it was a quasi-imagistic rendering of time *through which* the image passed (*through*, in both senses of the word)? *Divertissement* passes the time, the empty time of boredom, but not in a vacuum. Images pass in and for modern music. It is already an abyssal 'image' into which images are drawn. Two aspects coincide here: the quasi-image of musical rhythm, discussed above, and the extra-musical image. As Adorno says of language in music, 'signifying intentions flood into' it. In fact, Adorno comes to a similar conclusion where the image is concerned, in his *Beethoven*:

> The dispute over whether music can portray anything definite, or is only a play of sound-patterns in motion, no doubt misses the point. A far closer parallel is the dream, to the form of which, as Romanticism well knew, music is in many ways close... Images of the objective

> world appear in music only in scattered, eccentric flashes, vanishing at once; but they are, in their transience, *of music's essence*.[81]

Adorno is reluctant to connect this dream world of music to the real world, in the manner of Bloch, perhaps. Adorno's shift of position on the image tracks his shifting evaluation of the dream, from hostility towards Benjamin's appropriation of Klages and Jung to the recording of his own dreams.[82] Adorno declares in the above note, unpublished in his lifetime: 'I believe the images flitting past to be *objective*, not merely subjective associations.'[83] Adorno can nevertheless retain his overall resistance to psychology here: musical fantasy is not internal but external. The meaning of music must relate to the imagistic character of the social world in which it is experienced.

If the commodity form privileges the image, then the imagistic character of music cannot be separated from this process. Indeed, 'commodity music' means no less than the rationalisation of the imagistic character of music amidst a society of the spectacle. The 'fetish character' must be said to extend to the context of musical listening. There is of necessity a space of fantasy and of phantasmagoria. This aspect of commodity music is left largely untouched by Adorno. But insofar as the context of *each* of the 'spheres' of music today is the city – or rather, what Simmel called 'metropolis' – then this context is one that already privileges the image. The environment is not accidental to the identification given the affinity between identity and *eidos*. This context even constitutes the commodity-being of music itself. The fractured experience of modernity – including its visual experience – is then ideologically massaged by commodity music, synthesising its disparate forms of the city (including class antagonism) into a unified whole. Music's affectivity – that which, according to Adorno, is responsible for its exemplary commodity character – concerns the need to feel that everything is in its place, in the 'non-dwelling' of the metropolis (see Chapter 4). It is in this sense that we can say Schopenhauer unwittingly predicted the truth of commodity music. For, commodity music goes beyond the *principium individuationis*, beyond the 'representation' of 'Ideas'. Early romantic fantasy is absolutised in Schopenhauer's high romanticism. Fantasy becomes bourgeois escapism. Commodity music presents an expropriated environment *as* appropriate – as a 'proper place'. It presents *Erlebnis* as *Erfahrung*, rather than transforming the one into the other. But these are not binary opposites. The two spheres of musical experience 'must be thought of together'. Modern music, like commodity music, speaks the language of fantasy. Where commodity music is receptive to the image, modern music seeks to appropriate this reception productively.

Ever since his 1933 book review, Adorno returned at several junctures to Ernst Kurth's *Musikpsychologie* (1930). Kurth had sought to understand the relationship between the 'inner' and 'outer' aspects of musical listening. How, he asked, does the compositional structure relate to the experience of spatial depth and collectivity, traditionally associated with the live performance? They are distinct yet intimately connected phenomena. The composition 'determines' the spatiality of the musical experience. Adorno does not consider this spatiality in terms of architecture. And yet, musical space:

> springs from the collective implications of all music, the character of something that embraces groups of human beings, which gradually carried over to the sound as such. The phenomenon can only be described in analogies, but can be perceived very distinctly.

Adorno finds this relationship obscure yet fundamental: 'the spatial quality *adheres to* the harmonic structure and the instrumental sound.'[84] For Kurth, the question about space is equally a question about the image. Neither in his review nor in subsequent writings does Adorno acknowledge the important section on the '*Bewegungsbild*', the dynamic image. Though music offers no 'visual image', its 'dynamic sequence' gives rise to an '"image".' Music's 'after-image' – a term borrowed from eidetic psychology – pertains to the phenomena of high and low, line and rhythm. Counterpoint is at once harmonic and rhythmic. The musical work is no mere succession of atomised notes.[85] The emphasis of '*Gestalt* psychology' upon the whole makes *its* theoretical application to music appropriate. It is this whole, even or especially as a negative whole, that *adheres* music to space. The work of music constitutes a '"simultaneous" dynamic image'. It is experienced as one, at once, in an 'instant [*Augenblick*]'. And yet, the work is temporal. Kurth conceives of a 'contradiction [*Widerspruch*] of the temporal and non-temporal unity'.[86] He aligns the *Augenblick* with the non-temporal. Despite his interest in inter-disciplinary education, it is surely unlikely that Kurth had read the recently published *Being and Time*. For Heidegger, the '*Augenblick*' was not the 'now' but 'an authentic Present [*Gegenwart*] or waiting-towards [*Gegen-wart*]' that 'permits us *to encounter for the first time* what can be "in a time"'.[87] Equally contrary to Bergson's 'crass dichotomy', Kurth's '*Widerspruch*' *acknowledged* the contradiction of musical time.

The dynamic image is constitutive of the work of modern music. The simultaneity of this image is its (by no means *authentic*) *Augenblick*. Adorno's thesis on music and the 'graphic arts' can be read as a historical materialist radicalisation of Kurth. Music's tendency toward the image is inseparable from, though not identical with, the imagistic character of its emergence.[88] The modern musical work effectuates a quasi-simultaneous image. Adorno hears in contemporary music a peculiar repetition, a mimesis, of the image. Its temporal character is no longer immanent to the intrinsic musical language, but is instead imposed on to it extrinsically:

> To this extent [the new music] obeys the romantic principle against which it is rebelling, by pursuing the spatialisation of time in a merely fictitious [*fiktiv*] manner, treating time without consideration, as if it were space, with all the inconsistencies that characterise the magician's act.[89]

Non-temporalising music is not modern music. And yet, it is precisely here, in the most unlikely of places, that a certain resistance to detemporalisation is proposed. Adorno describes *Moses und Aron* as '*musica ficta*... elevated to a different plane [*aufgehoben*]'. The figurative image *has become* music: 'The pictorial aspect of music is now shifted on to the individual figures, as if the non-pictorial might result from their demise.'[90] This is the result of Schoenberg's 'constructivist' totality, a non-image absolute in music. It is not the chronometric measure that produces this anti-rhythm image, but rather the 'establishing [of] sound relationships vertically' and the neutralising of harmonic meaning in a relentless 'twelve-tone technique' ('The simplest way to describe the general effect is to say that the music is dissonant from the first bar to the last, but that it does not sound dissonant for a single second.').[91] Its static rhythm is a function of the static tonality. Against Adorno's literal reading, however (in order to concur with him), Schoenberg's 'timbre' is not always 'integrated into the construction'. In the burning bush scene, for example, the murmuring voices do not indicate any positive totality. There is both fragmentariness and becoming. As we shall see, *Moses* is fundamental to Nono's understanding of space. In his essay, 'Notes on Music-theatre Today' (1961), Nono refers to the burning bush scene in terms of its understanding of the intrinsic musical space and the dispersal of the chorus singers on stage: 'Schoenberg has to find a new spatial dimension of the tonal [*Raumdimension des Klanglichen*] and introduce an element whose focus until now has been centred on the orchestra and on the stage.'[92] Nono recalls Kurth – with the difference that Nono does not aim at any unity of the two musical spaces.

We may therefore speak of a spatialising of time that temporalises, or a temporalising mimesis of detemporalisation (reification). Since music is the 'art of time', the issue of 'detemporalisation' remains acute with respect to music. The ageing of the new music is somehow symptomatic of the ageing of the world – perhaps this is why half of Adorno's writings are devoted to the medium.

Nono's mimesis

Adorno's critique of *Moses und Aron* must be understood in relation to his engagement with the Darmstadt summer courses. This engagement is preoccupied with the question of musical time and space by way of a series of binaries: becoming and stasis; young and old; and music and painting. An initial refusal of the younger generation of composers (including Boulez, Stockhausen and Nono) is followed by a more positive engagement from around 1957 onwards. 'On the Relationship Between Music and Painting Today' (c.1950) and 'The Aging of the New Music [*Das Altern der Neuen Musik*]' (1955–56) belong to the former position, whereas 'Vers une musique informelle' (1961), 'The Relevance of Wagner for Today' and 'Some Relationships Between Music and Painting' (1965) belong to the latter. Crucially, Adorno's re-evaluation stems from a *re-evaluation of the status of space in the new music*. An account of this repositioning, in parallel to his repositioning of Wagner, can elucidate Adorno's thesis on the two spheres of music, and hence the foregoing notion of musical experience as constituting a dialectical 'image'.

One of the charges levelled by 'The Aging of the New Music' was the confusion of preformed material with musical experience. This criticism was both philosophical and music-critical in nature. In philosophical terms, if the conception is too determinate – worked out in advance – then the work is over before judgement (critical listening) has been called upon. As has been said, free judgement not only takes time but is equally a form of temporalisation. Adorno connects this aesthetic principle to music in particular. He discerns in both the later Webern and the young composers the attempt to outdo Schoenberg in the sphere of development and rhythm, leading to total or integral serialism (the organisation of all parameters using this principle). But in negating all previous musical forms – including thematic development and variation – they are alleged to have negated temporalisation altogether. Adorno pushes the two critiques, philosophical and musical, together: non-temporalisation is a consequence of the over-reliance upon preformed material. This pre-war tendency has continued into the music of the youth, whose music is accordingly not new but old: 'young people no longer trust in their youth'.[93] Since Adorno addresses 'the new music' as such, there are two levels of ageing: that of the individual works and that of the conception of music on which they rely. New music itself is 'falling into contradiction with its own idea'.[94]

The problem of music is the problem of time. This is why Adorno focuses on forms of development and, moreover, on the relationship between 'the temporal art of music' and thc 'spatial art of painting'.[95] The two essays on this relationship illuminate the adjustment in Adorno's stance on space in the new music. In the earlier texts, Adorno held that new music had slipped into a pastiche of modern painting, resulting in a form of stasis. Adorno had in mind the visual and spatial senses of 'drawing up' the composition – including latter-day pointillism, of which Nono's *Polifonica–Monodia–Ritmica* (1950) remained an example. The reference of musical 'pointillism' to painting was, ever since Schoenberg's *Klangfarbenmelodie*, explicit. Reginald Smith Brindle thus comments upon the 'almost static atmosphere' of the opening to *Polifonica*. But in Adorno's thinking at this time, the 'static' is solely pejorative:

> The basis of this serialism is a static idea of music: the precise correspondences and equivalences that total rationalization requires are founded on the presupposition that the identical element that recurs in music is indeed actually equivalent, as it would be in a schematic spatial representation.[96]

Nono is included among the *enfants terribles* in Adorno's contemporaneous essay 'New Music Today' (1955) – they include 'Boulez in France, Stockhausen in Germany, and Maderna and Nono in Italy. Objective construction is now supposed to encapsulate all elements mathematically, in particular rhythmic ones; the aim, to put it drastically, is the liquidation of composition in each composition.'[97] The sense that Adorno was not ready to *listen* to the young generation was nevertheless concretised in a response by Heinz-Klaus Metzger, the theorist of the young composers – which, appropriately enough, appeared in the 'Young Composers' issue of their journal, *Die Reihe*. Its title, '*Das Altern der Philosophie der Neuen Musik*' (The Ageing of the Philosophy of New Music, 1958) fuses Adorno's titles, '*Philosopie der Neuen Musik*' and '*Das Altern der Neuen Music*'. Metzger accuses Adorno of not keeping pace with the concept of new musical material in a manner that Adorno's own philosophy of new music would demand. Adorno was to take Metzger's critique to heart, and by 1961 would confess that 'informal music' is but an expression for 'Metzger's term – an *a-serial* music'.[98] The reason why Adorno takes Metzger seriously is that they share an identification of musical time as being the crux of the matter. But Metzger takes Adorno to task on his conflation of space with stasis, and stasis with non-temporalisation. The performance can remain experientially non-identical to the score whilst at the same time borrowing something distinctively spatial from it. Metzger cites Adorno's own phrase only to turn it against its author: 'There are indeed cases in present-day production in which a "schematic spatial presentation" takes on an unusual value.'[99] This somewhat vague 'unusual value' finds particular meaning, going beyond Metzger's own musical preferences, in *Il canto sospeso* (1956).

At best, Adorno may have heard recorded extracts of *Il canto sospeso* in 1957, when Stockhausen gave the '*Musik und Sprache*' lecture that Nono took to have misrepresented his work. This would account for Adorno's acquaintance with at least its programme. For the reference to *Il canto sospeso* is unmistakable from the 'Vienna' essay of 1960:

> The fact that [the most recent composers] compose settings for revolutionary texts, the diaries of anti-fascists under sentence of death, or surrealist shock verses, is appropriate to the music, just as the dream-like convulsions of [Schoenberg's] *Erwartung* can be said to fit what is admittedly a comparatively harmless text.[100]

On the surface, Adorno places little importance here upon the programmatic content and context of *Il canto sospeso*. The 'sung' letters, written by anti-fascists facing execution, are valuable as examples of expression rather than for their confrontation of the listener with the gravity of the historical event. But Adorno's emphasis on expression is by no means dismissive of the work's historical significance. Expression names the artwork's mimetic resistance to a reified society. Being mimetic, the artwork is non-identical, and to that extent constitutes an act of resistance to the identical – including the perpetuation of fascism. Expression and mimesis are two of the most important categories of *Aesthetic Theory*. Art 'is modern art through its mimesis of the hardened and alienated'.[101] Mimesis and expression are not thereby behavioural or psychological categories but rather social and even ontological ones. The artwork embodies a dialectic of rational construction and mimetic expression.[102] Again, Benjamin is a crucial source: in texts dating from the 1930s, Benjamin defined mimesis as original appropriation, a prototype being child development.[103] Mimesis is the freedom of becoming where reification is the imposition of stasis, mirroring the above opposition between youth and aging in Adorno's music criticism. Given the proximity of mimesis and expression, the importance of Adorno's *expression* of waiting in vain should not be underestimated.

If Adorno heard fragments of voices and texts from *Il canto sospeso*, he would not have heard its instrumental sections. Yet these sections both anticipate and respond to Adorno's concerns about the new music. The fourth part follows the concluding line of the third, falling into silence: 'Your son is leaving, he will not hear the bells of freedom....' Strings enter with extremely long durational values. Pre-empting sentimentality, however, small instrumental groups including percussion abruptly interrupt those strings. These interruptions serve to heighten the 'static' character. We can say that the work is simultaneously an exponent of pointillism, each instrument sounding only few notes before passing on to the next, and an *Aufhebung* of pointillism, in that Nono's polarisation leads to a paradoxically moving stasis. A sense of unfolding is eked out (not the escape from time, as Stockhausen claimed of his own music), anticipating Nono's later use of the fermata. What we experience, therefore, is not an aging of the new music, but rather a mimesis – and hence becoming – of that aging, a microcosm of broader, social reification. In response to the 'detemporalisation of time', a work like *Il canto sospeso* presents a 'temporalisation of detemporalisation'. Not only are Adorno's complaints about the crossover from technique to experience misplaced, but the response is anticipated: the 'mimesis of the hardened and alienated'. Becoming – in other words, temporalisation – may be achieved as mimetic stasis, the temporalisation through space suggested by the same Metzger whose 'a-serial' music would later be endorsed by Adorno.

The integral serialism of *Il canto sospeso* would already guarantee its failure in Adorno's theory (recalling his critique of *Moses*). Yet Adorno may have underestimated Nono's inventive use of the technique – the composer used the all-interval 'wedge' series, 'generated by jumping between chromatic scales in opposite directions from a nodal pitch'. 'From such raw materials', David Osmond-Smith notes, Nono 'could stamp out the shapes – often bristlingly architectonic – to which his immersion in the visual abstraction of post-war painting made him feel akin' (the reference is surely to Nono's comrade, Emilio Vedova).[104] The 'elementary' nature of Nono's material gave him more freedom rather than less, since there was no pretence towards mystical games whose answer remained forever hidden. Nono transcends the preformed row through systematic interruption (*sospeso* means both 'suspended' and 'interrupted'), meaning that the interruption is not itself preformed but rather, in Adorno's terms, mimetic. 'Even back then', Nono later explained, 'I was not writing what the press called totally organised music…[C]omposing was never for me merely the concretisation of preformed structures. Improvisatory moments always played a part; I left decisions open until the last instant.'[105]

We recall that Adorno eventually acknowledged the mimetic approach to painting in his revised stance on Wagner. *In Search of Wagner* cited the transformation scene of *Parsifal*: 'You see, my son, time here becomes space.'[106] But whereas this had previously signified reification, the post-war Adorno takes this 'spatialising' tendency to have productive possibilities:

> In the most recent music, which draws so near to painting and the graphic arts, the trend toward the static becomes quite marked – here, too, something is fully realized that Wagner had envisioned earlier…Colour itself became architectonic…[as] a new kind of construction.[107]

In the context of three contemporaneous Darmstadt talks on 'The Function of Colour in Music', Adorno's remark about Wagner invokes a new possibility in new musical spatialisation. This double possibility of music is signalled in 'On Some Relationships between Music and Painting': 'The convergence of music and painting…opens up the possibility of crass infantilism, at least in music; it is possible to stave off this element only to the extent that it reflects it within itself, as an expression of decay, and composes it out, so to speak.'[108] However negatively, Adorno here acknowledges the productive possibility of the spatial in music – if we take 'expression' in Adorno's full sense of the term. Against his previous verdict, Adorno now considers the productive aspects of music's spatiality in terms of colour and *écriture*.

In spite of their somewhat awkward personal relationship, an historical and philological affinity between Adorno and Nono can be shown in relation to Lukács' concept of reification. Looking back on the period, Nono's student Helmut Lachenmann commented that it was 'in a work like *Il canto sospeso* that one can see the beginnings of the gap – now a gulf – between composers like Stockhausen and Nono'. Lachenmann recalled that his teacher had been accused of giving up on the avant-gardist path: 'as a West German composer put it in 1960…Nono had "ground to a halt"'.[109] But this 'grinding to a halt' is not pejorative for Lachenmann:

> Structural purification of a new, terse expressiveness which is almost archaic in quality, and thus liberated from its conventional reification – this was what Nono had 'ground to a halt' in. Or, perhaps one should say…Nono in the late fifties had remained clinging to a rough, inhospitable landscape of naked signs from which others were striving to find their way to more homely surroundings – forwards, backwards or sideways…In those days Nono did not move further on – he went deeper.

Nono's student does not refer to wilfully mystical depth here. Rather, 'the processes of structuring and differentiation were ultimately determined by their function of driving music into *space*'.[110] Such driving of music into space became a temporalisation *through* space. Lachenmann confirms that his concept of reification derives from Lukács.[111] In a line that characterises 'On the Fetish-Character' and 'The Aging of the New Music', the commodity form, stated Lukács, 'degrades time to the dimension of space'.[112] Adorno changed his verdict on the relation between the arts of time and space, now suggesting that music may paradoxically find its salvation in painting, without being painting. Something of this relation can be sensed in Adorno's use of the term *informel*, a movement in post-war painting throughout Europe, including Adorno's Frankfurt.[113]

In a conversation about Nono, Metzger and Rainer Riehn noted in 2003 that Helmut Lachenmann 'has often asked us why [Theodor] Adorno never discussed Nono'. Riehn reflects that Lachenmann is mistaken, insofar as Adorno was 'forcefully engaged' with [Nono's] *Varianti* (1957), which he mentioned publicly in 1966. The talks in question are 'The Function of Colour in Music'. The context of the reference to Nono is once again the relationship between music and painting, specifically colour. Adorno recalls the *Varianti* in relation to his violinist friend Rudolf Kolisch and his 'crisis of strings' thesis (Kolisch in fact commissioned and performed the *Varianti*).[114] Adorno and Kolisch were taken with Nono's deconstruction of the violin's 'beautiful tone' and his expansion of its possible timbres. Together with the other, later essays, these lectures display Adorno's tentatively new position on music's relationship to painting. Referring to the 1966 lectures, musicologist Alistair Williams has spoken of 'Adorno's conviction that sound colour becomes a crucial part of structure when music, as he puts it, has "cut its connecting cables" (*Verbindungsdrähte*), by which he means when it has dispensed with established methods of organizing components such as pitch and rhythm.'[115] Frustratingly, Adorno does not explicitly identify this expanded conception of form as a valid response to the problem of stasis, even though stasis is explicitly related to painting in the previous texts. The non-connection of colour to time is surprising given that, as Williams notes, Adorno's lectures were motivated by György Ligeti's essay 'Form in the New Music' (1966), in which the new form is defined as 'the product of an imaginary spatialisation of the temporal process', and that Ligeti's *Atmosphères* (1961), a work with profound temporal implications, appears in Adorno's 'Function of Colour' talks.[116]

Nono's late fermata

That which has been regarded as a 'late turn' in Nono concerns his musical politics: 'I had the need to think anew my whole work and my whole existence as a musician today and as an intellectual in this society, to discover new possibilities of knowledge and creation.'[117] Nono had become wary of the 'ideological' and had avowedly turned 'inwards'. But Osmond-Smith reminds us that Nono's work of the 1980s onwards 'continued to resonate with the perception that social evolution is achieved by subverting subjective priorities'.[118] The continuation of a theme from *Il canto sospeso* can be traced to the late work, concerning the ongoing problem of temporalisation and spatialisation.

The work for string quartet, *Fragmente-Stille* (1981) marked the beginning of the 'new Luigi Nono'. The surprisingly new feature was its fragility – a departure from the strident theatrical-political works of the 1960s and 70s. But this was a strident fragility. The way in which Nono invited the musicians to determine the length of each fermata, for instance, was new – or rather, said the detractors, *old*: a return to subjectivist expression. But this was, to use Lachenmann's phrase, a 'terse expressiveness'. The integration of material is the secret of the fermata in Nono's late work. The fermata is not ornamental but rather is of the rhythm itself – in the performers' production of musical time. Here lies the affinity to *Il canto sospeso*. Nono's fermata – the term comes from the Latin *firmare*, to stop – is a coming-to-a-standstill. In their interpretation of *Fragmente-Stille*, Nono asked the Arditti Quartet to play the fermatas ever longer.[119] At stake was not contemplative slowness but rather a quasi-spatial immersion. The composer now reversed the insight from his 'Notes on Music-theatre' essay: the 'use of a non-geometrised space... runs up against the dissolution of normal time, of the time of narration and of visualization'.[120] This is not an opposition of chronometric time to musical time, however. There remains a distant pulse to *Prometeo*, which employs traditional measure. Adorno's single concrete suggestion for an 'informal music' concerned a distancing of 'pulse', which 'could augment rhythmic flexibility to a degree as yet undreamed of.'[121] The obscure relationship of chronometric time to musical time is exaggerated in Nono's late work, giving rise to Adorno's 'passage of time that is holding its breath'. Nono's major late work, *Prometeo*, involved a collaboration with the Venetian philosopher Massimo Cacciari. Cacciari compiled the libretto from fragments of Hesiod, Hölderlin, Benjamin and himself. In a conversation reproduced for the 1984 programme, Nono and Cacciari raise the issues of space and the image in relation to music. Music, Cacciari suggests, proposes a certain resistance to the image amidst 'a civilization placed under the sign of the *ideîn*, of knowledge envisaged with *ideîn*'.[122] The unidirectional performance, centring attention upon the stage and performer, aims at an identification of an image by means of music, not in spite of it. But *Prometeo* has no single group of soloists to focus upon, no narrative action. There is a compulsion towards the invitation of the music to listen rather than to look. But this thought invites the same criticism that can be made of Adorno's remark in *Composing for the Films*. To pit listening against sight is to conceive of an autonomy of the individual senses. But music is already imagistic. To listen is to see, though not in an equivalent manner.[123] Nono and Cacciari align listening to the abstract and sight to representation. As with Adorno, language is the privilege of music. Only images are forbidden. Perhaps *Prometeo* constitutes a peculiar abstraction of its own, however. The fragmentary figurations of *Prometeo* – of the texts, the music, the text-music – are absorbed into its spatial singularity. Indeterminacy is determined where distraction is concentrated. This absorption, recalling Adorno's 'adherence' of inner to outer musical space, constitutes both an acknowledgement of the image and a promise to 'go beyond' it.

In their conversation Nono and Cacciari respond with a notion of sound that initially comes close to the Stockhausen's mysticism. Cacciari is aware that in considering how music might oppose the image, he must paradoxically think of it, recalling Adorno, in terms of colour. Composers like Scriabin lapsed into a 'symbolic system'. What, wonders Cacciari, would a non-symbolic, non-representational music be like? Cacciari steers his friend away from an overly empirical response, a 'natural' idea of sound-colour, towards two alternatives: 'silence' and 'multiple geometry'.[124] Nono is undoubtedly interested in these alternatives. Where the latter is concerned, *Prometeo* offers a 'mobile sound' of 'multi-directional listening'. As we have seen, Nono believes that the spatial characteristics cannot be separated from the temporal ones. But Cacciari takes this correspondence more literally than does the composer. In a sense, *Prometeo* eludes Cacciari's theoretical grasp on this point, something that might be explained by Nono's background in the Darmstadt debates.[125]

Turning around the dialectical image

For Benjamin, the 'image is dialectics at a standstill'. The 'genuine' dialectical image appears in a 'flash...suddenly emergent'.[126] In the 'Theses on the Philosophy of History' (1940), Benjamin claims that the dialectical image of history 'flashes up at the moment [*Augenblick*] of its recognisability, and is never seen again'.[127] But unlike the moment, the image, when understood in its intrinsic relation to space, reminds us that detemporalisation endures, as empty time. And it is this sense of stasis that *Prometeo* mimetically incorporates so as to wait upon another time. The *Augenblick* inheres in the fermata. This *Augenblick* may be understood in Benjamin's sense, to the extent that it is a mimesis of mythic commodity time. But it is also to be understood in Heidegger's sense, in that another temporality is proposed by way of its temporalising. Adorno had questioned Benjamin's Jungian and Platonic 'dream image' of the future, 'as Utopia'.[128] The question of *what* the dialectical image gives rise to is, in one sense, the problem of Bergson, another important source for the later Benjamin. The 'ur-phenomenon' is not originary in the sense of Heidegger's 'temporalising'. Heidegger's *Augenblick* is the disclosing of possibility out of, and into, the facticity of history. By contrast, that which originates in Benjamin's *Augenblick* is 'the image of history in itself.'[129] For, in 'the dialectical image, what has been within a particular epoch is *always, simultaneously,* "what has been from time immemorial".'[130] At this level of Benjamin's thought, the image is not progressive in any Kantian or Hegelian sense, but rather 'simultaneously' mythical. The 'immemorial' is eternal, but not as transcendent of the finite. Its infinity must instead be thought of in terms of the mythic repetition of a concrete singularity. This repetition is occasioned by, and gives rise to, history. It is this conjunction of mythic time with historical time that Benjamin tentatively formulates in the most ambitious 'convolute' of the *Arcades Project*: 'On the Theory of Knowledge, Theory of Progress'. Can a phenomenon be historically singular and immemorial? Perhaps it is the *Augenblick* itself, in excess of itself: 'What is "always the same thing" is not the event but the newness of the event, the shock with which it eventuates.'[131] Benjamin's 'imagistic' *Augenblick* marks a vertical instant *in* historical time, and remains to this extent chronometrically overdetermined. At the same time, the dialectical image is not sufficiently determined chronometrically. For Benjamin no longer acknowledges, as he did in the *Trauerspiel* book, that the chronometric tends towards the imagistic. Benjamin had proposed that the baroque 'slow procession' constituted a 'choreographic' rendering of time.

The foregoing account has attempted to elucidate the meaning of an expression of waiting in vain. The mimesis of detemporalisation suggests a form of waiting *upon*. Its protest against a reified totality, and its acknowledgement of alternative political spaces, suggests a waiting *for*. Adorno's own example of this expression was Berg's music drama. Nono departs from Berg's paradigm of waiting in that the rhythm of the Second Viennese School is, as Stockhausen observed, premised upon a critique of verticality in harmony and cadence – it is those unresolved chords that Adorno has in mind when he speaks of an expression of waiting in vain in *Wozzeck* and *Lulu*. In the post-war avant-garde, the horizontal, explicitly temporal dimension of music comes to be addressed by Nono and others. And yet, even this tendency follows in the spirit of Berg: in his 1929 essay on *Wozzeck*, Adorno suggests that Berg articulates Büchner's words in a tragic-ironic opposition to words, so as to bring out the contemporaneity of hope. The 'reflection [*Reflex*]' of this '*Trauerspiel*' is 'clouded in the light of tragic irony'. Perhaps Adorno's notion of a music that 'counts the minutes to death' already anticipates Nono's late fermata.[132] For there remains, of necessity, a tragic-ironic moment in the mimesis of detemporalisation. Hence, the 'Fetish Character' essay closes with a remark that pits stasis against becoming, but not as an unresolvable antinomy:

> As little as regressive listening is a symptom of progress in the consciousness of freedom, it could suddenly turn around in art, in unity with society, should it ever leave the road of the always identical.[133]

There is an inner logic of mimesis here. The 'turn around [*umzuspringen*]' happens 'suddenly', out of regressive listening. Something other than music is given rise to, 'in unity with' a society to come.

4
Invincible in the Wasteland? Music, Space and Utopia

Negativity in Cacciari and Adorno

The 'spatial' temporalisation of *Prometeo* considered in the previous chapter cannot be separated from its spatial environment. Where both 'spheres of music' are concerned, this environment is today pre-eminently urban. During the 1970s, Massimo Cacciari engaged with some of the classical theoretical reflections on the metropolis within the German sociology of the first third of the twentieth century. In this research, Cacciari conceived of an 'architecture of nihilism' as constituting the 'tragic' acknowledgement of and resistance to the capitalist 'project'.[1] Although Nono's music may be said to elude his philosophical grasp, much of Cacciari's thought about architecture proves to be useful in understanding that music, as will be shown. Furthermore, Cacciari's Nietzschean research into German sociology allows for a fruitful dialogue with Adorno and with Heidegger – even though Cacciari himself only discusses the latter writer explicitly. Specifically, the category of the tragic is at stake in the temporal-musical mimesis discussed above, just as it will be at stake in the spatial-architectural mimesis outlined below. Cacciari was well aware of the musical character of the architectural – increasingly, perhaps, through his conversations and collaborations with Nono.[2] Yet Cacciari did not explicitly call upon his earlier research when writing about and for Nono in the 1980s. Nor did he draw upon a long-standing, though marginal literature on 'music and space'. Nono's late work can nevertheless be understood as a new response to the problems raised by Cacciari, whose architectural paradigm was limited to the epoch of those classic reflections. It will be suggested in what follows that *Prometeo* asks a question of the meaning of place in relation to notions of utopia. This was always a part of its programme – the figure of Prometheus representing both the tragedy of humanity and the possibility of overcoming the tragedy. The text, compiled by Cacciari, refers to Benjamin's 'weak messianic force' as a name for this possibility. But the current interpretation departs from existing interpretations of *Prometeo*, including Cacciari's. In spite of the recognition of space as being central to this work, no attempt has been made to situate this concern within the problematic of modernity or capitalism. If the time of modernity impinges upon its space, and vice versa, then *Prometeo* can be said to express this double impingement. An expression of waiting in vain, *Prometeo* equally constitutes a practical corrective to Adorno's conception. A productively tragic-mimetic waiting confronts the vanity of waiting in vain.

Cacciari's reflections on 'non-dwelling' come close to Adorno's critique of origins – including the mythic home that would be utopia once over. Adorno attributes this archaism to Heidegger, with justification. But one irony of 'Adorno and Heidegger' is that it is the latter thinker who systematically confronts the metaphysics that underpins the utopian concept of place: the will to identity from absolute difference. Moreover, it is possible that, in spite of his idea of natural history, Adorno participates in this 'ontotheological' schema. For his part, Heidegger must rely upon a history of metaphysics that does not acknowledge *its* possibly ontotheological ruse. Both Heidegger and the later ('Heideggerian') Cacciari risk a certain valorisation of waiting without the awaited – an open waiting that closes in on itself and which invites those regressive infinities associated (above) with Adorno. A revised idea of natural history might nevertheless be directed against the latent pessimism of Cacciari's tragic negativity – if, that is, the post-Hegelianism of Adorno's Promethean tragic is equally emphasised.

The structure of this chapter breaks down into four parts. The first will reconstruct Cacciari's research into the metropolis and tragic negativity in order to suggest that the question of negation is already implicated into the questions of place and utopia. This will have recourse to other philosophies of the tragic. Cacciari's tragic negativity and Adorno's negative dialectic can each be viewed as productive forms of mimesis. Second, as something of an *intermezzo*, the marginal yet significant literature of music and space will be reconstructed in order to introduce an affinity between the concepts of music, space and utopia. Thirdly, Adorno's concept of aesthetic autonomy will be read according to the preceding narratives in order to stress the spatial permutations of art. This critique will be mounted from the standpoint of Nono – who, fourthly, will propose an alternative understanding of the relationship between art, space and politics.

The metropolis and tragic negativity

Cacciari's essay 'Metropolis' takes Simmel's 'The Metropolis and Mental Life' (1903) as its point of departure. The metropolis is 'a determinant moment of modern existence'. The metropolis differs decisively from the city. It is 'the phase, or the problem, of the rationalisation of all social relations, which follows that of the rationalisation of the relations of production.' These rationalisations cannot do without the metropolis – 'there is an objective reason' for it, as the singular expression of economic, political and social space.[3] A productive tension pervades Cacciari's concept of the metropolis. On the one hand, it is the real capitalist metropolis. On the other hand, the metropolis is an ideal – the progressive yet impossible realisation of what Cacciari's colleague Manfredo Tafuri called, in *Architecture and Utopia* (1973) the 'project'. Cacciari partly follows Tafuri's critique of the ideological syntheses manifested in the architectural projects of the enlightenment (in France, England and the USA).[4] He does not, however, follow Tafuri's tendency to conflate the avant-garde with the project *tout court*. Cacciari initially seeks to expose the ideological implications of Simmel. The end of the nineteenth century gave rise to an ideal of *Aufklärung* in Germany – by way of a restoration of Kant and Goethe – which was bound to notions of individual cultivation or *Bildung*. 'The Metropolis and Mental Life' is a thesis on individuation in the metropolis: the 'intellectualisation [*Vergeistigung*]' of 'mental life [*Geistesleben*]'. According to Simmel, the 'intellect [*Verstand*]' is 'intensified' as a 'protective organ' against the stimulation of 'nervous life [*Nervenleben*]'.[5] Nervous stimulation threatens to 'uproot' the individual (the Kantian synthesis of the sensuous manifold is clear). The resulting 'reserve... assures the individual of a type and degree of personal freedom to which there is no analogy in other circumstances [because] the individual gains a freedom of movement'.[6] Cacciari highlights the 'synthesis' of Simmel's closing remark: 'it is not our task to complain or condone, but only to understand'.[7] For Cacciari, the synthesis and totality of the metropolis, an aggregate of free individuals (of seemingly no particular class) 'recuperates the value of community... in order to reaffirm it in society'.[8] This leads to the second aspect of Simmel's ideology. The metropolis is in reality a perpetually becoming ideal, or a regulative idea. It simultaneously posits and proscribes its utopia, in bad faith. Following Nietzsche's critique of metaphysics, Cacciari suggests that the ideal of the metropolis is willed by, and as, the real metropolis.[9]

For Simmel, the intellect names the productive schematism of 'continuous "innovation"'. But as Cacciari observes, the life of the nerves and the intellect must stand in a reciprocal relationship, meaning that the intellect and not only intuition risks passivity: 'The *Nervenleben* is a *condition* of the intellect – an internal condition of its power, its dominion, completely integrated within it.' For the 'life of the nerves' is complicit in the reproduction of the commodity form and its attendant relations of production in the metropolis. Cacciari is at one with Adorno here, who describes this reciprocal movement in terms of memory and forgetting. For Simmel, this process 'dissolves individuality into the current of impressions and reintegrates these, precisely by virtue of their constitution, into the overall process of *Vergeistigung*.'[10] As the manifestation of the convergence between *Vergeistigung* and the exchange process, the metropolis naturalises estranged relations of production (or, relations that reproduce estrangement). The metropolis represents itself as place, as the familiar home promised in its name: 'mother-city'. The real-ideal synthesises the contradiction that individuation based upon exchange relations does not produce the good life of the *polis*, but rather blocks it. The metropolis is the phantasmagoria of home, 'the futility of the search for the *unicum*'.[11] Cacciari's critique of the '*unicum*' can be understood according to his ambitious genealogy of modernity. Cacciari is initially careful not to subsume Kant (on whom he wrote his doctoral thesis) into the narrative of *Vergeistigung*. He is aware of this tradition through the figure of Schiller, whom he sharply distinguishes from Schiller's contemporary, Goethe. Schiller represents not only the will to identity but also a determination of that will *as* infinite longing. Novalis famously declared that 'philosophy is really homesickness, an urge to be at home everywhere'.[12] In light of Cacciari's thesis, Novalis simultaneously expresses the problem of modernity *and* its solution. Philosophy is always in danger of being a form of consolation, at least so long as philosophy is understood as an autonomous mode of reflective existence, a utopia of its own making. The 'urge to be at home everywhere' determines 'home' *as* 'everywhere' and, so long as it remains philosophical, nowhere. If longing is infinite then utopia is placed beyond this world. The question of music holds a privileged position in this romantic metaphysics.

Having criticised Simmel the liberal, Cacciari now credits him with having appropriated a Goethean-tragic approach to modernity:

> Simmel's most outstanding perception is his recognition of the most appropriate expression of such an ideology *in the form of negative thought*. If the blasé type fully reflects the structure of the Metropolis, it is not because he is fully consistent with it or because he is a mere

reflection of it, but rather because he understands it from the perspective of his own inability to go beyond it, that is, from the perspective of his own negated individuality.

The 'blasé' is an abstraction from use value: 'the money economy and the domination of the intellect stand in the closest relationship to one another. They have in common a purely matter-of-fact attitude in the treatment of persons and things.' As Cacciari puts it, the 'monetary economy formalises economic relations, just as the intellect formalises psychic relations and movements'.[13] The blasé-type is Robert Musil's *Man Without Qualities*. But 'negative thought' is the self-consciousness of this abstraction. And negative thought is tragic rather than dialectical. For it does not presume any gradual progress. That would be to repeat the ideology of *Vergeistigung* itself. It is here that tragic negativity can be contrasted with dialectical negativity. This contrast has been understood as a mythic, pessimistic tragic repetition as versus the historical and progressive understanding of the tragic. But this opposition is complicated for two reasons. Firstly, Cacciari's tragic negativity is already historical, or is at least a productive understanding of the tragic. Secondly, Adorno's historical conception of negation comes close to – and must even coincide with – the tragic moment of the dialectic itself.

What is Cacciari's concept of negation? In the essay 'On the German Sociology of the City at the Turn of the Century', Cacciari draws out the negative thought of Simmel, whom he now situates in relation to Max Weber. Weber's critique of Tönnies' nostalgic 'Community and Society' (1887) is read against the backdrop of *Thus Spoke Zarathustra* (1882). Although Weber's 'The City' comes much later (1911–13), Cacciari draws upon Weber's latent Nietzscheanism.[14] Weber had confronted the dominant metaphysical assumptions of the *Geisteswissenschäfte* – of, notably, the Baden neo-Kantian historian Friedrich Rickert.[15] A crisis in the cultural sciences arose from the question of their metaphysical grounding. For Rickert, a regulative horizon of truth could be assumed to validate and unify the science of history. But for an anti-metaphysician such as Weber, this assumption remained merely an assumption. Weber attributed an ensuing epistemic crisis to the withering of the theological presuppositions of that metaphysics.[16] 'Disenchantment' arose from the tragedy that rationalisation by science leads to the impotence of that science.[17] Weber's response was the attempted 'value free [*wertfrei*]' perspective. This does not mean a relinquishment of the problem of value – as in Simmel's 'it is not our task to complain or to condone'. Cacciari's imagined dialogue between Simmel and Weber instead proposes an *active* nihilism: 'it is precisely this tragic, value free character of the negative that most accurately expresses the form and function of the metropolis'.[18]

The value-free perspective has three moments: (1) A self-consciousness of the historical conditions of the cultural sciences.[19] (2) A 'Goethean' hypothesis of the 'ideal-type', which is 'formed':

> by the one-sided accentuation of one or more points of view and by the synthesis of a great many diffuse, discrete, more or less present and occasionally absent concrete individual phenomena, which are arranged according to those one-sidedly emphasised viewpoints into a unified *analytical* construct. In its conceptual purity, this mental construct cannot be found anywhere in reality. It is a *utopia*.[20]

Weber's self-conscious disenchantment is exhibited in this tragic-ironic reference to 'utopia'. And yet, the ideal-type aims at knowledge, and is thus grounded in a positive *evaluation* of 'enlightenment'. The parallel to Nietzsche's *Genealogy* is clear. The ideal-type acknowledges a tendency, and in so doing challenges it, opposing it with another possibility – hence, revaluation through evaluation.[21] The ideal-type is a productive mimesis. The value-free perspective is the productive mimesis of scientific objectivity. This tragic reversal in the meaning of utopia, which Weber merely hints at, is a reversal of the contemporaneous, classicist interpretations of Goethe. Meinecke and others interpret the Goethean trope of contradiction (in *Elective Affinities*) as 'at once problem and solution, question and answer, lack and fulfilment ... from the perspective of the Schillerian utopia'. Conversely, Nietzsche and Weber recognise that 'in Goethe the tragedy is the impossible utopia of the artistic representation's total ascendancy over modern social relations'.[22] In Adorno's terms: modern art is semblance as dissonance. Finally, (3) Weber foregrounds the 'commitment' and 'character' of the scientist, as a 'heroic' calling.[23] The three moments of the value free perspective share the characteristic of *distance*. According to Löwith, 'What this doctrine demands is not the elimination of guiding "value ideas" and interests, but their objectification, so as to provide a basis for us to distance ourselves from them.'[24] This is the distance of the blasé-type, of Zarathustra. Distance is the freedom from and of value judgement. But not as negative, abstract freedom. The distancing gaze cannot lose sight of its object, just as the scientist cannot objectively relinquish the problem of value. Conversely, the distance of the gaze is produced in the re-valuation itself.[25] The concept of distancing promises to overcome an antithesis of immanence and transcendence. It is no coincidence that Adorno had Weber in mind when conceiving of his dissonant nominalism. Though distancing is most obviously imagined spatially, it is equally a temporal concept: 'dissonantly musical' waiting as the historical possibility of nearness, the awaited.

Book Three of *Zarathustra* provides Cacciari with a literal instance of tragic negation in the metropolis. Zarathustra finds himself outside of the '*Großstadt*'. A dwarf appears to him as 'the spirit of gravity':

> Everything that rises must fall – you hurl a stone high into the air, and it will strike you – yet this pessimism, at bottom, is characterised by an ideal of perfect equilibrium. This pessimism regarding the direction of life's movements is only the equilibrium and the fulfilment of Schopenhauer's nirvana, which we later find in *Parsifal*. This pessimism is countered by the idea of the eternal return.[26]

Like the dwarf, the ape mistakes the 'eternal return' for equilibrium. He urges Zarathustra to curse the metropolis and return to the mountains: 'Rather spit on the city's gate and turn back.'[27] For Cacciari, this moment refers to the nostalgic return proposed by Tönnies, criticised in 'The City'. Zarathustra 'instead, gazes a long time upon the Metropolis, and remains silent'. His silence is tragic in that there is knowledge in excess, in the acknowledging gaze: 'the tragic vision illuminates the destiny of the Metropolis.'[28] Zarathustra concurs with the blasé-type – 'there is nothing to make better, nothing to make worse' – but ultimately promises to go beyond him. Zarathustra neither remains at the city gate, nor does he return home. He does not *resent*: 'Where one can no longer love, one should – *pass by!*'[29] Zarathustra's perspective encompasses two moments: 'repeating' (in the acknowledging gaze) and 'going beyond' (in the excessive knowledge). Cacciari emphasises the historicity of Nietzsche's eternal return over its cosmological interpretations.

The conceptual pairs of progress and repetition, and history and fate, can be read into the contrasting interpretations of tragedy in modern philosophy – indeed, *as* the inception of modern philosophy itself.[30] Heroic resistance to the gods' power brings something of the gods' power to the mortals. For Benjamin, therefore, the tragic death is 'an ironic immortality'.[31] Human knowledge encompasses a finite limit that is acknowledged and experienced in its repetition. Divine knowledge is repeated in this appropriation, an appropriation of the power of recurrence itself. It is the meaning of this liminal repetition that is disputed in the philosophies of the tragic. For, the tragic is not necessarily pessimistic. The principle thinkers to conceive of the tragic as productive, Hegel and Nietzsche, are conventionally opposed – though in light of the discussion of *Aufhebung* in Chapter 2, an affinity should not be surprising. According to the Nietzsche, the nihilism of Zarathustra demands an awareness that 'repeats... as going beyond.' The 'going beyond' is the transgression of the tragic cycle.

Tragedy was one of the first models Hegel used to confront the antinomies of Kant and Fichte. In his essay *On the Scientific Ways of Treating Natural Law* (1802–3) Hegel displaced a negative concept of freedom, which situated the individual against abstract, universal law, with a positive, finite conception of freedom, as mediated in (or as) the 'absolute idea of ethical life [*Sittlichkeit*]'. According to Hegel:

> *Tragedy* consists in this, that ethical nature, in order not to become entangled with its inorganic nature, separates the latter from itself as a fate and opposes itself to it; and by acknowledging this fate in the struggle against it, ethical nature is reconciled with the divine being as the unity of both.

In Hegel's Hellenocentric schema, Greek tragedy is the historical emergence of the *notion* of spirit, since spirit is the self-consciousness of the contradiction of finite and infinite *as* contradiction. Modernity is thereafter the determinate unfolding of spirit. In more structural terms, the dialectic must *encompass* the tragic – though it is surely going too far to say, as Peter Szondi does, that for Hegel, 'the tragic and the dialectic coincide'.[32] Hegel and Nietzsche share a productive understanding of the tragic, against Schopenhauer. There is a promise of going beyond.[33] From either end of the nineteenth century, these thinkers are motivated, as Löwith knew, against the stasis of bourgeois society.[34]

Cacciari comes close to Benjamin's sketch for an interpretation of the later Nietzsche in the *Arcades Project*. Eternal recurrence is the time of novelty. Where Adorno tends to find only stasis and death in this repetition of the same, Benjamin finds a rupture of the new.[35] 'On eternal recurrence: "The great thought as a Medusa head: all the features of the world become motionless, a frozen death throe".'[36] Benjamin undoubtedly sees Nietzsche as a product of his age: 'The notion of eternal return appeared at a time when the bourgeoisie no longer dared count on the impending development of the system of production which they had set going.'[37] But if Benjamin were only interested in historicising Nietzsche, then he would not have included the following citation: 'we have created the weightiest thought – now *let us create the being for whom it is light and pleasing*!'[38]

Why does Cacciari go to Nietzsche and not to Benjamin's colleague, Adorno? Cacciari does 'not intend to go into a discussion of the various "critical theories".'[39] His early essay 'On the Genesis of Negative Thought' sought 'a rigorous systematisation of an anti-dialectical thought.'[40] Of course, Adorno shares Cacciari's aversion to synthesis. The 'anti-dialectics' of negative thought is comparable to the 'anti-system' of negative dialectics. Adorno comes close to Cacciari's Nietzschean reflections to the extent that he posits ideal-types as hypothetical extractions of historical tendencies. And like Cacciari, these ideals name certain limits that regulate the real – even though they cannot themselves be realised. Adorno's 'absolute commodity' is one such ideal-type.[41] Hence, Cacciari's formulations closely resemble the 'Fetish Character' essay:

> the whole system becomes clear: the *Nervenleben* corresponds to the continuous and relentlessly innovated transubstantiation of exchange value into use value – that is, it corresponds to the necessary instance in which exchange value becomes real value.[42]

Cacciari's 'transubstantiation' recalls the 'quid pro quo' of Marx and Adorno (a 'theological nicety'). Adorno and Cacciari each consider the real implications of this ideal, a limit that is experientially demarcated and raised to the level of self-consciousness in art.

Mimesis and rationality

For Adorno, 'mimesis' in art acknowledges and goes beyond a rational limit, manifested in the 'constructive' aspect of the work. 'Art is a stage in the process of what Max Weber called the disenchantment of the world, and it is entwined with rationalisation.'[43] Mimesis, like the tragic, thereby constitutes a productive repetition of the limit. Unlike in Cacciari however, mimesis and rationality are *themselves* dialectical limit concepts: 'The dialectic of these elements is similar to dialectical logic, in that each pole realises itself in the other, and not in some middle ground.' Thus, 'construction gains expression through coldness' – that is, through its non-expressive limit.[44] On the basis of the conceptual affinities between Adorno and Cacciari, and in the light of the philosophies of the tragic in Hegel and Nietzsche, Cacciari's 'negative thought' may not be so 'anti-dialectical' after all. Conversely, Adorno's concept of negation seems far from being neo-Kantian. Modern art, insofar as it is modern, must acknowledge and transgress limits. This is because, according to Adorno, the incessant rationality manifested in capitalist society renders most past forms of art obsolete once the rational limit that they resisted is fully developed. The acknowledgement of an advanced *ratio* appears in the mimetic repetition of the constructive limit in the most advanced art. As in the case of the demise of the tragic hero, there is no possibility of going beyond limits without acknowledging them momentarily. As 'Vers une musique informelle' makes clear, there can be no assumption that such limits *will indeed* be overcome. For, 'It is self-evident that nothing concerning art is self-evident anymore.'[45] This is crucial for understanding Adorno's negative dialectic. From the standpoint of experience, the dialectic faces a single limit, not a series of limits stretching into an expected future, since such limits only become acknowledged *as* limits *after* negating existing ones. There is no presumption of progress in Adorno's dialectic – no *Vergeistigung*.

Hegel had various ways of stating the progressive nature of spirit. The sociality of reason must be 'real', not 'abstract'. That there has been progress – that there has been a series of determinate negations – reveals the series to be inherently progressive. Each historical shape of consciousness manifests a *true* moment in the unfolding of world-spirit. For Adorno, this quasi-inductive approach cannot hold, given the course of recent history. It was suggested in Chapter 1 that this seeming disavowal of progress leads to the problem of positing. The problem of progress and (infinite) regress returns once again. For if it is the case that, in rejecting a progressive dialectic, Adorno unwittingly embraces a neo-Kantian infinite task, then this would lend a passive nihilistic meaning to his upholding of the *Bilderverbot*. That is to say, Adorno would thereby uphold the ban on *both* the representation *and* the presentation of utopia. He would idealise utopia as no-place ever, a 'never-place'. Adorno is partly saved from this fate by his idea of natural history. But in a passage from *Dialectic of Enlightenment*, Adorno and Horkheimer slip from the disavowal of concrete origins to a disavowal of concrete goals:

> The fact that – despite the fascist lies to the contrary – the concept of homeland [*Heimat*] is opposed to myth constitutes the innermost paradox of epic. Precipitated in the epic is the memory of an historical age on which nomadism gave way to settlement, the precondition of homeland. If the fixed order of property implicit in settlement is the source of human alienation, in which all homesickness and longing spring from a lost primal state, at the same time it is toward settlement

> and fixed property, on which alone the concept of homeland is based, that all longing and homesickness are directed. Novalis's definition according to which all philosophy is homesickness holds good only if this longing is not dissipated in the phantasm of a lost original state, but homeland, and nature itself, are pictured as something that have first to be wrested from myth.[46]

The origin – *Heimat* – is the goal. But Adorno and Horkheimer invite the reverse possibility: the goal is the origin, 'a lost primal state' from which 'longing spring[s]'. The concept of *Heimat* here arises from the experience of its loss. But what is lost was itself *Heimatlos*: nomadism, which Adorno and Horkheimer tend to determine as exile. A 'paradox' of *Heimat* and *Heimatlos* is sustained here. But this antinomy tends to synthesise its self-contradiction, in the most Kantian of ways, in its suggestion that *Heimat* is the unending longing of nomadism for settlement, settlement for nomadism, and so on, *ad infinitum*. Adorno wants to preserve a longing for home, as utopia. But it cannot be 'wrested from myth' because myth is itself the regressive, cyclical infinity of longing. Utopia is thereby idealised, as it is in Novalis. 'Nature' *remains* the unconditioned. At the same time, Adorno and Horkheimer posit nature *as* that which must be reconciled with history, as history's alienated other. This ontotheological schema is no more apparent than in Adorno's essay on Hölderlin.[47]

The disavowal of utopia is arguably connected to the absence of a phenomenology and politics of space in Adorno's writings. If utopia is no-place, then it can be placed in the present as little as it can be placed in the past or the future. Cacciari does not oppose this position, and in many respects repeats it. For Cacciari does not offer a positive utopia, here and now. Rather, following Nietzsche and Heidegger, he radicalises the problem, the negativity of *its* non-place, into the nihilism of *Vergeistigung* itself. It is here that an avowedly 'anti-dialectical' response becomes more promising than a 'dialectical' one. Cacciari suggests that there is a compulsion to consider the problem of space, since the existing social space is complicit with the passive nihilism generated by the 'project' itself. The tragic acknowledgement of this nihilism is the possibility of a new place.

Non-place and non-dwelling

Not unproblematically, Cacciari construes the problem of the metropolis as a problem *for* architecture. His exemplary architect of nihilism is Adolf Loos. In *Aesthetic Theory*, by contrast, Loos – who makes up most of the few references to architecture – stands for functionality over mimesis. Architecture cannot be autonomous:

> The purely constructed, strictly objective artwork, which ever since Adolf Loos has been the sworn enemy of everything artisanal, reverses into the artisanal by virtue of its mimesis of functional forms: Purposelessness without purpose becomes irony.[48]

Elsewhere, Adorno offers a more sympathetic view of Loos.[49] But for Cacciari, purposelessness without a purpose is ironic *and* tragic. Loos exposes the structural limits of *Vergeistigung*. Instead of 'dialectics', his multiple 'dialects' eschews the traditional syntheses – of modern and traditional, industrial and craft – associated with the contemporaneous *Werkbund* and *Werkstätte* architectural movements. The former presented the 'immediate use value' of handicraft as 'pure value corresponding to precise a priori forms, forms constituting artistic creativity.' Such forms purported to lie beyond exchange relations. The contradiction that their use value was in fact transubstantiated exchange value, and that one language is many, was suppressed: 'Use value, in its capitalist sense, has no "autonomous" quality to manifest.'[50] This claim to autonomy extends to, or from, the metropolis itself. The metropolis is valorised according to its boundaries, against what the metropolis is not. Under conditions of global capital, the metropolis now occupies a diffuse 'empire' (to borrow a category from Cacciari's erstwhile comrade). At the same time, the spatial and architectural specificity of the metropolis cannot be relinquished. The limit is once again real and ideal. The metropolis as place stands in contradiction with the exchange relations that reproduce it. This is because pure space is an ideal of the metropolis itself. Its claim to place is made through an ideological valorisation of an empty space of appropriation, and hence of primitive accumulation. This *tabula rasa* is already hinted at in Simmel – 'transforming the world into an arithmetical problem and of fixing every one of its parts in a mathematical formula'.[51] Cacciari reads Simmel's arithmetic in terms of a geometric, an allusion to the rationalist systems perhaps. This shift of emphasis within the mathematical constitutes, at a specific level, a critique of Cartesian space – of space as Cartesian, as against the spatial – and, at a general level, a critique of the ideologically rationalist foundations of social and political space. The metropolis presents itself as a place at the same time as it forecloses the possibility of any different place. It is no surprise, therefore, that Cacciari is drawn both to Heidegger's critique of

Cartesian space and to Heidegger's later reflections upon the possibility of 'dwelling' amidst the 'homelessness of modern man'.[52]

In *Being and Time*, Heidegger observed that the *'res corporea'* of Descartes' *Principia Philosophiae* (1644) is determined as *'substantia'*: 'Substances become accessible in their "attributes", and every substance has some distinctive property from which the essence of the substantiality of that definite substance can be read off.' 'Which property', asks Heidegger, 'is this in the case of the *res corporea*?':

> Extension – namely, in length, breadth, and thickness – makes up the real Being of that corporeal substance which we call 'world'... Extension... must already 'be' before any other ways in which Being is determined, so that these can 'be' what they are.[53]

Extension is the essence of substance, against which all other attributes are, precisely, accidental. A substance without attributes would remain substantial, because the *res corporea* is essentially *res extensa*. If the *res* is an extended thing then how is its extension, its essence, to be determined? 'That which is accessible in an entity through mathematics, makes up its Being'.[54] Heidegger does not question the reliability of mathematics, but rather the attempt to render its ontic findings as ontological. Heidegger's phenomenological alternative to Cartesian space goes under the heading of 'The Spatiality of Being-in-the-world'. 'Being in space' might be defined as a 'position in "world-space".' Locations 'in' space are relative to each other by measured extension. Heidegger proposes an alternative conception of distance here, as *'de-severance* [*Entfernung*] and *directionality'*.[55] 'Nearness' does not coincide with measured distance. Neither is it 'anti-realistic'. 'Things' are 'equipment', disclosed according to the ends to which they are 'assigned' and 'referred' by way of an expectation of determinate possibilities (including 'letting-alone'). Calculating measurement would be one such possibility. But that remains a distinctive possibility of Dasein as *already de-severing*. Dasein, the *'Fragwürdig'*, is 'scientific' in the broadest possible sense. Hence, the spatial is the condition for the possibility of space, and not vice versa. The determination of place as idealised space then renders place an ideal impossibility. Importantly, this ideal is regulative. It is not that place *is* space (today) but rather that the *project* forecloses the possibility of another, collectively self-determined place. In terms of Heidegger, of course, it closes down possibility as such. The determination of Being as quantifiably extended substance leads to the nihilism of 'modern technology'.

The concepts of place, dwelling and home share connotations of the local, the community and the family (the familiar, *heimlich*). According to Cacciari, Loos negates these connotations in his homes. He gives voice to the contemporary near-impossibility of place, and to the contradiction of space and place. Loos' homes are anti-homes. One of Cacciari's arguments about these homes concerns the relationship between interior and exterior:

> the bourgeois, philistine concept of the home – the concept of a totality of dwelling, of a reciprocal transparency between interior and exterior... is logically false. The home is in reality a plurality of languages that cannot be reduced to unities by the deterministic logic of nineteenth century positivistic utopianism... The architect remains true to his calling as long as he gives maximum voice to these differences and lets them appear in full.[56]

This multiplicity exceeds the binary of interior and exterior, into the 'silence' beyond dialects. By treating the boundary of inner and outer abysmally, Loos both resists the 'natural' boundaries of the home and keeps open the possibility of a different dwelling. Possibility thus originates in nihilation. In his reading of Wittgenstein's '*oikos*' (designed for his sister), Cacciari suggests that 'all that remains' after the determination of place as space is this silence of possibility. Such silence must be given voice – it must become eloquent. The negation of the metropolis through an affirmation of an alternative utopia is the only impossibility, for Loos, since the 'metropolitan context... negates the interior values' of 'place'. The architecture of nihilism does not oppose the metropolis with another place. It might at least open the possibility of thinking another place.

It is here that Cacciari both repeats a problem in Heidegger and follows Heidegger's response to that problem – albeit with a polemical reversal. In *Being and Time*, the nothingness of '*Dasein's* impossibility', death, is that which provokes the question of Being. Heidegger's early, active nihilism can be characterised as a call to questioning. This gesture appears in Cacciari's account of the abstracted blasé-type. The emptiness of the man without qualities plummets him into the call for decision. But Cacciari ironises 'authenticity [*Eigentlichkeit*]' by suggesting that *Der Mann ohne Eigenschaften* is the *modern* possibility of authenticity, even though the structure of nihilation and possibility remains, meaning that Cacciari is susceptible to some of the other objections to *Being and Time* (other than the concept of authenticity). Questioning is seemingly without content here. Loos risks the abstract over the determinate negation by asking non-questions. There is nowhere to 'go beyond' to.

Heidegger's *Kehre* involved the attempt to confront this problem of questioning for its own sake. The 'enigma [*Rätsel*] of Being' is not infinitely irresolvable. On the basis of his readings of Hölderlin, Heidegger suggests that 'we must try to bring the enigma as enigma closer to us' – in, that is, an unprecedented manner.[57] An instance of Heidegger's turning can be found in 'Building Dwelling Thinking' (1951). Heidegger proposes another non-Cartesian concept of 'space [*Raum*]':

> A space is something that has been made room for, something that has been freed, namely, within a boundary, Greek *peras*. A boundary is not that at which something stops but, as the Greeks recognised, the boundary is that from which something *begins its essential unfolding*. That is why the concept is that of *horismos* that is, horizon, the boundary…*Accordingly, spaces receive their essential being from places* [Orte] *and not from 'space'.*[58]

Heidegger's 'boundary' is equivocal. On the one hand, a nostalgic, provincial conception of dwelling can be discerned – belonging to the locality, which for Heidegger is not just any locality. The 'clearing away [*Räumen*]' is a dispersing, yet the 'place' that it places is a 'gathering [*Versammeln*]'. 'Place always opens a region in which it gathers the things in their belonging together.'[59] That which does not belong or is not proper (the metropolis, no doubt) lies beyond the horizon of Heidegger's *Ortschaft*. Heidegger's declaration on 'Why We Remain in the Provinces' is given its due in *The Jargon of Authenticity*.[60] On the other hand, 'boundary' signifies that space is bounded, not unbounded, as with the Cartesian *res* (whose extension cannot be limited by *any* qualities). Space is finite for the finite human being: 'To be a human being means to be on the earth as a mortal. It means to dwell.' Hence Heidegger connects dwelling to finitude. This is no longer the existentialism of 'Being-in-the-World' because dwelling is both a questioning and a response. Dwelling cannot, today, be brought about solely by building new buildings, or by returning to such buildings as the 'farmhouse' of Heidegger's Black Forest. There is a circular, or circling problem of dwelling, building and thinking according to Heidegger: 'Only if we are capable of dwelling, only then can we build.'[61] But the circle is not solely vicious, to the extent that the problem of dwelling appears in the impossibility of dwelling. In terms of Cacciari's nihilism, the idealisation of place not only raises the question of the meaning of place – this position would correspond to existentialism. It also hints at a response to the problem. What dwelling would be presents itself in the contemporary negation of dwelling. It is in this sense that Cacciari speaks of 'non-dwelling' as 'the essential characteristic of life in the Metropolis'.[62] Cacciari mostly opposes Heidegger's preoccupation with dwelling as 'locale', but he equally radicalises Heidegger's unique awareness of the problem of dwelling as constitutive of the problem of nihilism itself. Hence, Heidegger's equal and opposite preoccupation with the '*unheimlich*' as '*unheimisch*' – that which is without place, the abyssal un-ground of Being in its concealment.[63] This constitutes Heidegger's ontological opposition to the 'onto-theo-logical' grounding of Being – the post-lapsarian longing for reconciliation with nature.[64]

Cacciari sympathises with Heidegger's critique of Cartesian space, as constituting the metaphysical ground of *Gestell*: 'cities then become, in exact accordance with their present image, a total…occupation-plundering of space.' Cacciari associates the 'spatial delimitation that one encounters in the history of the city' with 'a loss of place' or '*Ent-ortung*', de-placement. And yet, Cacciari had already noted that the projection of the categories of place or home into the contemporary situation is anachronistic. That would be precisely the interpretation of decadence as decline that Cacciari opposes in his essays on the 'posthumous people' of *fin-de-siècle* Vienna.[65] Cacciari is at other times sensitive to this problem of nostalgia. How 'can one conceivably combat *Entortung* without making the Angel's gaze towards the past a mere act of nostalgia and consolation?'[66] The anti-utopia of Loos provides the clue, once again:

> Loos' architecture does not seek the rationalisation of 'pure' places, but is aimed at showing the endless contradiction between the thought-out space of calculation, the equivalence of the exteriors, and the possibility of place, the hope of a place. The Loosian house preserves this hope, just as the gaze of Benjamin's Angel preserves the 'glimmers' of the past. That which can be shown is not the 'redemption' of place, but the dissonance existing between the equivalence of techno-scientific space and the characteristic of space as a game of a combination of places, where things are gathered and dwell with man. This dissonance must be composed: even the extreme dissonances must be the object of composition.[67]

The composition of the contradiction contains within it the 'hope of a place'. Cacciari's understanding of nihilism is not completely nostalgic here. The determination of place as space does not call for a return to local places. Rather, the progressive determination of *Vergeistigung* must be radicalised and ultimately overcome, in a manner akin to the 'twisting-free' of metaphysics encountered above. Cacciari's non-dwelling can be termed, against his stated intentions, 'dialectical'.

It then becomes clearer as to why Cacciari had drawn upon the cosmopolitan implications of non-dwelling in Simmel. Following Benjamin's interpretation of Simmel, Cacciari suggests that the 'adventure [*Abenteuer*]' is not simply affirmative – *of* negative freedom – but is rather, in light of Hölderlin and Nietzsche, the possibility of the journey. For Simmel, Cacciari *and* Nono, 'Venice' is an allegory for this possibility: 'That Venice has been and will be the *city of adventure* is just the most perceptible expression of the deepest destiny of its image: it cannot be a home for our soul, cannot be anything but adventure.'[68] For Nono, this adventure, the determinate negation of home, is exemplified in the acoustico-spatial experience of Venice:

> the sound of bells spreads in different directions: some add to each other, are transported over the waters along the channel. Other sounds vaporise almost completely, or mingle in various ways with the other signs of the lagoon and the city.[69]

This remark merely hints at the way in which the negation of home is related to music. For music is not sound alone. A literature of music and space will be briefly reconstructed here in order to understand the way in which Nono's *Prometeo* is, to cite its sub-title, a 'Tragedy *in* Listening' or a 'Tragedy *about* Listening'.

Intermezzo: of music and space

That which Safranski calls 'the current era's ubiquity of music', which 'knows no bounds' recalls Cacciari's 'futile search for the *unicum*'. This is the paradox of the 'musical' adventure and journey. On the one hand, the 'ubiquity of music' satisfies the need to be at home everywhere in the world. On the other hand, the traversal of boundaries in multiple directions is the adventure of the blasé-type, the man without qualities, the wanderer – hence, the 'critique' of home itself. And music seems to hold a privileged position in this twisting from the no-place to the non-place, on account of its spatial peculiarities.

Before Schopenhauer had suggested that music goes beyond world space into an infinite space beyond, his master Kant had taken notice of music's transgression of boundaries:

> Music has a certain lack of urbanity to it. For owing chiefly to the character of its instruments, it scatters its influence abroad to an uncalled-for extent (through the neighbourhood), and thus, as it were, becomes obtrusive and deprives others, outside the musical circle, of their freedom ... The case is almost on a par with the practice of regaling oneself with a perfume that exhales its odours far and wide.[70]

The spatial ambiguity of music, expressed in the question, 'Where is it?', has traditionally been acknowledged in terms of a polarity between inner and outer. Kant remarks on the outer aspect of music here. But the same Kant would have to say that the art of time is accordingly the art of the 'inner sense' (as Schelling would).[71] How can music be *both* inner and outer? A distinction can be made within the outer between the sense of musical space and the space of the performance. But this is ultimately another 'inner-outer'. Kurth thus appealed to Kant's outer sense: 'With the outer world-image [*Weltbild*] we are bound to the intuition of space (as *a priori* origination); something thereof is also conferred upon the inner world image of music.'[72] Music gives rise to a 'strongly felt' 'analogy' to the 'outer'.[73] Music is *as if* space. It is an 'abstract [*Undeutlich*]' and 'enigmatic [*Rätselreich*] ... spatial presentation'.[74] But the space of the performance – the 'localisation' of the sound – 'has nothing to do' with the inner musical space. It is rather the 'opposite of the inner spatial presentation'.[75] This opposition must be returned to.

Hegel classified the forms of art according to the *Erinnerung* of spirit. Art is an externalisation, *Entaüsserung,* commencing with the most outward, symbolic art of architecture, and ending with most the inner, romantic arts of painting, music and poetry. Hegel's philosophy of music can be read according to the 'architecture' of the *Aesthetics* as a whole. Just as 'music acquires an especially architectonic character', 'romantic architecture' displays the 'most contrasting eurhythmy'. Hence, 'although [music] stands in contrast to architecture, it still has an affinity with it.'[76] This is the affinity of the first and the last, as well as the outer and the inner. Hegel echoes Schelling's definition of architecture as 'music in space ... frozen music'[77] – a dictum popularised by Goethe as 'muted music [*verstummten ... Tonkunst*]'.[78] Like Hegel, Bloch associated the outer with the architectural and the inner with music.

But the outer was, precisely contra- Hegelian idealism, collective utopia. This Hegelian structure would have come to Bloch from Lukács, who turned the dictum of Novalis into a statement on modern subjectivity. The 'urge to be at home everywhere' demonstrates that:

> philosophy, as a form of life or as that which determines the form and supplies the content of literary creation, is always a symptom of the rift between 'inside' and 'outside', a sign of the essential difference between the self and the world, the incongruence of soul and deed.[79]

In Bloch's appropriation of Lukács, the 'musical' connotations of Novalis come to fruition. Bloch's intended title for *The Spirit of Utopia* was *Music and Apocalypse*.[80] According to Bloch's experimental synthesis of expressionism and constructivism, great music is the inner anticipation of an outer collective. The 'ornament' is the inner expressed through the outer, an 'exteriorised interiority'. The movement of the 'I who I will be', recalling Hegel, is the movement towards the 'We'.[81] In Bach's Passions, Bloch hears 'the fusion and balance of the lyrical and the structured in an essentially *architectonic*, Gothically architectonic harmony and counterpoint, which acts as the particular house, the so to speak spatially constitutive system of this lyricism.'[82] For Cacciari, following the anti-ornament of Loos and Webern, Bloch's '*Antizipation*' would be more romantic *Sehnsucht* – longing *for* a projected utopia. Adorno's utopian anticipation is, by contrast, dissonant. An expression of waiting in vain does not anticipate the awaited in the sense of expectation. It is, however, clear that in spite of his criticisms of Bloch's aesthetics of music, Adorno's aesthetic theory owes much to the *Spirit of Utopia* (by way of Benjamin, perhaps) – in terms of its dialectic of expression and construction, but also in the sense that the artwork has an inner, autonomous character only insofar as it is outwardly manifested. The artwork is a 'monad'. This inner-outer paradigm, a form of which is found in the opposition between autonomous and political art, is in fact questioned by Nono.

Nono's spaces of resistance

Politically, the charge of resignation against Adorno concerns the fact that his theory of 'the totally administered society' obscures more immediate problems and opportunities in the world. Reification often seems to be the most fundamental problem for Adorno, according to which imperialism and exploitation are symptoms (notwithstanding his references to Apartheid and Vietnam). Undo reification and these issues will resolve themselves (structurally, a truism). In the previous chapter, we saw Nono's latent awareness, via Lachenmann, of this German-speaking tradition of reification-critique – as sensed in his mimetic treatment of time in *Il canto sospeso*. But Nono, who joined the Italian Communist Party in 1952, saw the problems of fascism, imperialism and exploitation as fundamental. These issues remained pertinent to the specific politics of Italy after the war – the watchword of Nono and the neorealists was 'resistance'.[83] Nono's twofold affinity to critical and activist traditions serves to situate him fascinatingly in relation to the classic German-language Marxist aesthetics debates (which included Adorno, Benjamin, Brecht, and Lukács) and their continuation in contemporary 'art and life/politics' debates.

From the time of Nono's move away from the increasing mysticism of the 'Darmstadt school' around 1960, Nono became interested both in the technology of music and in political music theatre. Nono's first political '*azione scenica*', *Intolleranza 1960*, deployed an entire section of the instrumental section of *Il canto sospeso*, discussed above – contradicting any sudden break with the Darmstadt period. Thus, Nono continued to experiment with musical time, but now in the context of real spaces of resistance. *A floresta è jovem e cheja de vida* (The Forest is Young and Full of Life, 1965–66), scored for soprano, three reciters, clarinet, copper plates and eight-channel tape is one such example. The texts, selected by Giovanni Pirelli, document liberation struggles from around the world. Its title comes from the words of an Angolan freedom fighter: 'they cannot burn the forest because it is young and full of life'. An immediate and crucial difference from *Il canto sospeso* is that these are explicitly contemporary struggles. Much like Adorno, Nono regarded fascism as an ongoing danger in central Europe, but some within the economic miracle of West Germany had mistaken *Il canto sospeso* for a cathartic farewell to a past problem. Where *Il canto sospeso* was well received on its première (by its 'bourgeois' audience, as Metzger was at pains to point out), the 1960s works were often received with far more difficulty – *La fabbrica illuminata* (1964) being censored by Italian radio for its protest against factory working conditions.[84]

A floresta opens with the words of a repair mechanic from Bergamo: 'As Marx said, we are in prehistoric time.' But a second difference to *Il canto sospeso* is that Nono's spaces of resistance now exceed the European context, given the international struggles cited. Nono is attracted to magnetic tape for its capacity both to bring the contemporary world into music and to take music out of the concert hall back into the world, including the factory.[85] Moreover, the acerbic sonorities of the tape medium remains appropriate to an anti-sentimental realism. In *A floresta*, Nono carves out a barren landscape from which sites of political struggle rise and fall. That which sounds the most bereft of life promises to be full of life. This promise is to be understood in terms of hope, and not expectation. As with *Il canto sospeso* promise is combined with mourning. *A floresta* in no way regards its revolutionary spaces as utopias. It is their present activity of resistance that might rather be termed 'utopian'. In one respect, this electronic work of music-theatre (the speakers were originally actors from the Living Theatre company) cannot be compared with the non-electronic, serial *Il canto sospeso*. But the continuity lies in its polarisation of duration through the dramatisation of timbral relations, constituting a newly 'spatialised' time. The tape medium allows Nono to exaggerate this process, not being limited to the all-too-human confines of live instrumental production (or, rather, it is precisely the crossover between the live instruments and the recorded ones that presses the new technology back to the social context). The reworked instruments and voices, combined with the copper sheets and the *Flatterzunge* of the clarinet (its 'rasping') emphasises this contrast between a quasi-spatial continuum and the movements of protest. What is new, therefore, is the interaction of the inherent spatialisation – the mimetic stasis considered in the previous chapter – and the real spaces of resistance, introduced programmatically (a written programme that accompanies the performance as part of the work). Resistance to reification is brought into conjunction with resistance to imperialism. *Against* Adorno, Nono knows the socially representational limits of 'absolute' music – despite Adorno's 'politics' of expression. *With* Adorno, Nono upholds that 'absolutist' moment of the *Zeitkunst* as a crucial element of his overall music-theatre. Nono's exploration of both spaces of music, 'inner' and 'outer', are theorised in his slightly earlier 'Notes on Music Theatre Today'. Anticipating *Prometeo*, Nono refers to an electroacoustic *cori spezzati*. Nono arranges the loudspeakers spatially to achieve this new idea of space. What results is another level of spatial interaction, between the polarised, static-eruptive music and its movement about the performance space. The effect is one of pulling the listener's attention out of the stage, out of the concert hall, and into a world of concrete problems – problems that, according to Nono's music theatre, this engaged consciousness might at least begin to address. Nono's avant-gardism thus differs from that of Adorno, for whom the task of art is to negate the existing space and not to propose solidarity with any new one. For the critical theorist, the artwork shows 'that the world could be other than it is'.[86] This 'other' remains perpetually negative, and the neglect of concrete spaces, in art as well as in political situations, no doubt remains a problem for him.

When, in *Aesthetic Theory*, Adorno states that the modern artwork is 'the determinate negation of a determinate society', the author plays on a double sense of 'determinate': logical and political. Society is determinate (already determined) in the sense of being fixed. But the all-too-unified world is determinately negated by the disruptive 'unity' of the advanced artwork, albeit as 'semblance'. What is paradoxically unified in the artwork is that which has become disenchanted: experience (*Erfahrung*). As Adorno knew well, Hegelian logic states that 'determinate negation', unlike 'abstract negation', gives rise to something new in the process of mediation. This 'something new' would be the alternative objectification to reification. Hence, Nono's critique of formalism at the end of the 1950s leads him to a music-theatre that brings these possible objectifications (all too 'empirical' for Adorno) into aesthetic experience itself. Yet, equally true to Adorno, Nono is aware that this remains an *aesthetic* experience – as semblance – and not an immediately 'revolutionary' act. Nono goes beyond Adorno here by acknowledging the positing as well as negating character of determinate negation: the critique of reification must suggest other spaces for life if that critique of reification is not to be merely abstract, if it is really to resist the determinate society.

Prometeo and the place of the artwork

For *Prometeo*, Nono brought back his *cori spezzati*. The singers, speakers, chorus, solo strings, solo winds, glasses, orchestral groups and live electronics were arranged spatially about the audience. A productive tension reigns in this work between the musical space and the space of the performance, which the former occupies. What is the nature of this occupation, and how is it productive? The French-language editor of Nono's writings has suggested that 'the music composes the space'.[87] But how can such space be composed in an already composed space – in the case of the premier, the deconsecrated San Lorenzo church?

The spatial experience of *Prometeo* can initially be described in terms of Adorno's sense of an 'adherence to the harmonic structure'. Adorno was aware, in his additional 'or the instrumental sound', that a new space promises to emerge out of the disintegration of traditional harmony. In Wagner, 'colour itself became architectonic'. Nono does not valorise colour over structure, sound over music. The harmonic material of *Prometeo* is polarised between close intervals, including micro-intervals, and expansive ones (the 'Promethean' fifth being a constant) amidst similarly polarised pitch and dynamic ranges. Nono exploits a fundamental characteristic of music, described in great detail by Kurth: height and depth.[88] There is no *legato* rising and falling of voices, however. Nono interrupts linear articulation and anticipates the problem of atomisation by way of 'the smallest transition'. This is supposed to counter the 'dramaturgy of contrasts' that characterised most bourgeois music, especially opera, as a mode of *representation*.[89] Similar figures are thus repeated in different instrumental groupings, such that the transition of texture and colour challenges the 'figurativeness' that Adorno attributed to *Moses*. For Cacciari, 'to eliminate all figurative appearance... has been the greatest problem for Nono in the general conception (but perhaps also in the "musical thought") of his work.'[90] As was suggested, Nono does not so much eliminate figurativeness as sublate it.

This attempted sublation is explained by Nono and Cacciari in terms of the problematic affinity between representation and space:

> In parallel to the cemeteries, asylums and prisons, the theatres and concert halls are built... The concentration and homogenisation of space, the disappearance of the multi-spatial possibility of the musical event, is closely related to the obvious reduction of polyvocity, of the multivocal possibility of 'directions' in listening. Inside these convoluted constraints, listening and the space of listening coincide; are apprehended together. All this during what one could perhaps call 'the bourgeois era' of listening.

Cacciari traces the emergence of the institutional spaces of music in 'parallel' to these other institutions. The 'constraint' of music implies that unconstrained music, outside of or against this 'era', offers a potential for resistance, to a 'civilization placed under the sign of the *ideîn*'.[91] Nono and Cacciari suggest that the 'multi-spatiality' of music derives from its capacity to estrange what is listened to from the listening. This refers not only to the abstraction of music (which, as we have seen, is quite amenable to representation) but also to an estrangement of the music from the locality of its production. This estrangement is ideologically cut short with the cult of the performer. What we see is what we hear. The inner-outer relation can be understood in terms of a distinction between the necessity of the spectacle – whereby the inner and outer are collapsed – and the possibility of the non-spectacle, according to which the meaning of the outer is in some way suspended by the inner.

The claim for this potential in music is nevertheless a fraught one insofar as it relies upon an empirical acoustics. As Kant observed to his distaste, sound crosses space, even walls. Nono speaks of a 'mobile sound' that 'does not fill the space, *but discovers it*, unveils it. And this provokes an unexpected and unpredictable *being in the sound, not to begin* to perceive, but to feel part of the space, to *play*.'[92] This play is not harmonious. It is a *Trauer-spiel*. Nono's 'tragedy in listening' can be understood as a continuation of Cacciari's 'negative thought'. The space of the performance is determined by the geometric space of the metropolis. Given Cacciari's Foucauldian language, the San Lorenzo perhaps constituted a 'heterotopia'.[93] But aside from what precisely is meant by heterotopia, this would only be the case insofar as *Prometeo* productively contradicted the real space of the San Lorenzo. According to Cacciari, a manifestation of negative thought 'repeats' as 'going beyond' the real-ideal space of the metropolis. The blasé, the wanderer, is the productive mimesis of the ideal space, the bad utopia.

As a manifestation of negative thought, the 'mobile sound' of *Prometeo* is the 'figure' of the wanderer, and that 'in which' the music wanders is the geometric space. As Nono makes clear, this mobile sound is produced in the disclosing of the space – including the performance space. Negative thought repeats and goes beyond the present space, the space of the present. Going beyond as mimesis offers no world transcendence. *Prometeo* radicalises the abstraction in the name of a second concreteness. Neither does it valorise *its own* musical space, in the sense of absolute music: 'to me, "symphony" means constructing a world' (Mahler).[94] The mobile sound of *Prometeo* refers incessantly to the performance space, without ever valorising it. It is 'here and now' that the spatial and temporal dimensions of *Prometeo* converge. Nono's fermata dwells on the performance space, its incontrovertible reference, as an expression of non-dwelling. The listener wanders purposefully, much like the performers of another late work, *La lontananza nostalgica utopica futura* (1988–89). The fermata says that *what* is purposeful in the wandering is the transformation of *this* space. In the text of *Prometeo*, Cacciari truncates the final line of the unfinished *Moses*: 'But in the wasteland you shall be / invincible and shall achieve the goal: unity with God.' The wasteland ('*die Wüste*', the desert) is precisely not the abyss of empty universalised space. This desert resembles the abyss, as its mimesis – the fundamental difference being, perhaps, that even a desert occupies *this* world. It is equally *not* the abyss. This sense of transformation within the world, of this world, is captured in *Aesthetic Theory*:

> If Schopenhauer's thesis of art as an image of the world once over bears a kernel of truth, then it does so only insofar as this second world is composed out of elements that have been transposed out of the empirical world in accord with Jewish descriptions of the messianic order as an order just like the habitual order but changed in the slightest degree.[95]

Adorno's reference to the 'messianic order' hints at how *Prometeo* extends beyond Cacciari's theoretical research. What is missing from Cacciari is the sense by which *Prometeo* produces the problem of space and utopia *as an artwork*. Conversely, and relatedly, a problem arises concerning negative *thought*, as to whether it can actually go beyond the contradiction that it tragically acknowledges. Negative thought threatens to hypostatise possibility as such, theoretically blocking *praxis*. This problem can perhaps be discerned in Cacciari's texts for *Prometeo*, none more so than in his appropriation of *Moses* – which, we recall, remained unfinished (the closing lines are not the closing lines). If the 'New Prometheus' is 'invincible in the wasteland', then why go beyond it, into the promised land? What is the promise of the wasteland? As was the case in the passage from *Dialectic of Enlightenment*, there is a tendency to melancholically valorise the wasteland and to proscribe promise.

Adorno is less sceptical about utopian promise in his aesthetic theory, however. Art constitutes a peculiarly radical kind of promise: 'As a musical composition compresses time, and as a painting folds spaces into one another, so the possibility is concretised that the world could be other than it is.' Is not this 'other than it is' more of the same 'possibility for its own sake'? The abstract negation of this place without the promise of another one? Adorno offers a speculatively positive moment of 'otherness' here. For although Adorno upholds the *Bilderverbot* on representations of utopia, the *utopian* meaning of the artwork consists in its autonomy, which Adorno accounts for with various categories, including 'coherence' and 'unity'. Although Adorno might be faulted for neglecting the spatial-utopian meaning of art, he does acknowledge its collective-utopian meaning, speculatively. The question of space in music is primarily the question of its 'collective implications'.

Further spatial implications of Adorno's aesthetic theory can be drawn out in relation to Nono. Art 'becomes social by its opposition to society, and occupies this position only as autonomous art'. An abstraction from 'empirical society' in 'an obscured form', the artwork both draws from empirical society and discloses the possibility of a different totality.[96] Adorno once again refers to the idea of the monad. The artwork determinately negates the ideological unity of the familiar world. It is 'the determinate negation of a determinate society' because its determinate unity and coherence displaces the existing unity and coherence. The utopian meaning of art is to imagine 'the totality as something that could be completely different'. In this sense, the artwork must remain outside of itself. The inner is inner qua different outer. As with the Jewish mystical teaching, the two outers, empirical society and utopia, cannot be absolutely distinguished. Adorno's account of autonomy can be taken to address the question, which he otherwise tends to remain silent over, about the space and place of the artwork. There is a utopian meaning of art insofar as 'place' appears in it negatively, 'only' as semblance. But *Schein* is itself internally contradictory. Place does not appear as *true* in the artwork. The artwork is *not* a place (whether a utopia or a heterotopia). And yet, Adorno seems to draw upon associations of place with autonomy, appropriation and naming. These are not simply bourgeois concepts of property and appropriation. The monad is the negating-mimesis of the bourgeois individual, not the bourgeois individual itself. The monad is not individualistic because it systematically refers to a 'totality as…completely different' – according to which the individual would equally be completely different also. When Adorno comes to consider what this different totality would be like – or rather, what it would be like to consider this totality – it is precisely a concept of place, or place-name, that is invoked. These are places from the memory of promise, from childhood. 'What metaphysical experience would be, to those who eschew the reduction of this to presumably religious primal experiences, comes closest to how Proust envisioned it, in the happiness promised by the names of villages like Otterbach, Watterbach, Reuenthal, Monbrunn.'[97] Does Adorno keep to his 'tragic' reading of Proust? ('Proust remarks on the caesura which voyages make in the course of life by "leading us from one name to another name".')[98] Or does the supposedly universal trope of a happy childhood rather uphold the nostalgic longing for home – that which Michel de Certeau termed the 'original spatial structure' of 'the mother'?[99] In any case, if Adorno does value a concept of place, then it is not explicitly spatial. Hence, perhaps, the near absence of architecture in his aesthetic theory, combined with his valorisation of modern music (as the Hegelian other of architecture). With his absolutist evaluation of modern music, Adorno tends towards the undialectical – where this dialectic of music and space has been recognised from Kant and Hegel to, more recently, Jacques Attali.[100] Modern music must make this demand of the dialectic, as happens in *Prometeo*.

The musical space of *Prometeo* manifests the 'inner' moment of its autonomy. But this moment cannot be sustained without the space of the performance – its heterogeneous moment. Although Adorno stresses that the artwork takes elements from the existing world, and is thereby social, its original transformation of these elements constitutes a different unity. Hence, the heteronomous moment of the work is already mediated in its autonomy. While the musical space and time of *Prometeo* could therefore be understood as autonomous, this work simultaneously refuses to mediate the space of the performance into the musical space. Its mediation is its refusal to mediate. It does not propose the absolutism that Adorno sympathetically attributes to Mahler:

> When some well-intentioned person advised Mahler to darken the hall during the concert for the sake of the mood, the composer rightly replied that a performance at which one didn't forget about the surroundings was worthless.[101]

How does *Prometeo* problematise Adorno's *Aesthetic Theory*, therefore? In light of Cacciari's research, the problem of space is not simply one problem among others, just as space is not simply one attribute of place. It is the determination of place through idealised space – by way of the commodity form – that forces the question of place. Cacciari tentatively 'goes beyond' in his suggestion that the space of the metropolis opens up the possibility of a new dwelling. None of this features in Adorno's reflections upon the meaning of place or of utopia – in spite his Weberian fears about rationalisation. It is once again the space of this sociality that Adorno tends to neglect. *Prometeo* negates its medium – that which aims to be at home everywhere in the world. Like Adorno, Nono knows that the two spheres of musical experience must be thought of together. Hence, Nono optimistically suggests in the 1980s that the 'Walkman':

> makes it possible to understand and render comprehensible that sounds are not stable and transmitted on only one axis, but are in a situation of constant mobility in comparison to our [visual] perception, thus contributing to refine it... The [bourgeois] listening about which we spoke thus develops through modernity and inside it.

Prometeo 'reveals the space' insofar as the musical space comes into conflict with the space of the performance, as a play without resolution – the 'composing [of]... dissonances'. *Prometeo* aims to affirm both its place, as semblance, and the non-place of the performance. This dual manifestation of the same place is 'tragic' in the above sense – a 'Tragedy *in* Listening', but also a 'Tragedy *about* Listening', and hence social space.[102]

That semblance is contradictory is to say that 'the artwork is here and is not here', a place and no-place. Adorno recognises the attempted destruction of semblance in 'the most recent works', which are themselves works of semblance. Hence, the 'dialectic of modern art is largely that it wants to shake off its illusoriness like an animal trying to shake off its antlers.'[103] Adorno and Cacciari want to affirm this sense of the tragic contradiction in art. According to Cacciari, the error of the prevailing humanism of the late eighteenth-century was to take the promise of reconciliation for granted:

> the romantic 'prometheism' of the whole humanist tradition regarded [Prometheus] as not only the powerful voice of *technai*, but also as the one who brought to man the supreme *technē* that would enable him to liberate himself from divinity.[104]

Cacciari risks valorising the *im*possibility of reconciliation. But Nono's *Prometeo* draws Cacciari into a more 'productive', though indeed mystical position. Can Prometheus be at once tragic and utopian, unreconciled and reconciling? Prometheus is the anti-tragedy. In the version told by Aeschylus (Cacciari relies upon Hesiod), Prometheus must wait 13 generations to be released. The 13 generations stand for a radically indeterminate and thus non-conciliatory time of waiting. Prometheus remains tragic, but not indefinitely. Marx regarded Prometheus as 'the most eminent saint and martyr in the philosophical calendar.'[105] Utopia is neither expected nor relinquished in *Prometeo*. Its time, therefore, is neither the bad utopia of waiting without the awaited nor the bad utopia of merely expecting the awaited. There is, once again, a peculiar convergence of the temporal and the spatial. Nono was aware of this, with his dictum on the 'dissolution of normal time' as 'a non-geometrised space'. An expression of waiting in vain is already spatial. That waiting could and even must have a spatial character is not, it was suggested above, alien to the thought of Adorno. His late remark on 'the static character of films like Antonioni's *La Notte*' (1961) is prescient of a scene from the same director's *The Passenger* (1975), in which the dead reporter addresses the desert: 'So still. A kind of waiting'.[106]

Ever since Thomas More's invention, utopia has been an imagined place. Following Marx's anti-utopianism, Cacciari worries that utopia is precisely the no-place of u-topia *as* place. There is, it was suggested, an equal and opposite danger of revealing and then simply affirming this no-place, to the detriment of utopia *as* place. More himself played on the dual connotation of utopia: no-place and happy-place, eu-topia. In conversation with Adorno, Bloch remarks on the change in the utopia literature: 'At the very beginning Thomas More designated utopia as a place, an island in the distant South Seas. The designation underwent changes later so that it left space and entered time.'[107] But this shift from space to time cannot become absolute – no waiting without the awaited.

5
The Expression of Waiting in Vain

Adorno

The promise of metaphysics

In Chapter 1, it was suggested that the melancholy science of natural history can be understood as a philosophy of waiting-expression. The retrospective projection of Adorno's reflections on 'waiting in vain' back onto the earlier work (including the 1932 lecture) is philologically justified by the reappearance of the idea of natural history in the later work itself. Indeed, the English-language translator of 'The Idea of Natural History' observes that *Negative Dialectics* follows 'precisely the same plan' as the lecture – 'a critique of Heidegger is followed by the presentation of the central concepts of the form of the critique'. This parallel is nevertheless limited by the fact that the last 'model' of *Negative Dialectics* was motivated by the event of a genocide surely not expected back in July of 1932. Adorno's 'Meditations on Metaphysics' – 'after Auschwitz' – immediately follow the two sub-sections on natural history.[1] The last part of *Negative Dialectics* is in this sense not prefigured in the lecture, but rather can be said to begin where the lecture left off.

At the same time, Adorno's later version of natural history seems to proceed from the concluding remark of the earlier one, which was 'only an interpretation of certain fundamental elements of the materialist dialectic'.[2] In *Negative Dialectics*, Marx's mediation of nature and history is stressed alongside the mediations of Benjamin and Lukács – the latter two being relied upon exclusively in the 1932 lecture. Adorno attempts that which he had failed to demonstrate previously, in terms of a 'radical' and 'ontological reorientation of the philosophy of history'. *Negative Dialectics* no longer employs this language, which belies the early influence of Heidegger (or, perhaps, the 'jargon of authenticity' of the 1920s as a whole). Adorno had acknowledged Heidegger's attempt to overcome historicism in *Being and Time* – 'false stasis and formalism have been eliminated' – only to retract the compliment in his subsequent polemics. The later Adorno seeks a reorientation of the philosophy of history that is *not* ontological (though he stands by the lecture, which, 'in its broad outlines has retained its validity').[3] Neither can he depend upon philological sources alone, since that would not amount to a philosophical response – this was the problem with the lecture. Nor can it amount to a positivist sociology. The same applies to an anthropological approach – Adorno pits Marx against Feuerbach to this end, though not always consistently. Adorno knows that *his* form of historical materialism, *however* materialist, must contend with metaphysics, as the problem of (its) grounding. The idea of natural history is equivalent to 'the transmutation of metaphysics into history'[4] – the problem being that, on turning the page of *Negative Dialectics*, we read that, 'the capacity for metaphysics is debilitated because what happened smashed the basis of the compatibility between speculative metaphysical thought and experience [*Erfahrung*].'[5] The problem of metaphysics is not *resolved* by its transmutation into history, so long as the nature of this transmutation remains obscure. For the transmutation is already founded upon a philosophy of history that is itself metaphysical. The transition to the 'Meditations on Metaphysics' leaves a tension both within *Negative Dialectics* and within the thought of Adorno as a whole, not least because the question of metaphysics, of (its) grounding, is the abiding question of Heidegger. In a sense, Adorno returns to Heidegger's problem, and not only to the problem of Heidegger. Adorno and Heidegger each contend that the question of metaphysics 'after' metaphysics is a question about time and history. More precisely, this 'after' concerns a question about waiting.

Why is 'the capacity for metaphysics crippled' after Auschwitz? Metaphysics is no *Hinterwelt* for Adorno. The tradition of philosophical metaphysics is bound to history and culture:

> That it could happen in the midst of all the traditions of philosophy, art and the enlightening sciences, says more than just that these, as spirit, were not capable of seizing and changing humanity [*die Menschen*]. In each of these branches itself, in its emphatic claim to autarky, dwells the untruth. All culture after Auschwitz, including its urgent critique, is rubbish.[6]

Adorno here implies that the tradition of metaphysics has been historically European – German, even. The term 'midst' signifies a temporal *and* spatial proximity where these 'enlightening' forces are concerned. The latter proximity is an especially fraught notion given that other catastrophes in which Europe was culpable have occurred, and continue to occur, outside of its geographical and political boundaries. Hence, in his 1965 *Metaphysics* lectures, Adorno acknowledges the contemporary, anti-colonial struggles in Vietnam and South Africa alongside the 'word symbol' of Auschwitz, which nevertheless remains 'the most symbolic thing of all'.[7] We have seen that Adorno privileges an enlightened, historical moment that coincides with the historical moment of the enlightenment – represented in the figures of Kant, Hegel, Beethoven, Goethe and Marx. This moment remained an unfulfilled promise. Philosophy, 'which once seemed obsolete, lives on because the moment to realise it was missed' (Adorno uses Marx's term here: *Verwirklichung*).[8] The promise is tested after Auschwitz, for the promise is needed more than ever in the moment of its being broken. An equivocation over this promise of metaphysics is evident from Adorno's shift of emphasis from each of the twelve meditations to the next. Adorno writes that 'culture', not metaphysics, is 'rubbish'. And yet 'metaphysics is fused with culture'. Is not metaphysics then reduced to rubbish? Adorno is careful not to damn metaphysics, not least because he has not fully worked-out what will take its place. It is precisely Adorno's clue to what must displace it that will be followed up here and related back to the interpretations of waiting in vain in the previous chapters.

To damn metaphysics – and not simply negate it abstractly, in the sense of positivism – would already amount to a metaphysical judgement. Both the promise and the disappointment arising from its being broken are metaphysical. For the promise is *itself* metaphysics. This is the underlying thesis of Adorno's lecture course on metaphysics. Adorno makes two strategic decisions in these lectures. The first is to offer an introductory, though fundamental definition. For, *what* is it that is crippled? The second decision is to generalise the tradition of metaphysics under one name: 'metaphysics began with Aristotle'.[9] Like Heidegger, Adorno acknowledges that Aristotle never used the title, but that he nevertheless remains its author in spirit. Adorno faults Heidegger for his violent interpretations of Aristotle, but Adorno's interpretation is already mediated through the violent Hegelian interpretation of Eduard Zeller.[10]

Adorno is at one with Heidegger on the question of the origins of metaphysics when he states that, in contrast to Aristotle, Plato bequeathed a dualism to philosophy. The 'Ideas' are 'the true, the One, the essential', whereas 'the world of the senses' is 'absolutely without being'. Plato is the first metaphysician *only* to the extent that he asks about 'the cause of all things'. The ideas are 'the cause of appearances'. Adorno recognises the 'profound and lasting influence' of Plato upon 'later western philosophy'. But he does not, here at least, take up Nietzsche's thesis on the complicity between Platonism, modernity and nihilism.[11] Whereas, for Heidegger, Nietzsche's account of nihilism *is* the problem and history of metaphysics, Nietzsche included. Adorno and Heidegger are also in some agreement about a fall or crisis of metaphysics in the context of modernity, even though modernity is construed in radically different ways. For Heidegger, the crisis is that of modernity itself, whereas for Adorno, the crisis emerges in the wake of a specific event of modernity. There remains a fatalistic sense in which Auschwitz was always coming, nevertheless – that Auschwitz is a 'word symbol' for catastrophic history as such – when Adorno and Horkheimer suggest for instance that anti-Semitism is constitutive of the structure of the dialectic of enlightenment itself.[12] The bourgeois *ratio* must eliminate the principle of non-identity, as represented in a non-representable absolute, if it is to realise its principle of identity as real domination. If the dialectic of enlightenment is modernity then modernity is itself, as it is for Heidegger, the problem.

According to Adorno, Aristotle attempted to mediate where Plato proposed only a dualism. As a consequence, Plato's philosophy remains within the cyclical time of the Greek religion. Platonism is not metaphysics proper, the thinking of the whole. The ideas, which have no cause in the sensuous, must have sensuousness conferred upon them extrinsically in order for them to be individuated *as* ideas. Platonism is late polytheism. Aristotle, by contrast, attempts to mediate the divine – ultimately, God – and humanity. All of the metaphysical systems of Western philosophy attempt to succeed where Aristotle failed. Mediation is becoming. In Plato, the first cause is the prototypical 'idea' – meaning that the true Being is non-temporal – whereas, in Aristotle, the first cause is always already manifest *in* sensuous matter, '*hyle* [ὕλη]', as its final form, '*morphe* [μορφή]'. Being is (in) becoming:

> this world of sensible appearance is teleologically oriented towards these ideas, or pure possibilities, which are supposed to be contained within them. In Aristotle there is an expression for this relationship of the ideas or possibilities to the existent: ἓν κατὰ πολλῶν: that is to say, the One in the Many.[13]

Pure possibility is more precisely potentiality, ἐντελέχεια. The realisation of potentiality is not a possibility, but a certainty. It is the question of 'when?' and not 'if?' Aristotle's *Metaphysics* is full of promise in the fullest sense of the word, even though it does not yet bear any historical, let alone utopian self-consciousness. Metaphysics, mediation towards the highest, is promise. Adorno's history of ancient philosophy is already Aristotelian, in that Aristotle inaugurates the promise.

Adorno thus thinks of the promise of metaphysics in terms of history, including the history of philosophy. The 'proposition, that movement is the realization of the possible, already implies the Hegelian thesis of history as progress in the consciousness of freedom.' Of course, the promise is actualised discontinuously. The dialectic of enlightenment is the dialectic of promise and broken promise, progress and regression in the consciousness of freedom and unfreedom. Promise already has a maximal and a minimal signification: expectation and hope respectively. But in the 'Meditations', hope is thrown into disarray. This is why Adorno considers the possibility of waiting in vain.

The reason that Aristotle 'fails' in his mediation is that he merely displaces the problem of the many and the one from the first to the final cause, which is just as non-temporal as the Platonic forms themselves. This problem is initially muted in Adorno's account of metaphysics, but it becomes louder. There must be something that unifies all final forms, something final that is not itself a form – a mover, since All is Becoming, that is not itself moved. As Adorno puts it:

> everything that has not evolved or become what it is, and is therefore the oldest thing, which has always existed, is regarded as the condition of the possibility of any becoming – an idea taken over directly from Aristotle by Hegel; and in which the final cause, that is, the divinity, is seen as the 'unmoved mover' of all things. Aristotle's famous formulation of this doctrine of the unmoved mover is ἀκίνητον κινοῦν.[14]

The unmoved mover cannot be seen in itself but (only) in what (it) moves, as the one in the many. What if that which moves, seen historically, is catastrophic? At one point in his lectures, Adorno defines the 'principle of inertia' as 'radically evil'.[15] What kind of absolute are we talking about in this case, if we may continue to speak of the absolute *at all*? After Auschwitz, it 'could no longer be asserted that the immutable would be the truth and that what moves, the transient, would be appearance [*Schein*]'.[16] Again, Adorno does not leap to conclusions about the end of metaphysics: 'historical compassion…prevents one from presupposing such an immutability, and thus changes the contents of metaphysics.'[17] Auschwitz puts an end to expectant promise. This promise applies to the individual as much as it does to history. Adorno thus draws upon the idea that the individual is a microcosm of the whole. The individual is a whole in itself (the many in the one). This is a prominent idea of Neoplatonism. It recurs in Kant, as well as in Goethe and in his interpreters. These Goetheans include Benjamin, Dilthey and, indirectly, Heidegger.

Adorno reads Heidegger's 'Being-towards-death' as a desperate attempt to confer meaning upon that which has become meaningless – and not, as Heidegger saw it, as the recognition of the meaninglessness of traditional metaphysics. There is a philosophical-modernist struggle for contemporaneity between Heidegger and Adorno on this point:

> The current death metaphysics [of Heidegger] is nothing but the powerless solace of society over the fact that, through social transformations, human beings came to be deprived of that which was once supposed to have made death bearable to them: the feeling of its epic unity with a rounded life.[18]

Adorno does not reject the tradition of death metaphysics (and this will be crucial for his *comparison* to Heidegger). He upholds it, negatively, with the suggestion that the horrific nature of death in the camps has permanently unsettled the epic unity of a life that is supposed to end meaningfully in death – not only for the victims and survivors, but, indirectly, for all who belong to the history that made the camps possible: 'What the sadists in the camps told their victims – tomorrow you will be smoke rising from these chimneys into the sky – names the indifference, towards which history is moving, of the life of each individual.'[19] The knowledge of death as the end of life, a classical humanist distinction between human and animal, underlies what Adorno means by 'metaphysical experience'. After Aristotle, metaphysics is nothing if it is not experienced.[20]

Adorno seems to have Benjamin's 'The Storyteller' in mind when he writes that, 'Death and history, especially the collective history of the category of the individual [*Individuum*], form a constellation.'[21] Adorno emphasises the individual death – death and individuation – more than does Benjamin, for whom death is a generational and hence collective concern (Benjamin is interested in the dead and the unborn, whereas Adorno is interested in the problem of the good death.). Adorno's worry about the fate of the individual explains some of his sensitivity towards Heidegger's philosophy of death. It might be supposed Adorno would accuse Heidegger of individualism and interiority (as he did with the revival of Kierkegaard). Adorno does the opposite. The existential categories are formal-transcendental, and to that extent a symptom of 'depersonalisation'.[22] Given that Adorno rejects the responses to the 'fall' of metaphysics in scientific materialism, philosophical positivism and Heideggerian nihilism, what, in that case, *is* his response?

After metaphysics?

Does not Adorno 'witness' in concrete history that which was already declared philosophically decades before? As Lacoue-Labarthe puts matters: 'God died at Auschwitz.'[23] Adorno, who has much to say about death and Auschwitz, refrains from saying this in so many words. But he does anticipate the ensuing nihilism: 'Philosophy need not do without the word any more.'[24] This declaration is complicated by the fact that Adorno does not explicitly distinguish between passive and active nihilism, and because his most original response to the problem of metaphysics nevertheless constitutes – according to this interpretation – a form of post-active nihilism. Having outwardly excluded nihilism, Adorno retreats into the familiar territory of Kant. That four of the 12 meditations revolve around Kant suggests, along with the lengthy 'Metacritique of Practical Reason', that Adorno regards him as occupying the pinnacle of the metaphysical tradition. The problem of metaphysics is, in its purely philosophical form, a Kantian problem, a problem after Kant. If metaphysics has been put into question historically then an engagement with the thinker that put metaphysics into question structurally – for whom metaphysics *is* constitutively questionable – would seem inevitable.

Adorno's position on Kant is, on the surface, ambivalent because, while Kant refuses an affirmative absolute, thus siding with the negative, he thereby risks affirming that refusal absolutely. Kant's 'philosophy circles, probably just as every other one does by the way, around the ontological proof of God. With magnificent ambiguity, he left open his own position.'[25] At the same time, the 'authority of the Kantian concept of truth became terroristic with the ban on thinking the absolute'.[26] Adorno is aware of the problem of the regressive infinity within Kant's critique of pure reason. But this awareness tends to get lost amidst the focus upon the third antinomy alone. Kant's doctrine of the *mundus intelligibilis* is the prism through which Adorno views Kantian metaphysics as a whole. According to Adorno, Aristotle's 'doctrine of immutability ... has survived throughout the history of metaphysics, to the point that it became the subject of Kant's third antinomy.'[27] The problem of 'the intelligible character' is, for Adorno, the problem of the promise of metaphysics.

Like Schelling, Adorno observes that the third antinomy is doomed to a dualism of nature and spirit because Kant remained tied to a rationalist paradigm of causation. Kant employs a concept of the intelligible character in his practical philosophy that cannot have been derived from the theoretical work. The first *Critique* could only claim that 'freedom is at least *not incompatible with* nature'. It did not show how they *are* compatible.[28] As Adorno puts it:

> According to the critique of reason, this [spontaneity] could no more be spoken of positively than the transcendental causes of the phenomena of external senses, while without the intelligible character, the moral act in what is empirical, the effect on this – and thereby morality – would be impossible.[29]

Transcendental causes can more readily be shown to be necessary theoretically than practically. It is easier to describe and thus posit the unity of experience in terms of the former than in terms of the latter – this being the neo-Kantian distinction between validity and value. The problem is that of what and how much can be transcendentally deduced from the unity of experience (that is to say, *which* unity?). Adorno nevertheless abides with Kant's paradigm of freedom to the extent that the doctrine of the intelligible remains the sole condition of its possibility. Otherwise freedom is arbitrary (Hume) or necessary (Leibniz, Spinoza) – not true freedom in either case. Adorno is not interested in grounding the intelligible character in theoretical philosophy *at all* – by proposing a new paradigm of causation, for instance. The theoretical cannot ground the moral. Adorno argues *for* the intelligible character, of which 'there is nothing better amongst human beings', in another way. In order to do so, he takes up the metaphysical and Kantian 'unity of the person' as constituting 'the location of the doctrine of the intelligible', and then interprets this unity as the speculative whole of lived *Erfahrung*, not the unity of a formal structure.

Kant's conception of freedom is formalistic because it fails to mediate the empirical with the pure consciousness. His 'critique of Hume's concept of personality is ossified into a principle beyond individual people. He grasps the unity of consciousness independently of each and every experience [*Erfahrung*].'[30] But Adorno once again conflates the unity of experience with the experience of the 'person'. He is left with an individualism that he does not want – the result of combining the metaphysical 'whole' with an anthropological 'life'. This concept of experience nevertheless remains Adorno's way of mediating the empirical with the intelligible. It moves in the opposite direction to Kant's attempted mediation. Rather than the intelligible character being the condition for the possibility of the unity of individual experience, the unity of individual experience is now the empirical ground for the possibility of the intelligible character:

> If one were to wager as to what the Kantian X of the intelligible character owes its true content, which maintained itself against the total indeterminacy of the aporetic concept, it would probably be the historically most advanced, spasmodically flaring, rapidly extinguished consciousness, which is inherent in the impulse to do the right thing. It is the concrete, intermittent anticipation [*Vorwegnahme*] of possibility, neither alien to humanity nor identical with it.[31]

Adorno's interpretation of the intelligible character is experimental. Can what is posited out of experience, the intelligible X, simultaneously be the condition for the possibility of that same experience? Another problem is that the 'impulse to do the right thing' looks too existential for Kant, for whom doing the right thing is a matter of rational choice, not impulse. Where is reason here? Adorno seems to respond that the 'impulse' does not come *ex nihilo*, but is instead given as a historical possibility – both as a possibility *in* history and as a possibility *of* history. The right thing is the right history and is therefore social as well as individual (the unity of the social as the unity of 'persons'). Adorno does not dismiss Kantian reason. He displaces it onto the right history, which flares up intermittently – from out of the wrong history, presumably, because reason is (bound to) rationality – as the 'anticipation' of (its own) 'possibility'. Adorno thus conceives of a non-transcendent absolute in Aristotelian-Hegelian terms, albeit in an interrupted form: 'as the possibility of the subject, the intelligible character is, like freedom, a becoming, not a being [*ein Werdendes, kein Seiendes*].'[32]

Adorno attempts to ground metaphysical experience in the experience of the right history. The period book-ended by 1798 and 1848 experienced this moment of promise in Europe, but not its realisation. Adorno reads Kant as a key figure on the stage of this moment of promise. Adorno's own experience of anticipatory promise was no doubt formed culturally and politically during the 1920s. However intermittent it may be, metaphysical experience can only be spoken of in relation to a metaphysical *and* materialist philosophy of history. Adorno's philosophy of history remains Hegelian to the extent that it acknowledges a marginalised ruse of human reason at work in it. But Adorno does not follow Hegel's systematic grounding of history: the 'doctrine of the positive negation is precisely and strictly the point at which I refuse to follow Hegel.'[33] Adorno's metaphysics of history still remains to be explained, therefore, since the 'positive negation' is the very possibility of Hegel's history of progressive world-spirit. In *Negative Dialectics*, Adorno believes that he can insert his immanent critique of Kantian freedom into Hegel's 'history as progress in the consciousness of freedom'. It is true that Adorno shares with Hegel a critique of formal freedom in Kant. But for Hegel, the liberal paradigm of individual freedom remains formal. Hegel's attempted sublation of transcendental idealism proceeded from an objection to negative freedom.

The 'Metacritique of Practical Reason' undergoes a two-pronged autocritique in the 'Meditations on Metaphysics'. (1) If the anticipation of the intelligible character, metaphysical experience, is derived from a history of its anticipations – those of the historically most advanced periods – then this anticipation will have to withstand the reality of the least historically advanced or barbaric periods. Adorno is quite consistent when he writes that metaphysical experience, not metaphysics *as such*, is crippled after Auschwitz, to the extent that we are living though an age of immaturity. 'After Auschwitz' might then connote an historical phase, one that could be worked-through 'metaphysically'. Yet this word-symbol is of such magnitude for Adorno that it must 'transform the content of metaphysics' *itself*, including the metaphysics of history. This 'name stands for something unthinkable beyond the unthinkable, namely, a whole historical phase.'[34] Hence, (2) what of the intelligible world, the transcendental 'rationalisation' of the unmoved-mover? What of the promise of metaphysics? Adorno knows that the crisis of metaphysics includes Kantian metaphysics. His response in the last meditation goes under the heading of 'Self-reflection of Dialectics'. If dialectics is prefigured in the transcendental dialectic, as Adorno contends, then dialectics is Kantian metaphysics and the reflection of dialectics is the meditation on metaphysics. A comparable notion is at stake in Adorno's *meta*-critique of practical reason. The important question therefore concerns the meaning and possibility of this reflection, since this is what is supposed to be extra-metaphysical. Adorno disappointingly displaces the problem, however. For this paradigm of reflection is already Kantian, or Fichtean. In his return to the *mundus intelligibilis* in the eighth meditation, Adorno suggests that the resources for its retrieval are already contained *within* the transcendental dialectic: the 'logic of appearance' as negative dialectic. 'Therein the redemption of appearance [*die Rettung die Scheins*], the object of aesthetics, has its incomparable metaphysical relevance.'[35] This summation contradicts Adorno's previous attempt to ground the metaphysical experience of the intelligible character outside of Kantian idealism. And yet, at least Kant attempted to ground it, in the dialectic itself. Adorno invites the problem of the infinite regress in the antinomical structure of pure reason. In isolating the third antinomy, Adorno loses sight of its place in the overall *problematic* of the dialectic. Of course, Adorno might be seeking to revive Kantian reason through his heterodox interpretation of the intelligible character. But in that case, why return to the 'logic of appearance'? The intelligible must appear, as semblance. But this semblance is subject to an anterior antinomy that guarantees it must never appear.

As was seen, the younger Benjamin was attentive to the problem of the regressive infinity in Kantian metaphysics. Adorno's thesis that 'metaphysics migrates into micrology' amounts to a restatement of his dissonant nominalism, the 'anti-system' modelled upon Benjamin's constellational monad and Weber's ideal-type. Benjamin's Schellingian materialism lives on in Adorno's micrology, to the extent that the micro has any claim upon the macro, even, or especially negatively. Adorno's retrieval of the intelligible character through (meta-) reflection nevertheless remains, in much of *Negative Dialectics*, something of a performative contradiction. Adorno replaces that which has fallen, Kantian metaphysics, with more of the same Kantian metaphysics. Adorno's ambivalence over Kant becomes fixed into a Kantian antinomy of its own, which is similarly assumed to be productive ('given to us as a problem'). But the antimony of the antinomy is surely a tautology. The sense of inertia – precisely that which Adorno wants to resist – is exacerbated by Adorno's nostalgic presentation of the quandary. Metaphysics is crippled, but only metaphysics has the cure. Adorno expresses a sense of loss for a metaphysical experience that, perhaps, never was. Fortunately, aside from the micrology, the narrowly Kantian response is not Adorno's only response to the problem of metaphysics. 'Happiness and Waiting in Vain' appears as a possibility amidst the seeming impossibility of the 'Meditations'. The section is nevertheless intimately connected to Adorno's overall problem. The crisis of metaphysics is a crisis of promise. Kant's 'kingdom of ends' becomes the bad utopia of waiting in vain for an end that we already take to be beyond us. The problem of the regressive infinity is, it was suggested, intimately connected to the problem of the temporal series of conditions.[36] In *Minima Moralia*, Adorno defines the experience of this stretch of time into infinity as boredom. In-finite, because this time is alienated from finite experience. As a form of alienation, this boredom is no benign idleness: 'The man for whom time stretches out painfully is one waiting in vain [*der Wartet vergeblich*], disappointed at not finding tomorrow already continuing yesterday.'[37] In *Negative Dialectics*, the boredom of 'waiting in vain' is explicitly related to the problem of metaphysics. Art 'has demonstrated' the condition of waiting in vain in the absence of metaphysical expectation. Art does not tautologically reproduce waiting in vain however: in *expressing* (it), art says something else. In *Aesthetic Theory*, expression is closely related to mimesis, which is equally productive and poetic. The expression of meaninglessness is not abstractly negative for Adorno – a lament to what has been lost. It is the reverse: 'happiness' – hence the Proustian example of place names. In his concluding lecture on metaphysics, and in contrast to the concluding meditation, Adorno says that 'waiting in vain' is 'no doubt the form [*Gestalt*] in which metaphysical experience manifests itself most strongly to us.'[38] There can, it seems, be no doubt that 'waiting in vain' is central to Adorno's late work.

But how can 'waiting in vain' name *both* unhappy boredom *and* the happiness of metaphysical experience? This transformation is the work of (its) expression. In the lectures, it is the work of the '*Gestalt*', as *Gestaltung*. As Adorno says of Beethoven's 'expansive type', empty time is 'shaped', albeit as the semblance of what fulfilled time *would be*. As semblance of the awaited, not the awaited of itself, anticipation is here intermittent. Perhaps Adorno's 'intermittent anticipation' (of the intelligible X) pertains to the nature of the anticipation more than the discontinuity of historical progress. 'Waiting in vain does not vouchsafe what the expectation aims at, but reflects the condition, which has its measure in the denial.' Reflection takes on a different sense to Kantian-romantic reflection here. It is as tragic as it is ironic, since it acknowledges that which it is denying for the sake of its knowledge. An expression of waiting in vain does not negate anticipation, but is instead a new kind of anticipation. The expression of waiting in vain is original, not weakened anticipation. Adorno will not use the ontological terminology of 'origin', but there is an implicit notion of temporalisation of possibility in his concept of expression – if only as a negation of detemporalisation. As with Benjamin's 'weak messianic force', weakness is not a comparative to some former strength in the case of *intermittent* anticipation.

A tension nevertheless remains between Benjamin's metaphysics, at work within Adorno's thought, and Adorno's late confrontation with metaphysics. The problem of waiting in vain involves an extension of the radical historical indeterminacy of the 'when?' into the 'if?' This is why we ask, 'is that all?' But given that the 'expression' is not of itself in vain, Adorno does retain a moment of promise, in his quasi-messianic form of waiting. In the 'Finale' to *Minima Moralia*, Adorno acknowledges the necessity of the internal contradiction of impossibility and possibility arising from this philosophical messianism. On the one hand, '[t]he only philosophy which can be practised in the face of despair is the attempt to contemplate all things as they would present themselves from the standpoint of redemption.' But on the other hand, this possibility remains:

> the utterly impossible thing, because it presupposes a standpoint removed, even though by a hair's breadth, from the scope of existence, whereas we well know that any possible knowledge must not only be wrested from what is, if it shall hold good, but is also marked, for this very reason, by the same distortion and indigence which it seeks to escape.

Adorno does not resolve this antinomy, but rather, again in a Kantian vein, takes the 'as if' to be productive, *a priori*, thus siding with possibility against impossibility regulatively: the 'question of the reality or unreality of redemption hardly itself matters'. Taubes and Agamben have thus taken exception to Adorno's 'Finale'.[39] Conversely, Adorno's formulation amounts to a critique of these thinkers, in terms of an assumption of 'the messianic light' itself.[40] And unlike Agamben, Adorno internalises this problem, however inconclusively, into his 'Meditations'. Agamben gives no consideration to the 'Meditations', to 'waiting in vain' in particular, which is arguably 'more messianic' precisely because it is, as Agamben puts it, 'non-messianic'. Adorno's extension of the 'when?' into the 'if?' sharpens the problem and meaning of an expression of waiting in vain as being not in vain.

The expression of waiting in vain shares a sense of promise, as becoming, with the traditional idea of metaphysics, but without being traditional. This intermittent promise would even become metaphysical for the first time. It would express 'solidarity with metaphysics in the moment of its fall'.[41] The expression of waiting in vain can therefore be understood as Adorno's critique of anticipation in the intelligible character. This 'changes the contents of metaphysics itself'. The genitive in the expression *of* waiting in vain functions both subjectively and objectively. An expression of waiting in vain is not identical with waiting in vain, and in a crucial sense opposes it. This is the moment of hope against all hope that is to be found in philosophical messianism. But insofar as such messianism does not consider the relation to the second aspect of the genitive, it remains, in the last instance, overdetermined by traditional metaphysics (as Benjamin himself ruefully remarked, the theological tradition 'has to keep out of sight').[42] This is what is distinctive about Adorno's late expression of waiting in vain. For the expression is *of* waiting in vain, in the sense of belonging to waiting in vain. There is something of waiting in vain in the expression. The expression is a *kind* of waiting, the mediating event of waiting in vain 'into' the awaited.

It was suggested in the previous four chapters that the nature of this 'twisting free' (Heidegger) and 'turn around' (Adorno) should be elucidated by way of a philosophy of the 'musical'. The '*divertissement*' of musical time and the 'bad utopia' of musical space each implies waiting in vain. But musical dissonance names its expression, and, as musical, forms another kind of waiting. It is an-other waiting as not the representing willing of some-thing, nor of no-nothing. At the same time, it is both waiting and willing. The expression of waiting in vain was equally understood as a mimesis of detemporalisation, taking the example of Nono. This 'tragic ironic' mimesis is as spatial as it is temporal. The meaning and possibility of the expression of waiting in vain nevertheless remains somewhat philosophically under-articulated (in the previous two chapters, the means of argumentation was not purely philosophical but also proceeded by way of an interpretation of Nono). As was suggested, the recourse to the idea of natural history only remains coherent if its metaphysical grounding is confronted. The 'anti-metaphysical' thinking of the tragic might risk the wishful thinking associated with philosophical messianism. This remains equally the case within Heidegger's *active* nihilism – as he increasingly comes to realise. Some of the results of Heidegger's auto-critique can once again contribute to an understanding of the expression of waiting in vain.

Heidegger

Boredom as fundamental attunement

The 'fundamental attunement [*Grundstimmung*]' of 'profound boredom', which Heidegger introduces in *The Fundamental Concepts of Metaphysics*,[43] can initially be read in terms of the 'fundamental state-of-mind' described in *Being and Time*: '*Angst*'.[44] This shift in terminology anticipates a series of shifts in Heidegger's philosophy at this time, amounting to a sustained critique of the book that had brought him notoriety (as early as 1928,

Heidegger would report to Karl Jaspers, 'I no longer think of the fact that a short while ago I wrote a so-called book').[45] In *Being and Time*, state-of-mind (*'Befindlichkeit'*: literally, how Dasein finds itself) is 'a fundamental *existentiale*'. For, 'in every case Dasein always has some mood [*gestimmt ist*]' – especially, as we shall see, in the 'pallid, evenly balanced lack of mood [*Ungestimmtheit*].'[46] In the quasi-transcendental terms of *Being and Time*, state-of-mind is the condition for the possibility of *'Stimmung'*, mood. In *The Fundamental Concepts*, however, it is *'Grundstimmung'* that is fundamental though not ostensibly formal-transcendental. The fundamental attunement signals a departure from the latent Kantianism of *Being and Time*, recognised by Adorno in his 1932 lecture.[47] Heidegger's *existentiale* had performed the function of a category. This was not the Kantian category, for it was intended to elude the formal-transcendental structure of Kantian (and all post-Cartesian) metaphysics. Judging from *The Fundamental Concepts*, Heidegger now doubts whether this attempt was successful. Heidegger's response is to radicalise state-of-mind *into* the fundamental attunement. In what sense is this a radicalisation? And how does it address the problem of formalism?

Heidegger is drawn to the twofold sense of *Stimmung* as mood and as attunement, in the sense of a relation (paradigmatically, as we have seen, the tuning of a musical interval). Unlike state-of-mind, there can be no attunement *in general*: 'there is not merely one single attunement, but several'. This is because attunement is already a way of being-in-the-world, not a formal condition of its possibility: 'An attunement is a way, not merely a form or mode, but a way.' There are profound consequences to Heidegger's foregrounding of the fundamental attunement, within and beyond his thought. Adorno consistently accuses Heidegger of idealism, for the reason that the transcendental structure of Dasein, including the category of historicity, is foundationalist and thus non-historical. Heidegger naturalises the historical structure of Dasein. Existence becomes the timeless ground of time, or Dasein's self-temporalisation. But Adorno's critique is problematic for two reasons: (1) A historically attentive reading of *Being and Time* would suggest that anxiety *becomes* fundamental in relation to the history of metaphysical modernity. The philosophy of history in *Being and Time* short-circuits this reading to a great extent, because the *existentiale* is, *as* a 'category', anachronistically projected into the 'having-been'. If ideology and dogmatic metaphysics excluded, and continue to exclude, an authentic attunement of *Angst*, then authentic 'historizing' was, and remains, an impossibility – even for Heidegger's untimely poets. (2) Adorno's principle objection is that Heidegger repeats neo-Kantian historicism along with its epistemology ('critical idealism').[48] This leads to an impotence of critical history. But does Adorno's alternative philosophy of history succeed in overcoming neo-Kantianism, given the problems encountered in Chapter 1? We are once again faced with the conflict between existence and history. Does history ground existence or does existence ground history?

The Fundamental Concepts lectures already anticipate some of Adorno's criticisms, and point towards responses that both resonate with and challenge Adorno's alternatives. For the re-interpretation of state-of-mind as attunement impinges directly upon the twofold problem of formalism and history. Since the fundamental attunement is not ostensibly formal-transcendental, Heidegger must choose *one* fundamental attunement, of *today*: 'Profound boredom is the fundamental attunement of our contemporary Dasein'. As Miguel de Beistegui has observed, the 'fundamental disposition' of profound boredom renders the lecture-course an eminently transitional work. De Beistegui entitles this transition: 'Between Existence and History'.[49] Heidegger must support his claim for *the* fundamental attunement of contemporary Dasein with a philosophy of history that goes beyond the formal historicity of *Being and Time*, initially by way of a phenomenology of contemporary boredom. Heidegger attempts to show his students that they are fundamentally bored. With both anxiety and boredom, Heidegger proceeded from the everyday and determinate towards the enigmatic and indeterminate. In *Being and Time*, the way is prepared for the account of anxiety with 'fear', that everyday state-of-mind which discloses 'the "*thrownness*" of this entity', Da-sein, 'into its "there".'[50] Fear is determinate, intended towards 'something which we encounter within-the-world'. The first form of boredom, 'becoming bored by', is similarly determinate. With the example of waiting for a train, Heidegger suggests that we are aware both of *what* we are bored by and *that* we are bored by it. We are all too aware that we are bored because we repeatedly try, and repeatedly fail, to pass the time. In this non-passing of the time, time presses itself upon us, not as something external or invisible but rather as the burden of Dasein itself:

> What is at issue in boredom [*Langweile*] is a while [*Weile*], tarrying a while [*Verweilen*], a peculiar remaining, enduring... what is decisive in passing the time, and indeed in *what* it shakes off, namely boredom, is, after all, *time*. Passing the time is therefore a shortening of time that drives time on, namely the time that seeks to become long [*lang*]. It is thus an intervention into time as a *confrontation with time*.[51]

In the second example, 'being bored with', we go to a dinner party and only realise that we were bored afterwards. We cannot put our finger on what exactly bored us. We are bored by *'I know not what'*. Hence, 'in the first case we have a *determinate boring thing,* whereas in the second case we have *something indeterminate that bores us.*'[52] Crucially, the parallel between anxiety and boredom breaks down with the third case of boredom, 'profound boredom', because there were only *two* levels of fear: conditioned (fear) and condition of possibility (anxiety) in *Being and Time*. In boredom, by contrast, an increasing profundity or depth accrues from each form to the next. Hence, the 'second form of boredom has a peculiar *intermediate position.*'[53] At the same time, 'the third form is the condition of the possibility of the first and thereby also of the second.'[54] 'Profound boredom' is indeterminate: 'It bores one [*Es langweilt Einen*]'.[55]

What, then, distinguishes the second and third forms of boredom, given that each is indeterminate? Profound boredom is occasioned by the 'refusal' of 'beings as a whole'. Rather than pitting the determinate against the indeterminate, Heidegger now suggests that the *manifoldness* of boredom signifies that its determinacy is a question of *intensity* (or 'depth'). This is the departure from the 'two level' transcendental (and empirical) Kantianism. Even, or especially, the deepest boredom is the negative concern of 'beings as a whole' – not beings *in general* (Heidegger wants to wrest the *as such* from the *in general,* to displace transcendental with ontological difference). As was suggested above, Heidegger's description of profound boredom comes close to an idea of melancholy, which he names on two occasions in these lectures. In profound boredom, 'all and everything appears indifferent to us'.[56] The 'all and everything' signifies that profound boredom is bored with 'beings as a whole' – just as, in this respect at least, anxiety, attested to in 'anticipatory resoluteness', is the secret to an authentic '*Ganzseinkönnen*'. The experience of radical indeterminacy is Heidegger's way of showing that time is a question about the whole and that the whole is a question about time: 'what is at issue is the question of *what time itself is,* such that it can have a relation to things, and furthermore such that from out of such a relation something like boredom is possible as an *attunement* that attunes *us* through and through.'[57]

In contrast to determinate fear, that 'in the face of which one is anxious is completely indeterminate'; 'is not an entity within-the-world'.[58] What, in that case, are we anxious about? When anxiety is introduced in division I of *Being and Time,* only one of the three ways in which Dasein is anxious has been characterised: thrownness. The remaining two are 'Being-towards-death' and 'the call of conscience'. In all three 'phenomena', anxiety rises-up out of the abyss: 'The "nothing" with which anxiety brings us face to face, unveils the nullity by which Dasein, in its very *ground*, is defined; and this basis itself is a thrownness into death.'[59] And yet, Heidegger does not discuss 'Being-towards-death' in *The Fundamental Concepts* (he does, briefly, as an instance of how the 'ordinary understanding' fails to grasp a concept when it grasps at it too tightly).[60] Heidegger also declines to pursue the meaning of the expression 'we are *almost dying of boredom*'.[61] Boredom is clearly a question about finitude: 'being affected by time in boredom…is evidently a peculiar *impressing of the power of that time* to which we are bound.' And profound boredom is, like Being-towards-death, radically indeterminate: 'Along with the certainty of death goes the *indeterminacy* [Unbestimmtheit] of its "when".'[62] Nevertheless, the disappearance of Being-towards-death in the lectures has important consequences for Heidegger's evolving understanding of the concepts: world, whole, time and history. It paves the way for a complex relation to Adorno's 'waiting in vain'.

World, whole, history

What is fundamental about profound boredom is that its indeterminacy is such that it *tells of* the refusal of 'things as a whole'. The 'silent fog' becomes deafening:

> All telling *refusal* [Ver*sagen*] is in itself a *telling* [Sagen], i.e., a making manifest. What do beings in this telling refusal of themselves as a whole tell us in such refusal? What do they tell us in refusing to tell? It is a telling refusal of that which somehow could and was to be granted to Dasein. And what is that? The very *possibilities* of doing and acting. The telling refusal tells of these possibilities of Dasein.[63]

As with the call of conscience, this way of telling 'does not put itself into words at all, yet it remains nothing less than obscure and indeterminate.'[64] But in *Being and Time*, the 'resolute' harkening to the call of conscience was only half of the story about authenticity. Being-towards-death provided Heidegger with the 'anticipatory [*Vorlaufen*]' that, joined with 'resoluteness', became 'anticipatory resoluteness' (as we shall see, the anticipatory is to be sharply distinguished from anticipation).[65] In the *Fundamental Concepts*, by contrast, possibility is not aligned with futural temporalisation. The understanding of temporality accordingly differs in these two works, in contradictory ways. These contradictions must be noted in order to take the most progressive elements from both of these 'modernist' works in a more or less coherent manner.

In *The Fundamental Concepts*, the fundamental attunement concerns time in its inherent relation to world, as things-as-a-whole, rather than to things that are not yet, or might never be. In the above citation, Heidegger speaks of possibilities, but these are now things according to things-as-a-whole and, though Heidegger will never admit it, historical time as-a-whole. Possibility inheres in all three temporal horizons – in the 'single threefold horizon of time' – whereas, in *Being and Time*, possibility is the necessary privilege of the futural, for the indeterminate expectation of death, the anticipatory, is the ontological possibility of determinate possibility: 'The anticipatory makes Dasein *authentically* futural, and in such a way that the anticipatory itself is possible only in so far as Dasein, *as being*, is always coming towards itself – that is to say, in so far as it is futural in its Being in general.'[66] This is not the case in *The Fundamental Concepts*. In fundamental boredom:

> All beings withdraw from us without exception in every respect [*Hinsicht*], everything we look at and the way in which we look at it; everything in retrospect [*Rücksicht*], all beings that we look back upon as having been and having become and as past, and the way we look back at them; all beings in every prospect [*Absicht*], everything we look at prospectively as futural, and the way we have thus regarded them prospectively. Everything – in every respect, in retrospect and prospect, beings simultaneously withdraw. The *three perspectives* [Sichten] of respect, retrospect, and prospect do not belong to mere perception ... but are the perspectives of all *doing and activity* of *Dasein* ... There is a telling refusal of all beings simultaneously in 'what' and 'how' they are: *as a whole*, as we put it.[67]

A tension reigns within Heidegger's 'world' of the lectures, between beings *as such* and, in this instance, a *totality* of beings – past, present and future. The latter resembles a form of pantheism. In his lecture on natural history, Adorno cites Heidegger's 'most recent turn towards Hegel' as further evidence of an unacknowledged absolute idealism. Adorno's later critique of Hegel's 'detemporalisation' is equally applicable to Heidegger in this instance.[68] The evolution of Heidegger's whole from a phenomenological to a pantheistic-Aristotelian concept is ambiguous. The totality of the whole comes close to the scholastic-nominalist idea that every-thing has its unique time and place: *haecceitas*. This teaching of Duns Scotus interested the younger

Heidegger – ultimately, in relation to Hegel.[69] Adorno found this nominalism in *Being and Time*, in spite of its emphasis upon the '*pragmata*' of things.[70] Heidegger now states, in *The Fundamental Concepts*, that 'boredom is possible only because every thing, and more fundamentally every Dasein as such, has its time.'[71] This conservative ontology (in every sense) is not modern or post-metaphysical, but medieval and eminently metaphysical (even the Nazis would come to fear Heidegger's Jesuitic scholasticism). Such an ontology views its world as the natural order of things. Prefacing the lengthy discussion of boredom with a discussion of Aristotle's *Metaphysics*, Heidegger devotes the remaining lectures to a comparison between the worlds of stone, animal and Dasein. Heidegger's philosophy calls for him to rethink the meaning of nature, but he cannot do this so long as he remains confined to an ontology that modernity has rendered otiose. What was modern about *Being and Time*, by contrast, was its systematic presentation of possibility *as* possibility. It is a fragmentary, modernist system of freedom. Heidegger acknowledged, in the tragic sense, that the world is not the stable creation of a creator, into which we creatures are purposefully placed. Modernity dispels this natural order of things. So long as Dasein *is there, things could be otherwise*.

Heidegger remained too optimistic about the tragic in *Being and Time*, however. Or, he focused upon the hero to the neglect of the chorus. This problem is acknowledged in *The Fundamental Concepts*. The problem of 'world' concerns 'us', 'today'. But, in addressing this problem, Heidegger produces a new set of them. On the one hand, world signifies 'beings as a whole', tellingly refused in fundamental boredom. On the other hand, 'world-formation' means the 'un-concealment' of determinate possibility, illuminated in the '*Augenblick*' of the very same fundamental attunement.[72] Heidegger risks ending-up either with a one-world monism or a two-world dualism (the actual world and the possible one). If truth is the unconcealment of that which has refused itself then truth is the same old world, once over. The anomaly is especially acute in the first instance of the temporal horizon. How can the having-been, as something, both refuse itself and be disclosed as a possibility? This problem is symptomatic of Heidegger's equivocation over whether the resolutely disclosing *Augenblick* remains held open in the *Grundstimmung*, as the readiness to act upon possibilities, or is rather *Bestimmung*, the determinate act of itself. Sometimes it appears to be both.[73] But so long as we are political animals, we can do more about the to-come than about the having-been, however much the former must be related to the latter. As Heidegger had put it in *Being and Time*, '[o]nly so far as it is futural can

Dasein *be* authentically as having been. The character of "having been" arises, in a certain way, from the future.'[74]

Adorno anticipates these problems in his natural history lecture: (1) What does Heidegger mean by 'the whole'? And (2), how can the whole include both the possible and the actual? '[T]he project [*Entwurf*] of being...takes priority over the subsumed facticity; a facticity that is to be fitted in as an afterthought.'[75] Adorno picks-up on Heidegger's equivocation between the *totality* and the *as such*. In *Being and Time*, the whole 'is no longer held to be a systematic whole, but rather a structural whole, a structural unity or totality.'[76] Tellingly, Adorno does not pursue the problem of the *as such*. In *The Fundamental Concepts*, Heidegger wants the 'as' to correspond to 'the Being of beings', and thus to ontological difference. Whereas, Adorno often defines 'being' in a traditional manner: 'the question of ontology...is none other than what I mean by "nature".'[77] Adorno can thus accuse Heidegger of projecting Dasein, as spirit, *onto* nature, in an eminently German idealist gesture. Heidegger 'only offers an *apparent* solution to the problem of the reconciliation of nature and history'.[78] Adorno's possible determination of Being as nature nevertheless seems to remain, from Heidegger's perspective, at the level of an ontic misrecognition of the ontological. As we saw from the Heidegger-critique in *Negative Dialectics*, Adorno takes Heidegger's concept of Being to correspond to 'the cosmos'. But for Heidegger, the Being of beings cannot be totalised in this way, since the meaning of Being is time (ironically, this comes close to Adorno's contention that the absolute is 'a matter of natural history').[79] Adorno seems to miss this fundamental thesis in Heidegger, which is perhaps remarkable given Adorno's own interest in time and history. Even in the later polemics against Being-towards-death, Adorno does not confront Heidegger's rethinking of temporality (in any case, Adorno would not have been familiar with the 1929–30 lectures).

Heidegger's lapse into scholasticism – which Adorno *was* well aware of – coincides with an attempt to address the problems of idealism and solipsism in *Being and Time*. There was a diremption in the book between the whole and the world. The possibility of Being-a-whole was to be attested to in the face of that which radically individuates. Death is 'in each case one's own'.[80] How can the radically individuated also be the whole? The whole in *Being and Time* is the whole individual, but only according to an attempted redefinition of individual and individuation. Adorno is right to say that Heidegger neglects the individual: firstly, because this is precisely Heidegger's point. Dasein is not the 'person' (in this sense, Dasein has more in common with Hegelian spirit or Schellingian existence than it does with Kantian subjectivity – hence the interpretations of Dasein as the 'for-itself'). Being is never mine but is always, authentically, a determinate response to the question of Being. Without mineness, Being would remain unquestioned and hence forgotten. That Being belongs to no-one is another way of saying that authentic Dasein is authentic '*Mitdasein*'. Heidegger must admit that, '[r]esoluteness brings the Self ... into solicitous Being with Others [*fürsorgende Mitsein*].'[81] This sort of thinking is not unique to Heidegger, of course. For Adorno, '[h]umanity can be thought only through [an] extreme form of differentiation, individuation, not as a comprehensive generic concept.'[82] Adorno's speculative universal collectivity is nowhere to be seen in *Being and Time*, however. Heidegger needs a collective movement of history to give content to his historicity. Not the collective of humanity, but of the German nation. Nevertheless, *The Fundamental Concepts* lectures show that Heidegger begins to think about contemporary modernity ('contemporary Dasein') and collectivity ('our') prior to his ideological conversion to National Socialism (outwardly, at least). Heidegger at no point aligns the 'we' to the German nation in *The Fundamental Concepts*, but that was soon to change.

'*Ganzseinkönnen*' does not explicitly include a world, as 'things-as-a-whole' did in *The Fundamental Concepts*. In *Being and Time*, things are redefined as 'equipment' prior to the explicit introduction of the problem of authenticity. Being-in-the world (of 'public' things) is thus biased towards the everyday and inauthentic (except for a brief return to equipment at the end of the book). Heidegger alludes to this problem, his former deconstruction of the *res*, in the lecture course: 'It never occurred to me ... to try to claim or prove with this interpretation that the essence of man consists in the fact that he knows how to handle knives and forks or to use the tram.'[83] Heidegger now seeks to incorporate 'world' explicitly into the possibility of authenticity – except that, not only is the openness of resoluteness, *Ent-schlossenheit*, now emphasised over its mineness (openness to Being *as* the question of mineness) but equally, the problem of authenticity now concerns *us*. Indeed, Heidegger never really deals with the *Solitude* of his subtitle (which he calls 'individuation' in the lectures). If ontological questioning is to occupy the void left by metaphysics then it must question 'comprehensively', in a manner that 'includes the questioner'. Between 1929 and 1932, Heidegger experiments with a redefinition of metaphysics, because it has traditionally served to ask this question of the whole.[84] In Aristotle, *physis* means both 'nature' *and* 'nature of'.[85] Physics is already metaphysics. These are but hints of a different kind of 'comprehensive philosophizing' for

Heidegger, who now follows the middle Schelling in contending that any systematic philosophy of facticity must include a positive account of nature. The *Freiheitschrift* is cited towards the end of the lectures.[86] Heidegger's repetition of Schelling's incorporation of contemporary natural science also repeats its syncretism, however. Heidegger intends to show, against idealism, that Dasein and animals share a world, only by sharing, against naturalism, different intensities of world. Heidegger combines a pre-modern materialism with modern zoology – a true dialectic of myth and enlightenment. Nevertheless, the Schellingian problematic might be recuperated in the light of both the ontological post-metaphysics of *Being and Time* and Adorno's melancholy science of natural history, which, it was claimed above, partly belongs to that 'system of freedom' tradition. A historical – and 'musical' – concept of *Stimmung* is central to both philosophies. This sense of historical attunement promises to mediate the two positions in order to respond to the question: what is the relationship between the world of possibility and the world of the awaited? For this is the messianic question of waiting.

Adorno and Heidegger

Boredom and waiting

In *Being and Time*, we read of a determinate and an indeterminate kind of waiting. Death always lies ahead, as 'that which is not to be outstripped'. But since the end cannot be determined in its 'what?' or its 'when?' – since Dasein would in these cases be *'Nicht-mehr-da-sein'*, then death cannot be *expected* – authentically, that is. Expectation, *Er-wartung,* is determinate waiting, in the sense that we already have what we are expecting before us:

> To expect something possible is always to understand it and to 'have' it with regard to whether and when and how it will be actually present-at-hand. Expecting is not just an occasional looking-away from the possible to its possible actualization, but is essentially a *waiting for that actualization* [ein *Warten auf diese*]. Even in expecting, one leaps away from the possible and gets a foothold on the actual.[87]

Expectation *does not* wait, to the extent that the awaited is already 'present-at-hand', projected from the present into the expected future – or, conversely, projected from the expected future into presence. We await the train in expectation of it. We know, now and in advance, what it will be like for the train to arrive since we have waited for trains that have arrived in the 'having-been'. The perpetuating present holds apart the possible and the actual, as a *long while* – boredom. Heidegger maintains that, in his first example, 'it is waiting itself that is boring and that bores us, but boredom is not itself a waiting. Furthermore, not every waiting is necessarily boring. On the contrary, waiting can be full of suspense.'[88] Heidegger is surely alluding to the more nuanced account of waiting in his *Hauptwerk*. Read in the light of *Being and Time*, the first form of determinate boredom must *return* in order for profound boredom to *be* profound. *No indeterminate waiting without determinate waiting* (as Benjamin observed, 'he who waits... takes in the time and renders it up in altered form – that of expectation').[89] Heidegger is reluctant to define boredom as waiting because he wants to retain the theme of attunement. It is not obvious that waiting is an attunement. Nevertheless, Heidegger cannot avoid waiting, since what is at issue in profound boredom is time, and hence the futural.

The second example of boredom is defined in terms of the perpetuating present of expectation. What differentiates the first and second forms of boredom is not, therefore, the question of determinacy alone. Whereas in the first example we fail to pass the time, in the second we succeed in it completely. We did not even notice that we were bored. Hence, distraction is the flipside of boredom. Warding off boredom through distraction, from boredom, means negating its long while, and shortening its time:

> We make time *stand*. We let the time we have taken for the evening – our taking consists precisely in this – endure in such a way during the evening that in being there alongside and part of whatever is going on we take no note of its flow or its moments. The enduring of the 'during' swallows up, as it were, the flowing sequence of nows and becomes a *single stretched 'now'* which itself does not flow but stands.[90]

Is it any coincidence that the evening's distractions include 'listening to music' – given that the temporality of music is, at one fundamental level, that of the sequential 'nows' that becomes a single, stretched 'now'?[91] The 'old aim of secular music', suggests Adorno, was 'that of the *divertissement* that distracts from boredom'. Music is the art of nihilism *par excellence*, Heidegger will suggest. For both Adorno and Heidegger, distraction from boredom perpetuates a fundamental alienation – of, for Adorno, the specifically capitalist mode of production. But at the same time, the peculiar connection between boredom and distraction 'lives on in the relationship to the time of autonomous music', that is, to *musically modern* time. Autonomy and authenticity are not, in that case, the simple 'others' of distraction and inauthenticity. Heidegger's sense of the historically telling refusal of things-as-a-whole provides a philosophically argumentative way of understanding the '*Augenblick*' in Adorno's understanding of boredom, distraction, and waiting-expression.

The 'Continuous stream of "nows"' corresponds to that which Heidegger had previously termed the 'vulgar ... representation' of time. In the lectures, vulgar temporality is made present and not merely represented. At the dinner party, 'we are *entirely present*'. Heidegger's conception of the present is already less promising than it was in *Being and Time*. There, the privileging of the futural was situated in the *inauthentic* mode of Dasein: the everyday 'Present [*Gegenwart*]' is not simply the perpetuation of 'nows' but is rather 'the "waiting towards" [*Gegen-wart*]'.[92] This benign optimism about everyday temporality is a consequence of the existential structuralism of *Being and Time*. It undergoes a severe reassessment in *The Fundamental Concepts*. Expressionist anxiety is superseded by Dadaist boredom. It is the seeming impossibility of possibility that now confronts our contemporary Dasein, not the plenitude of heroic possibilities. This seeming impossibility is, understood in the light of Adorno's waiting in vain, twofold. Firstly, the impossibility of possibility names reification. Secondly, this totalisation is false consciousness. Unfreedom, impossibility, appears as freedom, possibility. The whole is such that it tends to become impossible to conceive of 'the totality as something that could be completely different'. Heidegger's reassessment of freedom in *The Fundamental Concepts* anticipates some of Adorno's criticisms of *Being and Time*. Heidegger's formal historicity had led him to abstract the meaning of death from its social and historical contexts – as if every age could and should be equally heroic. Adorno's critique of Being-towards-death makes sense precisely because the fall of metaphysics – of consoling promises of all kinds, including consolation for the absence of promise in forms of distraction – becomes unbearable, leaving talk of authentic Being-towards-death meaningless. The 'terror', *not* anxiety, about of death today is that 'of seeing how much the living resemble it'. Poets such as Trakl gave expression to this situation, Adorno suggests. The outlook of Heidegger, another reader of Trakl, is similarly bleak in the 1929–30 lectures. Could this be a reason why Being-towards-death disappears from Heidegger's work (until the 'mortals' of 'the fourfold')? Being-towards-death is, in its heroism, anachronistically 'pristine'. It does not finally shake-off the suspicion of solipsism – that it is *never* the whole. The analysis of fundamental boredom can, by contrast, illuminate the meaning of finitude in a way that confronts the existential solipsism. Neither Adorno nor Heidegger can do without a future-oriented conception of finitude. Death articulates this orientation phenomenologically (initially, through the death of others). For Heidegger, Being-towards-death is the way in which the question of Being *appears for* Dasein, as its question: 'Why is there Being and not nothing?' is no logical conundrum that invites a propositional answer (as it is given by Leibniz, to his own question). Though Adorno rejects Heidegger's ontology – the question of Being constituting a merely 'childish question' – he nevertheless understands *Erfahrung* in terms of a relation to death and to the whole (both individual and social).[93] For Adorno, the 'good life' would be one in which death was not terrifying. There is another affinity to Heidegger's 'death metaphysics' here: the expression of waiting in vain, the intermittent anticipation of possibility, is a kind of temporalised possibility, in a similar way that, for Heidegger, indeterminate waiting is grasped as the possibility of possibility. Each opposes expectation in the name of expectation.

If Heidegger's philosophy of boredom is read as a critical reconceptualisation of Being-towards-death, rather than as its mere surrogate – as the necessary critique of heroic solipsism and formal-transcendentalism – then it might be possible to understand waiting in vain in terms of profound boredom, as a temporalisation of possibility, and on the basis of Heidegger's initial account of originary temporalisation in *Being and Time*. Conversely, Adorno's metaphysical experience can be read, against Adorno, as a critique of Heidegger's 'metaphysics of death' rather than as its abstract negation. This approach would result in a twofold critique of metaphysical waiting (expectation) on the one side and ontological waiting (without expectation) on the other. Indeed, Heidegger's ontology provides a means of understanding the expression of waiting in vain as more failed promise. In that form, the expression would be in bad faith, since it would be the intermittent interruption of that which it had rejected: traditional metaphysical promise. On Adorno's side, the critique of 'anticipatory resoluteness' is the historical critique of 'trans-historical' existence (de Beistegui), and by extension, fundamental ontology.[94] It proposes that society can and must change – but not according to any pre-established harmony. This mutual critique promises to set up a post-metaphysical account of the expression of waiting in vain that retains the historical facticity in the idea of natural history. If the expression of waiting in vain is the interruption of anticipatory resoluteness then 'inauthentic' distraction becomes the interruption of authenticity, which accordingly becomes the possibility of another modernity, not a reaction to it. This interruption is not another form of uncritical messianism by the back door, however. Interruption here names the positive character of the waiting-expression, between metaphysics and ontology, history and existence.

One of Johann Peter Hebel's *Assorted Thoughts* (1811) reads: 'Boredom waits for death'.[95] Death cannot be expected, but it can be willed. Passive nihilism is the will to nothing. Willing and longing are forms of expectation. They actualise the impossible and make the actually possible impossible. Romanticism waits in vain insofar as it waits for an object of infinite willing and longing. Adorno stresses that an expression of waiting in vain is *not* 'a sphere of Romantic wishing', however.[96] In *The Jargon of Authenticity*, Adorno questions Heidegger's dismissal of all reflections upon death.[97] But such reflection is not necessarily the death metaphysics that concludes *Tristan und Isolde*. Adorno at one point even approves of Heidegger's alternative comportment: *Vorlaufen*. 'Only rarely do Heidegger's words contain as much truth as these.'[98] The anticipatory is, like the expression of waiting in vain, *not* expectation. *Vor-laufen* is the *running-ahead* of 'that which is not to be outstripped'.[99] The anticipatory holds open the greatest possibility *in* resoluteness. The *Augenblick* of the telling refusal of profound boredom must therefore be said to open up the greatest possibility in the mode of the anticipatory. There is an affinity between profound boredom and *Vorlaufen*, in terms of the shared indeterminacy of their waiting. This return of the futural into profound boredom means that the worlds of the existing and the possible are now temporalised, historically, and not confused unhistorically. The existing world is the world of contemporary Dasein and world formation is the waiting that belongs to the awaited.

In the early 1930s, Heidegger strategically retreated from the existentialism of *Being and Time* and advanced into what he perceived to be the actual possibilities of his time and place. The account of Being-towards-death nevertheless reminds the reader of *The Fundamental Concepts* that the greatest possibility is nothing without factical possibilities. This is the formal-transcendental problem that the fundamental attunement was intended to address. Profound boredom does not quite close its eyes to the world. The telling refusal is a squinting that seeks out the brightest of dim possibilities, possibilities that must be grasped. Where Heidegger makes his way through the fog, Adorno goes underground to make his point:

> For thought there is really no other possibility, no other opportunity, than to do what the miner's adage forbids: to work one's way through

> the darkness without a lamp, without possessing the positive through the higher concept of the negation of the negation, and to immerse oneself in the darkness as deeply as one possibly can.[100]

Just over two years after the lectures, Heidegger would become impatient with his indeterminate waiting. Heidegger would make a political decision. The problem of formalism could not be resolved immanently within Heidegger's system, and so the historical content had to come in from the outside. Waiting without expectation converges with decisionism. But what if Heidegger did not remain true to (his) waiting? What if the philosopher of waiting failed to experience waiting, or rather its *expression*? This would be on account of a misapprehension of the political economy of boredom and waiting – of 'contemporary Dasein'.

Waiting or destining?

Who is to say when is the right time for waiting and for no-longer waiting? Who, for that matter, is to say that boredom is the fundamental attunement of our contemporary Dasein? Heidegger gives the following response: *we* are. The telling refusal of factical possibilities *itself* signifies that profound boredom is the fundamental attunement of contemporary Dasein. The fundamental attunement simultaneously tells of this refusal. The reason that boredom, and not anxiety, is the fundamental attunement, is that 'what oppresses us most profoundly and in a concealed manner is the very *absence of any essential oppressiveness in our Dasein as a whole.*' This is not at all to say that there are no contemporary 'needs'. Heidegger is more attuned to the (culture of) crisis at the end of the 1920s than he would like to admit:

> everywhere there are disruptions, catastrophes, needs: the contemporary social misery, political confusion, the powerlessness of science, the erosion of art, the groundlessness of philosophy, the impotence of religion.[101]

But Heidegger is looking for a deeper, unifying need. This need is 'demanded', ontologically, *in* the telling refusal. What is more, distraction – though Heidegger only uses this term in *Being and Time* – *is* the telling refusal itself: 'This absence of oppressiveness is only apparently hidden; it is rather attested by the very activities with which we busy ourselves in our contemporary restlessness.'[102] Heidegger initially comes close to the 'philosophy of culture' that he dismisses, insofar as his claim about boredom relies upon empirical, cultural *evaluations*. But

Heidegger's 'empiricism' is of a particular kind here. The fundamental attunement is primarily 'attested to' not, for instance, in the evidence of an emerging culture industry, but rather in the attestation itself, which is already the experiential register of the social and cultural. The value of (the concept of) attunement now becomes clear: the fundamental attunement is an attestation of something fundamental, beyond the attunement (or, attunement *as* relating beyond). Indeed, who does not feel boredom today? There is, of course, a precedent for this notion of attestation, as a fundamental and historical condition – in the concept of alienation.

The fundamental attunement tells of contemporary Dasein *as* a unique historical situation. In a sense, the rise in importance of both autonomous and heteronomous music is part of the story of the fundamental attunement, since each makes a claim of a whole. Heidegger's musical description of *Stimmung* appears as more than a passing reference in light of his later characterisation of music and nihilism. The fundamental attunement of boredom anticipates Heidegger's account of the subject of metaphysical modernity as an affective subject that wills an object in its totality. In the earlier work, this false totality (false with respect to 'Being as a whole') is defined in terms of extreme depth, 'deep boredom', and in the later work, extreme height, the 'highpoint of humanity'. In both cases, of extreme depth and height, it is claimed that another whole becomes speculatively visible.

Heidegger subsequently moved away from historicity and towards 'destiny [*Geschick*]' or rather 'destining [*Schickung*]'. This philosophy of history, in the strong sense of *Geschichte*, is not yet fully in place in *The Fundamental Concepts* (as the lapse into scholasticism would suggest). Neither is it as yet the 'remembrance' and 'forgetting of Being'.[103] And yet, in the 1929–30 lecture course, Heidegger no longer imposes a formal structure upon history, but instead attempts to experience it from the qualitative standpoint of the contemporary. As with Adorno, destiny is now on the side of a notion of facticity, since profound boredom has crept up on us unawares – as if a Dasein of its own. This alien destiny, the wrong history, is the alienation of another destiny, the right history. That which Adorno calls reification, the 'naturalisation of history' is, to an extent, comparable to Heidegger's 'darkening of the world'. The 'refusal of things' is, at some level, comparable to a notion of reification (the refusal of things as the world becoming a thing). The attunement of *Trauer*, in allegorical *praxis*, allows for the possibility of arresting reification. During the 1960s, Adorno moves away from a 'purely derogatory' concept of reification (a move away from Lukács, for various reasons).[104]

This possibility of negating the negation looks more piecemeal in Adorno than it does in Heidegger. But the increasingly metaphysically fraught nature of the melancholy science brings Adorno, unwittingly perhaps, closer to Heidegger's terrain, such that the problem of the metaphysical grounding of the melancholy science becomes more acute. In *The Fundamental Concepts*, Heidegger cites and then rejects Oswald Spengler as a misreader of Nietzsche.[105] But what Adorno says of Spengler in the 1960s equally applies to Heidegger, who sought to colonise the space of these philosophers of crisis: 'After Auschwitz, a regression... has already *taken place* and is not merely expected à la Spengler.'[106] Heidegger is the philosopher of the problem of nihilism but Adorno is thrown onto this problem by the force of a history that Heidegger both failed to foresee and to remember.

For both thinkers, however, waiting in vain is alienation and the possibility of the negation of the negation, by way of its expression. For Adorno particularly, boredom is not an existential *a priori*. Boredom 'need not necessarily exist'.[107] As a historical phenomenon, it can change and even disappear. What does an *expression of* waiting in vain promise, in that case? The right history for Adorno; the right destiny for Heidegger. The problem of waiting is then indistinguishable from the problem of history *as* destiny. If the possibility of an expression of waiting in vain were solely contingent, then there would indeed be no awaited in the singular. Such waiting, before the 'endless multiplicity' of possibilities (Heidegger), *is*, in that case, constitutively in vain. Heidegger's turn from the historicity of *Being and Time* to contemporary Dasein sets up the turning from Dasein to Being. The wrong history is now 'the forgetting of Being' and the right history 'destining' through 'remembrance of Being'. We saw that, in his 'Letter on Humanism', Heidegger autobiographically dates his turning to his lecture-course 'On the Essence of Truth', which was given shortly after *The Fundamental Concepts*.[108] The turning is equally a turning to a notion of destiny that is intended to counter the bad infinity of an endless multiplicity of possibilities. This also gives a different sense to Heidegger's subsequent return to waiting, which is no longer solely phenomenological, but is now equally 'messianic'. In this connection, the inappropriateness (or mere absence) of a political orientation in Heidegger, including after his condemnation of militarism, may be filled (quite against Heidegger's wishes) by the historical materialist engagement with the 'messianic'.

It was suggested that Heidegger's heterodox 'turn to Hegel', decried by the younger Adorno, became strangely pronounced in his 'history of metaphysics'. The problem of metaphysics is that its interpretation of

Being, as object-dominating subject, becomes a totalising interpretation of *all possible* interpretations. The 'enframing' of the 'world picture' is, accordingly, a 'forgetting of Being' (*as* 'the mystery'). Profound boredom can be said to arise from the nothing that is left after the totalising interpretation, which nevertheless does not put an end to Dasein (which asks 'is that all?' – this asking is *not nothing*). This interpretation must nevertheless fail from the standpoint of the appropriating event, of 'Time and Being'. The necessity of this 'only' is structurally messianic – but without, outwardly at least, the ontotheological problems of uncritical messianism.

In *Negative Dialectics*, Adorno confronts the problem of fatalism implicit in Heidegger's later philosophy of history. Yet he neither mentions Heidegger's conception of destiny nor its possible relation to National Socialism. Rather, as we have seen, Adorno writes of Heidegger's attempt to 'justify subjugation to historical situations, as if it were the behest of Being itself.'[109] But this is mainly the critique of formalism once again – that which arguably *did* make possible Heidegger's 'decision'. It is as if Adorno had denied himself that critique because he had already branded Heideggerian historicity as ineffectual. It was the concept of 'destruction' (or 'deconstruction') and not historicity that 'led directly to barbarism and fascism'.[110] But ever since his curiosity about *Being and Time*, Adorno had shared Heidegger's imperative for a post-metaphysical philosophy of history; an imperative that becomes increasingly post-Hegelian for both thinkers, though in very different ways.

The contemporary 'demand' of Dasein is a privileging of the contemporary: 'This occurrence of a fundamental attunement itself and the very choice in question as an engagement of the philosopher's existence is rooted in the history of Dasein.'[111] Heidegger does not (yet) say it in so many words, but this 'history of Dasein' is a destiny of Dasein, because the occurrence of the fundamental attunement of profound boredom discloses the problem of metaphysics – of the whole – for the first time. The 'history of Dasein' no longer signifies historicity – that which 'brings history to a halt in the unhistorical' (Adorno). The genitive in 'history *of* Dasein' now functions in both senses. At the same time, Heidegger is not yet proposing what the whole will be: 'The possibility of a different kind of necessary grounding for metaphysics must remain open.'[112]

Adorno's idea of waiting in vain founders, it was suggested, upon its self-problematised metaphysical grounding. Heidegger's confrontation with metaphysics signals a response, to which Adorno must in turn respond. Both Heidegger and Adorno connect the waiting of boredom to a form of post-metaphysical waiting. Each connects a particular attunement to another possible historical whole, and to the whole as possibility of history. An expression of waiting in vain is the intermittent anticipation of the right history, since the expression, the act, seeks to bring about that history.

In *The Fundamental Concepts*, Heidegger makes an ontological claim on behalf of expropriated experience. He simultaneously acknowledges the impossibility of a heroic experience of Being-towards-death. The anti-hero is profoundly bored (*The Man Without Qualities*). But on Adorno's side, death remains the fundamental *problem* of experience. An expression of waiting in vain is the critique of anticipatory resoluteness, the authentic mode of Being-towards-death. This is equally the 'twisting free' of traditional metaphysics discussed in Chapter 2, since it combines the non-willing of the anticipatory with the willing expectation of the awaited. For Adorno, metaphysics *after* metaphysics means 'thinking beyond itself, into *openness*.'[113] Of course, this is not the 'clearing of Being', or 'the open' of Heidegger. And yet, in both cases, openness names the necessity of thinking out of metaphysical willing, as the possibility of confronting *its* nihilism.

Adorno and Heidegger each turn to the category of thinking, each in relation to waiting. The former maintains that 'thought' is consistent with a notion of determinate critique and not resigned quietism. And yet, since '*praxis* is delayed for the foreseeable future', such 'thought' once again conjures-up the spectre of the regressive infinity. It is telling that, in his radio-lecture 'Resignation', Adorno does not address the objections of his detractors to theory but rather turns the tables on their equal-and-opposite valorisation of *praxis*. The question of the mediation of theory and *praxis* – of, in a sense, waiting and awaited – is side-tracked. Adorno is left defending theory as the 'happiness' of the 'thinking person'.[114] It is not entirely facetious to compare this statement to Heidegger's 'piety of thought'.[115] Heidegger's 'thinking' makes no such claim of determinate negation, since this identity philosophy is part of the problem of metaphysics. Like Adorno, Heidegger questions the metaphysical distinction between theory and practice in itself. But Heidegger's 'task of thinking', after 'the end of philosophy', *does* threaten to valorise a waiting without expectation, sliding into the regressive infinity to which it was originally opposed. Man's 'essence [*Wesen*]', Heidegger will state in 1949, 'is to be the one who waits'.[116] Man is condemned to wait, for nothing. Notwithstanding Heidegger's speculative redefinition of 'essence', waiting comes to be in vain *after all* – '*Gelassenheit*' as 'being left empty [*Leergelassenheit*].'[117] In his *Spiegel* interview, Heidegger counters the charge of quietism with a notion of destining. Destining is the time of the awaited. Since Heidegger thinks the whole after metaphysics as the Being of beings, and as time, the destining of Being is the appropriating event of Being as time. The whole would then be experienced in a non-dominating comportment, since domination marks the non-time of presence:

> It is not a matter simply of waiting until something occurs to man within the next 300 years, but of thinking ahead (without prophetic proclamations) into the time which is to come, of thinking from the standpoint of the fundamental traits of the present age, which have scarcely been thought through. Thinking is not inactivity but is in itself the action which stands in dialogue with world destining [*Weltgeschick*].[118]

If the *active* elements of the 'thought' of waiting – in Adorno *and* Heidegger – are brought together within the historical materialist context, then the expression of indeterminate waiting, of waiting in vain, becomes the possibility of determinacy. An expression of waiting in vain is, in that case, not in vain.

Notes

Introduction

1. Simon Glendinning, *The Idea of Continental Philosophy* (Edinburgh: Edinburgh University Press, 2006), p. 12.
2. Cf. Wesley Phillips, 'The Future of Speculation?' *Cosmos and History*, 8 (2012), 289–303.
3. Theodor W. Adorno, 'The Actuality of Philosophy', trans. by Benjamin Snow, *Telos*, (1977), p. 130.
4. Theodor W. Adorno, *Negativ Dialektik* (Frankfurt am Main: Suhrkamp, 1966), p. 69.
5. *Adorno and Heidegger: Philosophical Questions*, ed. by Iain Macdonald and Krzysztof Ziarek (Stanford, CA: Stanford University Press, 2008), p. 5.
6. Cited in, Nicholas Walker, 'Adorno and Heidegger on the Question of Art: Countering Hegel?' in Macdonald and Ziarek, p. 87.
7. Adorno, *Negativ Dialektik*, p. 368.
8. Theodor W. Adorno, *Metaphysics: Concept and Problems*, trans. by Rolf Tiedemann (Stanford, CA: Stanford University Press, 2000), p. 143.
9. The translators render this term as 'destroying' or 'destruction', but there is also a sense of 'de-structuring' or 'deconstruction'. Martin Heidegger, *Being and Time*, trans. by John Macquarrie and Edward Robinson (Oxford: Blackwell, 2000), p. 41.
10. Gillian Rose, *Hegel Contra Sociology* (London: Athlone, 1981), chap. 3.
11. Martin Heidegger, 'Only a God Can Save Us', in *Philosophical and Political Writings*, ed. by Manfred Stassen, trans. by Maria P. Alter and John D. Caputo (New York and London: Continuum, 2003), p. 38.
12. 'Readers have taken constant offence at the violence of my interpretations. Their allegation of violence can indeed be supported by this text…Thinkers learn from their shortcomings to be more preserving.' Martin Heidegger, *Kant and the Problem of Metaphysics*, trans. by Richard Taft, 5th edition (Bloomington: Indiana University Press, 1997), p. xx.
13. Maurice Blanchot, *The Infinite Conversation*, trans. by Susan Hanson (Minneapolis: University of Minnesota Press, 1993), p. 123.
14. *Music and the Muses: The Culture of Mousike in the Classical Athenian City*, ed. by Penelope Murray and Peter Wilson (Oxford: Oxford University Press, 2004), p. 372.
15. Plato, *The Republic*, trans. by Desmond Lee (London: Penguin, 1955), p. 71.
16. Walter Benjamin, 'The Concept of Criticism in German Romanticism', in *Selected Writings, Volume 1*, trans. by David Lachterman, Howard Eiland, and Ian Balfour (Cambridge, MA: Harvard University Press, 1996), pp. 179–80.
17. Plato, *Timaeus and Critus*, trans. by H. D. Lee (London: Penguin, 1965), p. 48.
18. Adorno, *Negativ Dialektik*, p. 115.

19. See translators' introduction, in Johannes Kepler, *The Harmony of the World*, trans. by E. J. Aiton, A. M. Duncan, and Field (Philadelphia: American Philosophical Society, 1997), p. xvii.
20. Martin Heidegger, *The Fundamental Concepts of Metaphysics: World, Finitude, Solitude*, trans. by William McNeill and Nicholas Walker (Bloomington: Indiana University Press, 2001), p. 67.
21. Cf. John Felstiner, *Paul Celan: Poet, Survivor, Jew* (Yale University Press, 1995), pp. 28–30.
22. Jacques Attali, *Noise: The Political Economy of Music*, trans. by Brian Massumi (Manchester: Manchester University Press, 1985), pp. 101–2.
23. Rüdiger Safranski, *Nietzsche: A Philosophical Biography*, trans. by Shelley L. Frisch (London: Granta, 2002), pp. 101–2.
24. Much of Adorno's 1958 essay on *Endgame* is taken up with the attempt to distinguish Beckett from traditional (and literary) existentialism. In Beckett, 'Absurdity is relieved of the doctrinal universality which in existentialism, the creed of the irreducibility of individual existence, linked it to the Western pathos of the universal and lasting.' Theodor W. Adorno, *Notes to Literature*, ed. by Rolf Tiedemann, trans. by Shierry Weber Nicholsen (New York: Columbia University Press, 1991), i, p. 241.
25. Cited in, Bryan Magee, *Talking Philosophy: Dialogues with Fifteen Leading Philosophers* (Oxford: Oxford University Press, 2001), p. 74.

1 Melancholy Science as Dissonant System

1. Theodor W. Adorno, 'Resignation', in *Critical Models: Interventions and Catchwords*, trans. by Henry W. Pickford (New York: Columbia University Press, 1998), p. 289.
2. Theodor W. Adorno, *Minima Moralia: Reflections on a Damaged Life*, trans. by Edmund Jephcott (London & New York: Verso Books, 1978), p. 15.
3. Antonio Negri and Michael Hardt, *Empire* (Cambridge, MA: Harvard University Press, 2000), p. 217.
4. Giorgio Agamben, *The Time That Remains: A Commentary on the Letter to the Romans*, trans. by Patricia Dailey (Stanford, CA: Stanford University Press, 2005), p. 38.
5. Gillian Rose, 'From Speculative to Dialectical Thinking – Hegel and Adorno', in *Judaism and Modernity: Philosophical Essays* (Oxford: Blackwell, 1993), p. 61.
6. Gillian Rose, *Hegel Contra Sociology* (London: Athlone, 1981), p. 27.
7. Theodor W. Adorno, *Negativ Dialektik* (Frankfurt am Main: Suhrkamp, 1966), p. 15.
8. Gillian Rose, *The Melancholy Science: An Introduction to the Thought of Theodor W. Adorno* (New York: Columbia University Press, 1978), p. ix.
9. Sigmund Freud, 'Mourning and Melancholia', in *On the History of the Psycho-Analytic Movement. Papers on Metapsychology and Other Words*, trans. by James Strachey, The Standard Edition of the Complete Psychological Works of Sigmund Freud (London: Hogarth Press, 1964), xiv, p. 245.
10. The early Rose reads Benjamin's *Trauerspiel* book as a work of history. 'The melancholy portrayal of objects and persons in baroque drama conveys

the prevalent attitude to the natural world at the time'. She acknowledges Benjamin's motivation against neo-Kantianism, but understands this as an intra-Kantian gesture. Benjamin merely 'attempted to revise Kant's notions of experience and knowledge.' Rose, *Hegel Contra Sociology*, p. 22, p. 32; Rose, *The Melancholy Science*, p. 37.

11. Rose would later distinguish between mourning and melancholy in her unfinished, posthumously published *Mourning Becomes the Law* (Cambridge: Cambridge University Press, 1996).
12. Rose, *Hegel*, chap. 1.
13. Henry E. Allison, *Kant's Transcendental Idealism*, 2nd edn (New Haven: Yale University Press, 2004), p. 312.
14. Immanuel Kant, *Critique of Pure Reason*, trans. by Paul Guyer and Allen W. Wood (Cambridge: Cambridge University Press, 1999), p. 461.
15. Adorno, *Negativ Dialektik*, p. 238.
16. Adorno, *Negativ Dialektik*, pp. 25–7.
17. Kant, p. 513.
18. Kant, p. 592.
19. Or, the 'spurious infinity', since the infinite 'straight line' is an infinity (the mathematical infinity) but not the absolute infinity. Kant's distinction between a mathematical and a philosophical infinity does not pre-empt Hegel's attack. Negative, indefinite infinity (an 'indeterminately continued regress') is contrasted with the positive, mathematical infinity. The former names the non-finitude that accompanies the finite conditioned, negatively. But this throws Kant back onto the antinomy, and its infinite insolubility. G. W. F. Hegel, *Hegel's Science of Logic*, trans. by A. V. Miller (London: Humanity Books, 1969), p. 149.
20. Martin Heidegger, *Kant and the Problem of Metaphysics*, trans. by Richard Taft, 5th edition (Bloomington: Indiana University Press, 1997), p. 193.
21. Martin Heidegger, *The Fundamental Concepts of Metaphysics: World, Finitude, Solitude*, trans. by William McNeill and Nicholas Walker (Bloomington: Indiana University Press, 2001), p. 209.
22. Adorno, *Negativ Dialektik*, p. 29.
23. Walter Benjamin, *The Origin of German Tragic Drama*, trans. by John Osborne (London: Verso Books, 1998), p. 27. Translation amended.
24. Adorno, *Negativ Dialektik*, p. 32.
25. Adorno, *Negativ Dialektik*, p. 165.
26. Theodor W. Adorno, 'Music, Language and Composition', in *Essays on Music*, trans. by Susan H. Gillespie (Berkeley: University of California Press, 2002), p. 113.
27. Theodor W. Adorno, *Aesthetic Theory*, trans. by Robert Hullot-Kentor (London: Athlone Press, 1997), pp. 116–7. Hullot-Kentor translates 'Sprachcharakter' both as 'articulation' and as 'linguistic quality'.
28. Jacques Derrida, *Of Grammatology*, trans. by Gayatri Chakravorty Spivak (Baltimore: Johns Hopkins University Press, 1998), pt. II, 1–3.
29. Adorno, 'Music, Language and Composition', p. 113.
30. Theodor W. Adorno, *Notes to Literature*, ed. by Rolf Tiedemann, trans. by Shierry Weber Nicholsen (New York: Columbia University Press, 1991), p. 112.
31. G. W. F. Hegel, *Hegel's Phenomenology of Spirit*, trans. by A. V. Miller (Oxford: Clarendon Press, 1977), p. 395.

32. Karl Marx and Friedrich Engels, *The German Ideology*, ed. by C. J Arthur (London: Lawrence & Wishart, 1970), p. 51.
33. Walter Benjamin, 'The Storyteller: Observations on the Works of Nikolai Leskov', in *Selected Writings, Volume 3*, trans. by Harry Zohn (Cambridge, MA: Harvard University Press, 1996), p. 88.
34. Benjamin, 'The Storyteller', p. 154.
35. Benjamin, 'The Storyteller', p. 162.
36. Benjamin, *The Origin of German Tragic Drama*, p. 27.
37. J. W. Goethe, *Maxims and Reflections*, ed. by Peter Hutchinson, trans. by Elisabeth Stopp (London: Penguin, 1998), p. 16.
38. 'In adulthood, he stretched the sphere of the comprehensible, which he continued to reach out to. In maturity, the feeling of an impenetrability of the actual won more power over his soul once again. This is the natural course of middle age [*Lebensalters*]'. Wilhelm Dilthey, '*Aus Der Zeit Der Spinoza-Studien Goethes*', in Weltanschauung und Analyse des Menschen seit Renaissance und Reformation, *Gesammelte Schriften* (Vandenhoeck & Ruprecht, 1991), ii, p. 394.
39. Benjamin, *The Origin of German Tragic Drama*, p. 37.
40. Gottfried Wilhelm Leibniz, 'Principles of Nature and Grace', in *Philosophical Essays*, trans. by Roger Ariew and Daniel Garber (Indianapolis: Hackett Publishing, 1989), p. 212.
41. Adorno, *Aesthetic Theory*, p. 136.
42. Adorno, 'Music, Language and Composition', p. 114.
43. Adorno, 'Music, Language and Composition', p. 117.
44. Adorno, 'Music, Language and Composition', p. 114.
45. Gershom Scholem, *Walter Benjamin: The Story of a Friendship*, trans. by Harry Zohn (New York: New York Review Books, 2003), p. 48.
46. Bram Mertens, *Dark Images, Secret Hints: Benjamin, Scholem, Molitor and the Jewish Tradition* (Bern: Peter Lang, 2007).
47. Cf. Wesley Phillips, 'History or Counter-Tradition? The System of Freedom After Walter Benjamin', *Critical Horizons: A Journal of Philosophy & Social Theory*, 11 (2010), 99–118.
48. Walter Benjamin, 'On Language as Such and the Language of Man', in *Selected Writings, Volume 1*, trans. by Edmund Jephcott (Cambridge, MA: Harvard University Press, 1996), p. 64.
49. Benjamin, 'On Language', p. 65.
50. Benjamin, 'On Language', pp. 63–4. Translation amended.
51. Benjamin, 'On Language', p. 73.
52. Benjamin, *The Origin of German Tragic Drama*, p. 202.
53. Benjamin, *The Origin of German Tragic Drama*, p. 37.
54. Jürgen Habermas, 'Dialectical Idealism in Transition to Materialism: Schelling's Idea of a Contraction of God and Its Consequences for the Philosophy of History', in *The New Schelling*, trans. by Nick Midgley and Judith Norman (London: Continuum, 2004), pp. 64–5.
55. F. W. J. Schelling, 'Philosophical Investigations into the Essence of Human Freedom and Related Matters', in *Philosophy of German Idealism*, ed. by Ernst Behler (New York: Continuum, 1997), p. 223.
56. Schelling, 'Essence of Human Freedom', p. 220.
57. Schelling, 'Essence of Human Freedom', p. 271. Translation amended.

58. Schelling, 'Essence of Human Freedom', p. 258. Translation amended.
59. Martin Heidegger, *Schelling's Treatise on the Essence of Human Freedom*, trans. by Joan Stambaugh (Ohio: Ohio University Press, 1985), p. 89.
60. Theodor W. Adorno, 'On Some Relationships Between Music and Painting', trans. by Susan H. Gillespie, *The Musical Quarterly*, 1995, p. 77.
61. Benjamin, 'On Language', p. 73.
62. F. W. J. Schelling, 'Stuttgart Seminars', in *Idealism and the Endgame of Theory: Three Essays by F. W. J. Schelling*, trans. by Thomas Pfau (New York: State University of New York Press, 1993), p. 242.
63. Theodor W. Adorno, 'On the Contemporary Relationships of Philosophy and Music', in *Essays on Music*, trans. by Susan H. Gillespie (Berkeley: University of California Press, 2002), p. 140.
64. Slavoj Žižek and F. W. J. Schelling, *The Abyss of Freedom / Ages of the World* (University of Michigan Press, 1997), p. 125.
65. Schelling, 'Essence of Human Freedom', p. 222.
66. Schelling, 'Stuttgart Seminars', p. 230.
67. Giorgio Agamben, *Language and Death*, trans. by Karen E. Pinkus and Michael Hardt (Minneapolis: University of Minnesota Press, 1991), pp. 55–6.
68. Heidegger, *The Fundamental Concepts of Metaphysics*, pp. 182–3.
69. Heidegger, *The Fundamental Concepts of Metaphysics*, p. 67.
70. Žižek and Schelling, p. 147.
71. Habermas, 'Dialectical Idealism in Transition to Materialism', p. 55.
72. Scholem, p. 84.
73. Schelling, 'Stuttgart Seminars', p. 227.
74. Habermas, 'Dialectical Idealism in Transition to Materialism', p. 78.
75. Schelling, 'Essence of Human Freedom', p. 267.
76. Schelling, 'Stuttgart Seminars', p. 210.
77. Schelling, 'Essence of Human Freedom', p. 241.
78. Habermas, 'Dialectical Idealism in Transition to Materialism', p. 53.
79. Karl Marx, *Early Writings*, ed. by Lucio Colletti, trans. by Rodney Livingstone and Gregor Benton (Harmondsworth: Penguin, 1975), p. 422.
80. Jürgen Habermas, *Philosophical-Political Profiles*, trans. by Frederick G. Lawrence (London: Heinemann, 1983), pp. 67–8.
81. It was Engels, not Marx, who attended Schelling's lectures.
82. Habermas, 'Dialectical Idealism in Transition to Materialism', p. 79.
83. Schelling, 'Essence of Human Freedom', p. 230.
84. Alfred Schmidt, *Concept of Nature in Marx*, trans. by Ben Fowkes (London: New Left Books, 1971), p. 9.
85. Schmidt, pp. 37; 43–6.
86. Theodor W. Adorno, 'The Idea of Natural History', trans. by Robert Hullot-Kentor, *Telos*, 1984, p. 122.
87. Benjamin, *The Origin of German Tragic Drama*, p. 151.
88. Benjamin, *The Origin of German Tragic Drama*, p. 149.
89. Benjamin, *The Origin of German Tragic Drama*, p. 157.
90. Adorno, 'The Idea of Natural History', p. 117.
91. Adorno, 'The Idea of Natural History', p. 119.
92. Cf. Bob Hullot-Kentor, 'Introduction to Adorno's 'Idea of Natural History'', in Adorno, 'The Idea of Natural History', p. 104.
93. Adorno, 'The Idea of Natural History', p. 122. Translation amended.

94. Hegel was equally dismissive of the *Freiheitschrift*, though this time on methodological grounds: 'Schelling has made known a single treatise on freedom. It is of a deep speculative nature, but it stands alone. In philosophy, a single piece cannot be developed.' Dale E. Snow, *Schelling and the End of Idealism: The Horizons of Feeling* (New York: State University of New York Press, 1996), p. 142.
95. The 'external world... obtains its existence through self-consciousness' own externalisation and separation of itself'. Hegel, *Phenomenology of Spirit*, p. 294.
96. In his *Differenzschrift* (1801), Hegel states that, to speak of a 'limited' moment of reflection only becomes meaningful with respect to the 'connection' of reflection to 'the Absolute', as a totality of connections. There is no limit to infinite reflection. For Hegel, reflection, or rather reason, now connects the limited to the whole in a manner that determines both: 'reflection nullifies itself and all being and everything limited, because it connects [the limited] with the Absolute. But at the same time the limited gains standing precisely on account of its connection with the Absolute'. These (Spinozist) claims are only substantiated in the Phenomenolgy to the extent that the absolute remains a postulation here in the Differenzschrift. Hegel needs the phenomenology of (re)cognition in order to break out of the solipsistic shell of subjective reflection, critically. G. W. F. Hegel, *The Difference Between Fichte's and Schelling's System of Philosophy*, trans. by Walter Cerf (New York: State University of New York Press, 1988), p. 94.
97. Cf. Wesley Phillips, 'The Future of Speculation?', *Cosmos and History*, 8 (2012), 289–303.
98. Žižek and Schelling, p. 116.
99. Hegel, *Phenomenology of Spirit*, p. 49. Translation amended.
100. Rose, *Hegel*, p. 32.
101. Adorno, *Negativ Dialektik*, p. 115.
102. Theodor W. Adorno and Ernst Bloch, 'Something's Missing: A Discussion between Ernst Bloch and Theodor W. Adorno on the Contradictions of Utopian Longing', in *The Utopian Function of Art*, trans. by Jack Zipes and Frank Mecklenburg (Cambridge, MA: MIT Press, 1988), pp. 1–17.
103. Adorno, *Negativ Dialektik*, p. 99.
104. Adorno, *Negativ Dialektik*, p. 70.
105. Adorno, *Negativ Dialektik*, p. 83.
106. Rose, *Hegel*, p. 23.
107. Adorno, *Negativ Dialektik*, p. 70.
108. Kant, pp. 401–3.
109. Benjamin, *The Origin of German Tragic Drama*, p. 214.
110. Philippe Lacoue-Labarthe and Jean-Luc Nancy, *The Literary Absolute: The Theory of Literature in German Romanticism*, trans. by Philip Barnard and Cheryl Lester (Albany: State University of New York Press, 1988), p. 28.
111. Philippe Lacoue-Labarthe, *Musica Ficta: Figures of Wagner*, trans. by Felicia McCarren (Stanford, CA: Stanford University Press, 1994), pp. 62–3; 152f.
112. Walter Benjamin, 'The Concept of Criticism in German Romanticism', in *Selected Writings, Volume 1*, trans. by David Lachterman, Howard Eiland, and Ian Balfour (Cambridge, MA: Harvard University Press, 1996), p. 179. Translation amended.

113. Benjamin, 'The Concept of Criticism', p. 179.
114. Benjamin, 'The Storyteller', p. 154.
115. Carl Dahlhaus, *The Idea of Absolute Music*, trans. by Roger Lustig (Chicago & London: University of Chicago Press, 1991), pp. 1–17.
116. Dahlhaus, p. 6.
117. Friedrich von Schlegel, *Philosophical Fragments*, trans. by Peter Firchow (Minneapolis: University of Minnesota Press, 1991), p. 92.
118. Lacoue-Labarthe and Nancy, p. 93.
119. Eduard Hanslick, '"Content" and "Form" in Music', in *German Essays on Music*, ed. by Jost Hermand and Michael Gilbert, trans. by Geoffrey Payzant (New York & London: Continuum, 1994), p. 84.
120. Paul de Man, 'The Rhetoric of Blindness: Jacques Derrida's Reading of Rousseau', in *Blindness & Insight* (London: Routledge, 1993), pp. 132–3.
121. Andrew Bowie, *Aesthetics and Subjectivity: From Kant to Nietzsche* (Manchester: Manchester University Press, 1990), p. 222.
122. James Hodkinson, 'The Cosmic-Symphonic: Novalis, Music, and Universal Discourse', in *Music and Literature in German Romanticism*, ed. by Siobhán Donovan and Robin Eliott (Rochester: Camden House, 2004), p. 13.
123. F. W. J. Schelling, *The Philosophy of Art*, trans. by Douglas W. Stott (Minneapolis: University of Minnesota Press, 1989), p. 109.
124. Lacoue-Labarthe and Nancy, p. 8.
125. Benjamin, *The Origin of German Tragic Drama*, pp. 47–8.
126. Gottfried Wilhelm Leibniz, *The Monadology and Other Philosophical Writings*, trans. by Robert Latta (London: Oxford University Press, 1968), p. 250.
127. Gottfried Wilhelm Leibniz, *Discourse on Metaphysics*, §13, trans. by Jonathan Bennet, accessed at, www.earlymoderntexts.com/f_leibniz.html, on 23 November 2008. Cf. *The Monadology*, pp. 247–9.
128. Adorno, *Negativ Dialektik*, p. 167.
129. Adorno, *Negativ Dialektik*, p. 166.
130. Theodor W. Adorno, *Metaphysics: Concept and Problems*, trans. by Rolf Tiedemann (Stanford, CA: Stanford University Press, 2000), p. 101.
131. Adorno and Bloch, p. 4.
132. Adorno, *Minima Moralia*, p. 222.
133. Theodor W. Adorno, *Philosophy of Modern Music*, trans. by Wesley V. Bloomster and Anne G. Mitchell (London: Sheed & Ward, 1973), p. 85.

2 Twisting Free With/Of Wagner

1. Friedrich Nietzsche, *The Birth of Tragedy and The Case of Wagner*, trans. by Walter Kaufmann (New York: Vintage Books, 1967), p. 156.
2. Friedrich Nietzsche, *The Will to Power*, trans. by Walter Kaufmann and R. J. Hollingdale (New York: Vintage Books, 1968), p. 17.
3. Martin Heidegger, *Nietzsche: The Will to Power as Art / The Eternal Recurrence of the Same*, trans. by David Farrell Krell (San Francisco, CA: Harper, 1991), p. ix.
4. Martin Heidegger, 'Only a God Can Save Us', in *Philosophical and Political Writings*, ed. by Manfred Stassen, trans. by Maria P. Alter and John D. Caputo (New York and London: Continuum, 2003), p. 33.

5. Richard Wolin, *The Politics of Being: The Political Thought of Martin Heidegger* (New York: Columbia University Press, 1990), p. 133.
6. Martin Heidegger, *Nietzsche: The Will to Power as Knowledge and as Metaphysics / Nihilism*, trans. by David Farrell Krell (San Francisco: Harper Collins, 1991), pp. 116–7.
7. Cf. Martin Jay, 'The Frankfurt School's Critique of Marxist Humanism', in *Permanent Exiles: Essays on the Intellectual Migration from Germany to America* (New York: Columbia University Press, 1990), pp. 14–27.
8. Cited in Karin Bauer, *Adorno's Nietzschean Narratives: Critiques of Ideology, Readings of Wagner* (Albany, NY: State University of New York Press, 1999), pp. 117–18.
9. Theodor W. Adorno, 'Wagner's Relevance for Today', in *Essays on Music*, ed. by Richard Leppert, trans. by Susan H. Gillespie (Berkeley: University of California Press, 2002), p. 584.
10. Peter Heyworth, *Otto Klemperer: His Life and Times, 1885–1933* (Cambridge & New York: Cambridge University Press, 1996), i, pp. 278–9.
11. Theodor W. Adorno, Preface to *In Search of Wagner*. In a letter to Walter Benjamin on 22nd September 1937, Adorno wrote, 'The Wagner piece is beginning to take shape, after much collecting of materials and many discussions with Max [Horkheimer], and will be focused around the concept of progress and reaction.' Theodor W. Adorno and Walter Benjamin, *The Complete Correspondence, 1928–1940*, trans. by Nicholas Walker (Cambridge: Polity Press, 2003), p. 213.
12. Nietzsche, *The Case of Wagner*, p. 156.
13. Slavoj Žižek, 'Why is Wagner Worth Saving?' Theodor W. Adorno, *In Search of Wagner*, trans. by Rodney Livingstone (London: Verso, 2005), p. iix.
14. Adorno's own compositions of lieder, as well as his remarkable *Singspiel* fragment of 1932–3, point in the opposite direction.
15. Adorno, *In Search of Wagner*, p. 119.
16. Theodor W. Adorno, *Minima Moralia: Reflections on a Damaged Life*, trans. by Edmund Jephcott (London & New York: Verso Books, 1978), p. 172.
17. Hegel first developed his concept of love as spirit in his theological writings, for instance in his interpretation of the Last Supper. Spirit is the task of humanity itself, when it is left behind by the 'death of God', in the Ascension. G. W. F. Hegel, *Early Theological Writings*, trans. by T. M. Knox (Philadelphia: University of Pennsylvania Press, 1988), p. 251.
18. Jean Jacques Nattiez, *Wagner Androgyne: A Study in Interpretation*, trans. by Stewart Spencer (Princeton, N. J: Princeton University Press, 1993), p. 123.
19. Ludwig Feuerbach, *Thoughts on Death and Immortality: From the Papers of a Thinker, Along With an Appendix of Theological-Satirical Epigrams*, trans. by James Massey (Berkeley: University of California Press, 1980), p. 29.
20. Cited in Nattiez, p. 125.
21. Nattiez, chap. 5.
22. Richard Wagner, *Die Walküre*, act I, scene 3.
23. 'What is meant' by the idea of natural history, Adorno writes, 'is certainly not the anthropological concept of nature of Feuerbach, against which Marx aimed dialectical materialism, in the sense of a reprise of Hegel against the Left Hegelians.' Theodor W. Adorno, *Negativ Dialektik* (Frankfurt am Main: Suhrkamp, 1966), p. 347.

24. Adorno, *In Search of Wagner*, p. 120.
25. Adorno, *In Search of Wagner*, p. 88.
26. Adorno, *In Search of Wagner*, p. 24.
27. Nietzsche, *The Case of Wagner*, p. 157.
28. Adorno, *In Search of Wagner*, p. 45.
29. Adorno, *In Search of Wagner*, p. 21.
30. Adorno, *In Search of Wagner*, p. 88.
31. Adorno, *In Search of Wagner*, p. 37.
32. Theodor W. Adorno, 'Music, Language and Composition', in *Essays on Music*, trans. by Susan H. Gillespie (Berkeley: University of California Press, 2002), p. 122.
33. Nietzsche, *The Case of Wagner*, p. 170.
34. Friedrich Nietzsche, *On the Genealogy of Morality*, trans. by Carol Diethe (Cambridge: Cambridge University Press, 1994), p. 64.
35. Adorno, 'Wagner's Relevance for Today', p. 574.
36. Adorno, 'Wagner's Relevance for Today', p. 587.
37. Ernst Bloch, *Essays on the Philosophy of Music*, trans. by Peter Palmer (Cambridge: Cambridge University Press, 1985), p. 151.
38. Adorno, 'Wagner's Relevance for Today', p. 587.
39. Theodor W. Adorno, *Aesthetic Theory*, trans. by Robert Hullot-Kentor (London: Athlone Press, 1997), p. 15.
40. Charles Baudelaire, *The Painter of Modern Life and Other Essays*, trans. by Jonathan Mayne, 2nd ed. (Phaidon,, 1995), pp. 137–40.
41. Adorno, *In Search of Wagner*, p. 34.
42. Max Horkheimer, 'Egoism and Freedom Movements: On the Anthropology of the Bourgeois Era', in *Between Philosophy and Social Science: Selected Early Writings*, trans. by G. Frederick Hunter, Matthew S. Kramer, and John Torpey (Cambridge, MA: MIT Press, 1993), p. 109.
43. Horkheimer, p. 62.
44. Nietzsche, *On the Genealogy of Morality*, p. 92.
45. Adorno, *Negativ Dialektik*, p. 149.
46. Adorno, *Negativ Dialektik*, p. 15.
47. Horkheimer, p. 52.
48. Nietzsche, *On the Genealogy of Morality*, p. 13.
49. Horkheimer, p. 69.
50. I have opted for Kaufmann's and Hollingdale's more literal rendering of '*Selbstaufhebung*' as 'self-overcoming' over Carol Diethe's 'sublimating itself', for reasons that are explained in part II of this chapter. See: Friedrich Nietzsche, *On the Genealogy of Morals*, trans. Walter Kaufmann & R. J. Hollingdale (New York: Vintage, 1967), p. 73. Cf. Walter Arnold Kaufmann, *Nietzsche: Philosopher, Psychologist, Antichrist* (Meridian Books, 1965), p. 236.
51. Adorno, *In Search of Wagner*, p. 34. Emphasis added.
52. Adorno, *Aesthetic Theory*, p. 245.
53. Adorno, *Aesthetic Theory*, p. 21.
54. Horkheimer, p. 110.
55. Nietzsche, *On the Genealogy of Morality*, p. 128.
56. I have in mind both Louis Althusser's critique of Marx's early humanism and, turn, a critique of Althusser's structuralism.

57. Cf. Wesley Phillips, 'Adorno on Music, Space and Objectification', *European Journal of Social Theory*, 16 (2013), 122–30.
58. Adorno and Benjamin, p. 130.
59. Walter Benjamin, *Selected Writings, Vol. 4, 1938–1940*, ed. by Howard Eiland & Michael W. Jennings (Cambridge, MA: Harvard University Press, 2006), p. 265.
60. Walter Benjamin, 'The Work of Art in the Age of Its Technical Reproducibility', in *Selected Writings, Volume 3*, ed. by Edmund Jephcott and Harry Zohn (Cambridge, MA: Harvard University Press, 2002), p. 104.
61. The 'absolute substance which is the unity of what Spirit is – this absolute substance which is the unity of different independent self-consciousnesses which, in their opposition, enjoy perfect freedom and independence: the "I" that is "We" and "We" that is "I".' G. W. F. Hegel, *Hegel's Phenomenology of Spirit*, trans. by A. V. Miller (Oxford: Clarendon Press, 1977), p. 110.
62. Feuerbach, p. 37.
63. Adorno, *In Search of Wagner*, p. 27.
64. Adorno, *Negativ Dialektik*, p. 355.
65. Martin Heidegger, 'Letter on Humanism', in *Basic Writings*, ed. by David Farrell Krell, trans. by Frank A. Capuzzi and J. Glenn Gray (London: Routledge, 1993), p. 231.
66. Wolin, p. 132.
67. Wolin, p. 137.
68. Adorno, *Negativ Dialektik*, pp. 98–9.
69. Wolin, p. 136.
70. In spite of Adorno's numerous Heidegger-critiques, 'Genuine opponents [to Heidegger]...can scarcely be found in the philosophical efforts of the most recent decades.' Karl Löwith, *Martin Heidegger and European Nihilism*, ed. by Richard Wolin, trans. by Gary Steiner (New York: Columbia University Press, 1995), p. 35.
71. Dominique Janicaud, *The Shadow of That Thought: Heidegger and the Question of Politics* (Evanston, Illinois: Northwestern University Press, 1996).
72. Heidegger, *Nietzsche, Vols. 1 & 2*, p. 200.
73. Heidegger, *Nietzsche, Vols. 1 & 2*, p. 78.
74. Heidegger, *Nietzsche, Vols. 1 & 2*, p. 83.
75. Heidegger, *Nietzsche, Vols. 1 & 2*, p. 84.
76. Heidegger, *Nietzsche, Vols. 1 & 2*, p. 83.
77. Heidegger, *Nietzsche, Vols. 1 & 2*, p. 92.
78. Heidegger, *Nietzsche, Vols. 1 & 2*, pp. 98–9.
79. Nietzsche, *On the Genealogy of Morality*, p. 73.
80. Nietzsche, *On the Genealogy of Morality*, p. 76.
81. Nietzsche, *On the Genealogy of Morality*, p. 77.
82. Arthur Schopenhauer, *The World as Will and Representation*, trans. by E. F. G. Payne (New York: Dover Publications, 1966), i, p. 257.
83. Heidegger, *Nietzsche, Vols. 1 & 2*, p. 85.
84. Heidegger, *Nietzsche, Vols. 1 & 2*, p. 39.
85. Heidegger, *Nietzsche, Vols. 1 & 2*, p. 94.
86. Martin Heidegger, *The Question Concerning Technology and Other Essay*, trans. by William Lovitt (New York & London: Harper and Row, 1977), p. 326.
87. Heidegger, *Nietzsche, Vols. 1 & 2*, pp. 85–6.
88. Heidegger, *Nietzsche, Vols. 1 & 2*, p. 129. Emphasis added.

89. Nietzsche, *The Case of Wagner*, p. 192.
90. Nietzsche, *The Case of Wagner*, pp. 188–9.
91. Friedrich Nietzsche, *The Gay Science*, trans. by Josefine Nauckhoff (Cambridge: Cambridge University Press, 2001), pp. 240–1.
92. Nietzsche, *The Case of Wagner*, pp. 161–2.
93. Walter Benjamin, 'The Storyteller: Observations on the Works of Nikolai Leskov', in *Selected Writings, Volume 3*, trans. by Harry Zohn (Cambridge, MA: Harvard University Press, 1996), pp. 149–54.
94. Martin Heidegger, 'Words', in *On the Way to Language*, trans. by Peter D. Hertz (London & New York: Harper Collins, 1971), p. 148.
95. Martin Heidegger, 'The Origin of the Work of Art', in *Off the Beaten Track*, trans. by Julian Young and Kenneth Hayes (Cambridge: Cambridge University Press, 2002), p. 45.
96. Philippe Lacoue-Labarthe, *Musica Ficta: Figures of Wagner*, trans. by Felicia McCarren (Stanford, CA: Stanford University Press, 1994), p. 102.
97. Martin Heidegger, *Being and Time*, trans. by John Macquarrie and Edward Robinson (Oxford: Blackwell, 2000), p. 214.
98. Nietzsche, *The Case of Wagner*, p. 185.
99. Nietzsche, *The Case of Wagner*, p. 180.
100. Heidegger, *Being and Time*, p. 214.
101. Heidegger, *Nietzsche, Vols. 1 & 2*, pp. 185–6.
102. Heidegger, *Being and Time*, pp. 216–7.
103. Heidegger, *Nietzsche, Vols. 1 & 2*, p. 202.
104. Heidegger, *Nietzsche, Vols. 1 & 2*, p. 207.
105. Heidegger, *Nietzsche, Vols. 1 & 2*, p. 208.
106. Heidegger, *Nietzsche, Vols. 1 & 2*, p. 213.
107. Heidegger, *Nietzsche, Vols. 1 & 2*, p. 215.
108. Heidegger, *Nietzsche, Vols. 1 & 2*, p. 217.
109. Heidegger, *Nietzsche, Vols. 1 & 2*, p. 220.
110. Heidegger, *Nietzsche, Vols. 1 & 2*, p. 203.
111. Heidegger, *The Question Concerning Technology*, p. 45.
112. Heidegger, *Nietzsche, Vols. 1 & 2*, p. 208.
113. Michel Haar, *The Song of the Earth: Heidegger and the Grounds of the History of Geing*, trans. by Reginald Lilly (Indianapolis: Indiana University Press, 1993), p. 68.
114. Martin Heidegger, *Nietzsche: The Will to Power as Art/The Eternal Recurrence of the Same*, trans. by David Farrell Krell (San Francisco, CA: Harper, 1991), i & ii, p. 129 Emphasis added.
115. Karl Marx, *Early Writings*, ed. by Lucio Colletti, trans. by Rodney Livingstone and Gregor Benton (Harmondsworth: Penguin, 1975), p. 258.
116. Heidegger, 'Letter on Humanism', p. 239.
117. Heidegger, 'Letter on Humanism', p. 243.
118. Heidegger, 'Only a God Can Save Us', p. 44.
119. From 'Patmos', in Friedrich Hölderlin, *Poems and Fragments*, trans. by Michael Hamburger (London: Anvil Press Poetry, 2003), p. 567.
120. Heidegger's reference to Stravinsky is of course grist to Adorno's mill. In fact, the *Symphony of Psalms* marks an attempted disintegration of neoclassicism by way of montage construction. Martin Heidegger, *Denkerfahrungen* (Frankfurt am Main: Klostermann, 1983), p. 113.

121. Heidegger, 'Letter on Humanism', p. 244.
122. Martin Heidegger, *Discourse on Thinking: A Translation of 'Gelassenheit'*, trans. by John M. Anderson and E. Hans Freund (London & New York: Harper and Row, 1969), p. 59.
123. Heidegger, *Discourse on Thinking*, pp. 54–5.
124. Heidegger, *Discourse on Thinking*, p. 68.
125. Heidegger, 'Letter on Humanism', pp. 333–4.
126. Heidegger, 'Only a God Can Save Us', p. 38.

3 The Dialectical Image of Music

1. This is reflected in the fact that the essay is available to the English-speaking reader in two alternative collections: *The Culture Industry* and *Essays on Music* (see Bibliography).
2. Karl Marx, *Capital: A Critique of Political Economy*, trans. by Ben Fowkes (London: Penguin, 1976), i, p. 165.
3. Adorno states, not entirely accurately, that Marx 'defines the fetish-character of the commodity as the veneration of the thing made by oneself which, as exchange-value, simultaneously alienates itself from producer to consumer.' Theodor W. Adorno, 'On the Fetish Character in Music and the Regression of Listening', in *Essays on Music*, ed. by Richard Leppert, trans. by Susan H. Gillespie (Berkeley: University of California Press, 2002), pp. 295–6.
4. The 'veneration' that Adorno attributes to Marx seems to come closer to Freud's contention that the fetishist 'reveres his fetish'. Sigmund Freud, 'Fetishism', in *The Future of an Illusion, Civilization and its Discontents and Other Works*, trans. by James Strachey (London: Hogarth Press, 1964), p. 157.
5. Adorno, 'On the Fetish Character', p. 298.
6. Adorno, 'On the Fetish Character', p. 305.
7. Adorno, 'On the Fetish Character', p. 314.
8. G. W. F. Hegel, *Hegel's Phenomenology of Spirit*, trans. by A. V. Miller (Oxford: Clarendon Press, 1977), p. 55.
9. Theodor W. Adorno, *Hegel: Three Studies*, trans. by Shierry Weber Nicholsen, New edition (Cambridge, MA: MIT Press, 1994), p. 53.
10. Theodor Adorno to Walter Benjamin, November 10th, 1938, in *Aesthetics and Politics: The Key Texts of the Classic Debate Within German Marxism*, ed. by Ronald Taylor (London: New Left Books, 1977), p. 129.
11. Walter Benjamin, 'On Some Motifs in Baudelaire', in *Selected Writings, Volume 4*, ed. by Howard Eiland and Michael W. Jennings, trans. by Harry Zohn (Cambridge, MA: Harvard University Press, 2003), p. 343.
12. Walter Benjamin, 'The Storyteller: Observations on the Works of Nikolai Leskov', in *Selected Writings, Volume 3*, trans. by Harry Zohn (Cambridge, MA: Harvard University Press, 1996), p. 143.
13. Walter Benjamin, 'On the Concept of History', in *Selected Writings, Volume 4*, trans. by Harry Zohn, Howard Eiland, and Michael W. Jennings (Cambridge, MA: Harvard University Press, 2003), p. 392.
14. Adorno, 'On the Fetish Character', p. 305.

15. Hegel, *Phenomenology of Spirit*, p. 68.
16. Adorno, 'On the Fetish Character', p. 296.
17. Adorno, 'On the Fetish Character', pp. 392–3.
18. 'Perhaps the strict and pure concept of art is applicable only to music, while great poetry or great painting – precisely the greatest – necessarily brings with it an element of subject-matter transcending aesthtic confines, undissolved in the autonomy of form'. Theodor W. Adorno, *Minima Moralia: Reflections on a Damaged Life*, trans. by Edmund Jephcott (London & New York: Verso Books, 1978), p. 223.
19. Theodor W. Adorno, *Aesthetic Theory*, trans. by Robert Hullot-Kentor (London: Athlone Press, 1997), p. 21.
20. Theodor W. Adorno, 'Sacred Fragment: Schoenberg's *Moses und Aron*', in *Quasi una Fantasia*, trans. by Rodney Livingstone (London: Verso, 1992), p. 230.
21. Philippe Lacoue-Labarthe, *Musica Ficta: Figures of Wagner*, trans. by Felicia McCarren (Stanford, CA: Stanford University Press, 1994), pp. xvi–xvii.
22. Nigel Fortune, 'Monteverdi and the Secconda Prattica', in *The Monteverdi Companion*, ed. by Nigel Fortune and Denis Arnold (London: Faber and Faber, 1968), p. 183. There is of course a relationship to the image here – the rise of monody paralleling linear figuration in baroque painting.
23. Martin Heidegger, 'The Age of the World Picture', in *Off the Beaten Track*, trans. by Julian Young and Kenneth Hayes (Cambridge: Cambridge University Press, 2002), p. 67.
24. The deconstruction of presence is anticipated in the *Kantbuch*. Heidegger states that the concept of the understanding is the 'regulative unity' (not regulating unity) of a 'range of possibilities'. Heidegger does not want to do away with logic – he wants to loosen the grip, *Griff*, of the concept, *Begriff*. The dualism of intuition and understanding arises from a need to determine the concept as non-finite – as Kant puts it, 'never [to] be encountered in an intuition' (intuition being finite for Kant). The form-content problem is the finitude problem – in Kant's terms, the antinomy. But the schema refers both to the regulative unity and to the horizon of possibility; the 'intuiting look'. Hence, 'beyond the representation of [the] regulative unity of the rule, the concept is nothing. What logic refers to as a concept is grounded in the schema.' Heidegger cites Kant. The concept 'always refers immediately to the schema.' The subsumed object, by way of the schema-image, would equally be nothing. Martin Heidegger, *Kant and the Problem of Metaphysics*, trans. Richard Taft, 5th edition (Bloomington: Indiana University Press, 1997), p. 69. Emphasis added.
25. Theodor W. Adorno, 'On Some Relationships Between Music and Painting', trans. by Susan H. Gillespie, *The Musical Quarterly*, 1995, p. 69. Translation amended.
26. Theodor W. Adorno, *Negativ Dialektik* (Frankfurt am Main: Suhrkamp, 1966), p. 207.
27. Hanns Eisler and Theodor W. Adorno, *Composing for the Films* (London & New York: Athlone Press, 1994), pp. 20–21. The chapter from which this citation is taken was written by Adorno.
28. Adorno, *Minima Moralia*, p. 140.
29. Guy Debord, *The Society of the Spectacle*, trans. by Donald Nicholson-Smith (New York: Zone Books, 1994), p. 112.

30. Immanuel Kant, *Critique of Pure Reason*, trans. by Paul Guyer and Allen W. Wood (Cambridge: Cambridge University Press, 1999), p. 212.
31. Kant, *Critique of Pure Reason*, p. 239.
32. Kant, *Critique of Pure Reason*, p. 272.
33. Kant, *Critique of Pure Reason*, p. 156.
34. Theodor W. Adorno, *Kant's 'Critique of Pure Reason'*, trans. by Rolf Tiedemann (Cambridge & New York: Polity Press, 2001), pp. 133–4. Adorno promised a more detailed lecture on the schematism chapter, which was never given.
35. Heidegger, *Kant and the Problem of Metaphysics*, p. 63.
36. Kant, *Critique of Pure Reason*, pp. 273–4.
37. Martin Heidegger, *Being and Time*, trans. by John Macquarrie and Edward Robinson (Oxford: Blackwell, 2000), p. 45.
38. F. W. J. Schelling, *System of Transcendental Idealism*, trans. by Peter Heath (Charlottesville: University of Virginia Press, 1993), p. 137.
39. Andrew Bowie, *Aesthetics and Subjectivity: From Kant to Nietzsche* (Manchester: Manchester University Press, 1990), p. 38. Bowie develops the parallel between music and schematism in his essay, 'Adorno, Heidegger, and the Meaning of Music', in, ed. Tom Huhn, *The Cambridge Companion to Adorno* (Cambridge: Cambridge University Press, 2004), pp. 262–3.
40. Kant, *Critique of Pure Reason*, p. 274.
41. Kant, *Critique of Pure Reason*, p. 276.
42. Kant, *Critique of Pure Reason*, p. 272.
43. Kant, *Critique of Pure Reason*, p. 276.
44. Kant, *Critique of Pure Reason*, p. 464.
45. Arnold Schoenberg, *Moses und Aron*, act 1.
46. Cited in, Lacoue-Labarthe, p. 137.
47. 'Perhaps there is no more sublime passage in the Jewish Law than the commandment: Thou shalt not make unto thee a graven image, or any likeness of any thing that is in heaven or on earth, or under the earth, etc.' Immanuel Kant, *The Critique of Judgement*, trans. by James Creed Meredith (Oxford: Clarendon Press, 1978), p. 127.
48. Kant, *Critique of Pure Reason*, p. 163.
49. Kant, *Critique of Pure Reason*, p. 470.
50. Kant, *Critique of Pure Reason*, p. 275.
51. Heidegger, *Kant and the Problem of Metaphysics*, pp. 63–73.
52. The 'image' [*Bild*] of 'imagination' [*Einbildungskraft*] is taken in three senses: as the 'look' [*Anblick*], the specific image of a being 'at hand', and as a 'likeness' (a 'photograph' or a 'death mask'). The 'pure look' defines intuition [*Anschauung*]. It is 'the horizon of the letting-stand against [*Gegenstehenlassen*].' Heidegger, *Kant and the Problem of Metaphysics*, pp. 63–4.
53. Heidegger, *Kant and the Problem of Metaphysics*, p. xvii.
54. Martin Heidegger, 'The Origin of the Work of Art', in *Off the Beaten Track*, trans. by Julian Young and Kenneth Hayes (Cambridge: Cambridge University Press, 2002), p. 22.
55. Adorno, 'On Some Relationships Between Music and Painting', p. 66.
56. Schelling, *System of Transcendental Idealism*, pp. 134–9.
57. F. W. J. Schelling, *The Philosophy of Art*, trans. by Douglas W. Stott (Minneapolis: University of Minnesota Press, 1989), p. 109.

58. August Wilhelm Schlegel, *Vorlesungen Über Philosophische Kunstlehre* (Leipzig: Theodor Weicher, 1911), pp. 224–7.
59. Schelling, *The Philosophy of Art*, pp. 110–11.
60. Theodor W. Adorno, *Beethoven: The Philosophy of Music*, trans. by Edmund Jephcott (Cambridge: Polity Press, 1998), p. 8.
61. Curt Sachs, *Rhythm and Tempo* (New York: Dent, 1953), p. 12.
62. Adorno, *Beethoven*, p. 112.
63. Adorno, 'On Some Relationships Between Music and Painting', p. 66.
64. 'The cognitive powers brought into play by this representation are here engaged in a free play, since no definite concept restricts them to a particular rule of cognition'. Kant, *The Critique of Judgement*, p. 58. Emphasis added.
65. Adorno, *Aesthetic Theory*, p. 136.
66. Kant, *The Critique of Judgement*, p. 59.
67. Theodor W. Adorno, 'Vers Une Musique Informelle', in *Quasi una Fantasia: Essays on Modern Music*, trans. by Rodney Livingstone (London & New York: Verso, 1992), p. 312.
68. Henri Bergson, *Key Writings*, ed. by Keith Ansell-Pearson (London & New York: Continuum, 2002), p. 60.
69. 'We call the temporal attribute of entities within-the-world "within-time-ness" [*die Innerzeitkeit*]. The kind of "time" which is first found ontically in within-time-ness, becomes the basis on which the ordinary conception of time takes form. But time, as within-time-ness, arises from an essential kind of temporalizing of primordial temporality. The fact that this is its source, tells us that the time "in which" what is present-at-hand arises and passes away, is a genuine phenomenon of time; it is not an externalisation of a "qualitative time" into space, as Bergson's Interpretation of time – which is ontologically quite indefinite and inadequate – would have us believe.' Heidegger, *Being and Time*, p. 333.
70. Hussurl considers the 'tone' as the being the 'temporal object' of immediate consciousness, the preceding tones the having-been objects, and the expected tones the anticipated objects. Music (the melody) is the analogy for time itself. And as in Bergson, the 'tone' is the analogy for the 'now' that is in time. Edmund Husserl, *On the Phenomenology of the Consciousness of Internal Time*, ed. by Martin Heidegger, trans. by John Barnett Brough (Dordrecht & Boston: Kluwer Academic Publishers, 1991), pp. 24–5.
71. Adorno, *Beethoven*, p. 90.
72. G. W. F. Hegel, *Hegel's Philosophy of Nature: Being Part Two of the 'Encyclopedia of the Philosophical Sciences' (1830)*, trans. by A. V. Miller (Oxford: Clarendon Press, 1970), p. 35. Cf. Hegel, *Phenomenology of Spirit*: 'History, is a conscious, self-mediating process – Spirit emptied out into Time', p. 492.
73. Adorno, *Negativ Dialektik*, p. 327.
74. Ludwig Feuerbach, *The Fiery Brook*, trans. by Zawar Hanfi (Minnesota: Anchor, 1972), pp. 57–8.
75. Wilhelm Heinrich Wackenroder, 'The Marvels of the Musical Art', in *German Essays on Music*, ed. by Jost Hermand and Michael Gilbert (New York: Continuum, 1994), p. 36.
76. E. T. A. Hoffmann, 'Beethoven's Instrumental Music', in *German Essays on Music*, ed. by Jost Hermand and Michael Gilbert (New York: Continuum, 1994), pp. 60–1.

77. Theodor W. Adorno, 'On the Contemporary Relationships of Philosophy and Music', in *Essays on Music*, trans. by Susan H. Gillespie (Berkeley: University of California Press, 2002), p. 138.
78. Adorno, 'On the Contemporary Relationships of Philosophy and Music', p. 139.
79. Adorno, 'On Some Relationships Between Music and Painting', p. 66.
80. Perhaps the historical case study would be Mozart's divertimento in B-flat, the *Gran Partita*.
81. Adorno, *Beethoven*, pp. 7–8.
82. Theodor W. Adorno, *Dream Notes*, ed. by Christoph Gödde and Jan Philipp Reemsta, trans. by Rodney Livingstone (Cambridge: Polity, 2007).
83. Adorno, *Beethoven*, pp. 7–8.
84. Adorno, 'On the Contemporary Relationships of Philosophy and Music', p. 150.
85. Ernst Kurth, *Musikpsychologie*, 2nd edn (Bern: Krompholz, 1947), pp. 85–7.
86. Kurth, p. 96.
87. Heidegger, *Being and Time*, pp. 387–8.
88. This is not to say that the goal of modern music is its origin. It does not negate 'expendable conventions', in pursuit of its essential medium. In contradistinction to Clement Greenberg, Adorno suggests that the arts converge in a manner that cannot be assumed to be progressive. For Adorno, music has historically lagged behind painting, in that it sought to imitate it, catching up only in the twentieth century. It had been late since the late renaissance of the stile rapprasentativo. Greenberg argues, by contrast, that painting and literature took music, which matured early, for their model. 'Because of its "absolute" nature, its remoteness from imitation ... music had come to replace poetry as the paragon of art. It was the art which the other avant-garde arts envied most, and whose effects they tried hardest to imitate.' Clement Greenberg, 'Towards a Newer Laocoon', in *Art in Theory, 1900–2000*, ed. by Charles Harrison and Paul Wood (Oxford: Blackwell, 2000), p. 565.
89. Adorno, 'On Some Relationships Between Music and Painting', p. 67.
90. Adorno, 'Sacred Fragment', pp. 231–2.
91. Adorno, 'Sacred Fragment', p. 237.
92. '*Notizen zum Musiktheater heute*', in Luigi Nono, *Texte: Studien zu seiner Musik*, ed. Jürg Stenzl (Atlantis, 1975), 64.
93. Theodor W. Adorno, 'The Aging of the New Music', in *Essays on Music*, ed. by Richard Leppert, trans. by Susan H. Gillespie (Berkeley: University of California Press, 2002), p. 191.
94. Adorno, 'The Aging of the New Music', p. 181.
95. Theodor W. Adorno, 'On the Relationship Between Painting and Music Today', in *Night Music: Essays on Music 1928–1962*, trans. by Wieland Hoban (London: Seagull Books, 2009), p. 415.
96. Adorno, 'The Aging of the New Music', p. 188.
97. Theodor W. Adorno, 'New Music Today', in *Night Music: Essays on Music 1928–1962*, trans. by Wieland Hoban (London: Seagull Books, 2009), pp. 398–9.
98. Adorno, 'Vers Une Musique Informelle', p. 272.
99. Heinz-Klaus Metzger, 'Intermezzo I: Just Who Is Growing Old?' ed. by Karlheinz Stockhausen and Herbert Eimert, trans. by Leo Black, *Die Reihe*, 4 (1960), p. 73.

100. Theodor W. Adorno, 'Vienna', in *Quasi una Fantasia: Essays on Modern Music*, trans. by Rodney Livingstone (London: Verso, 1992), p. 219.
101. Adorno, *Aesthetic Theory*, p. 21.
102. Adorno, *Aesthetic Theory*, pp. 44–5.
103. See, 'On Astrology' (1932), 'Doctrine of the Similar' (1933), and 'On the Mimetic Faculty' (1933), in Walter Benjamin, *Selected Writings, Vol. 2, 1931–1934*, ed. by Howard Eiland & Michael W. Jennings (Cambridge, MA: Harvard University Press, 2005).
104. David Osmond-Smith, *Break-out from the Concert Hall: Luigi Nono and the New Music*, Concert Program (Queen Elizabeth Hall, London, 2005), p. 3.
105. Cited in, Jeannie Maria Guerrero, 'Serial Intervention in Nono's Il Canto Sospeso', *Society for Music Theory*, 2006 <http://mto.societymusictheory.org/issues/mto.06.12.1/mto.06.12.1.guerrero.html> [accessed 2 February 2010].
106. Cited in, Theodor W. Adorno, *In Search of Wagner*, trans. by Rodney Livingstone (London: Verso, 2005), p. 88.
107. Theodor W. Adorno, 'Wagner's Relevance for Today', in *Essays on Music*, ed. by Richard Leppert, trans. by Susan H. Gillespie (Berkeley: University of California Press, 2002), p. 594.
108. Adorno, 'On Some Relationships Between Music and Painting', p. 68. Emphasis added.
109. Helmut Lachenmann, 'Touched by Nono', *Contemporary Music Review*, 18 (1999), p. 19.
110. Lachenmann, pp. 20–1.
111. Lachenmann, p. 27.
112. Georg Lukács, *History and Class Consciousness. Studies in Marxist Dialectics*, trans. by Rodney Livingstone (London: Merlin Press, 1971), p. 89.
113. Adorno mentions the Frankfurt informel painter Bernard Schultze, but unfavourably. His preferred moment of modernist painting is Picasso's synthetic Cubism – the later essay on music and painting is dedicated to Picasso collector Daniel-Henry Kahnweiler. Moreover, the term 'musique informelle' was chosen by Adorno 'as a small token of gratitude towards the nation for whom the tradition of the avant-garde is synonymous with the courage to produce manifestoes.' Hence, the name does not refer to the specific manifesto of art informel (namely Tapié's *An Other Art*). Adorno, 'Vers Une Musique Informelle', p. 272.
114. *Luigi Nono*, ed. by Heinz-Klaus Metzger and Rainer Riehn (Munich: edition text + kritik, 1981), pp. 304–5.
115. Alastair Williams, 'New Music, Late Style: Adorno's "Form in the New Music"', *Music Analysis*, 27 (2008), p. 196.
116. György Ligeti and Carl Dahlhaus, 'A Debate on Contemporary Music', in *Contemplating Music: Essence*, ed. by Carl Dahlhaus and Ruth Katz, Source Readings in the Aesthetics of Music (Hillsdale, NY: Pendragon Press, 1992), iii, p. 795.
117. Jürg Stenzl, *Luigi Nono* (Reinbek bei Hamburg: Rowohlt, 1998), pp. 97–8.
118. Osmond-Smith, p. 4.
119. Irvine Arditti, *Nono's Fragmente-Stille…*, Concert Program (Queen Elizabeth Hall, London, 2007), p. 7.

120. Michele Bertaggia, 'Prometeo – Conversation Entre Luigi Nono et Massimo Cacciari', in *Programme Luigi Nono* (Paris: Contrechamps, 1987), p. 138.
121. Adorno, 'Vers Une Musique Informelle', p. 322.
122. Bertaggia, p. 134.
123. Cf. Jonathan Rée, *I See a Voice: A Philosophical History of Language, Deafness and the Senses* (London: Harper Collins, 1999).
124. Bertaggia, pp. 134–46.
125. In his essay on *Prometeo,* Cacciari refers to the 'tempo' of 'The Master of the Game' as, 'the a-rhythmic succession of the punctual', according to which,the past is nothing more than *having-been*... and the present is a space from which we throw ourselves 'all together' into the future; or, as Michelstaedter used to say, we 'enfuture' ourselves. On the other hand, the tempo of the Master is polyphonic; his dimensions are given simultaneously; the past of such a line, of such thought, of such speech, may be the future of any other. The present is not a space common to 'all', but the irreplaceable instant, fugitive, clear and living, of the Unique. Like a New Angel, he chants the instant, but this instant, precisely, is unique and non-reproducible, and by the very fact of this uniqueness and of this unrepeatable quality, it never-ceases-to-be; it is *necessary*. To think necessity and creation simultaneously, snatching something from the instant – the fugitive nature of the instant – that which can break the 'movimentum', is infinite temporality, the 'development' from one being to another, as from death to death: this is what constitutes the unique quality of the Master of the Game, his 'weak messianic force'. Massimo Cacciari, 'Verso Prometeo', in *Programme Luigi Nono,* (Paris: Contrechamps, 1987), p. 153. Translation by Adeline Mannarini.
126. Walter Benjamin, *The Arcades Project,* trans. by Howard Eiland and Kevin McLaughlin (Cambridge, MA: Harvard University Press, 2002), p. 462.
127. Benjamin, 'On the Concept of History', p. 390.
128. Theodor W. Adorno to Walter Benjamin, August 2, 1935; Taylor, p. 111.
129. Rolf Tiedemann, 'Dialectics at a Standstill', in Benjamin, *The Arcades Project,* p. 940.
130. Benjamin, *The Arcades Project,* p. 464.
131. Benjamin, *The Arcades Project,* p. 686.
132. Theodor W. Adorno, '*Die Oper Wozzeck*', in *Musikalische Schriften V,* ed. Rolf Tiedemann, vol. III, *Gesammelte Schriften* (Frankfurt am Main: Suhrkamp Verlag, 1986), p. 479.
133. Adorno, 'On the Fetish Character', p. 314.

4 Invincible in the Wasteland? Music, Space and Utopia

1. This research is represented in English in, Massimo Cacciari, *Architecture and Nihilism: On the Philosophy of Modern Architecture,* trans. by Patrizia Lombardo (New Haven: Yale University Press, 1993).
2. Cacciari writes of 'the shadowy possibility of consonance between music and monumental architecture.' But the affinity of music and architecture is dependant, here, upon an association of 'nothing' with 'silence', and 'being' with 'listening', recalling Heidegger's phonocentric 'call to thinking'. Massimo Cacciari, 'Eupalinos or Architecture', *Oppositions,* 1980, p. 111.

3. Cacciari, *Architecture and Nihilism*, p. 4.
4. Manfredo Tafuri, *Architecture and Utopia: Design and Capitalist Development*, trans. by Barbara Luigia La Penta (Cambridge, MA: MIT Press, 1976), chap. 1.
5. Georg Simmel, 'Metropolis and Mental Life', in *On Individuality and Social Forms*, ed. by Donald Levine, trans. by Edward A. Shils, pp. 325–6.
6. Simmel, p. 332.
7. Simmel, p. 339.
8. Cacciari, *Architecture and Nihilism*, p. 12.
9. Matters are more complex than Cacciari gives credit here. Nietzsche attributes the ascetic ideal of 'intellectualisation [*Vergeistigung*]' to Kant, among other 'ascetic priests'. But the language of *Vergeistigung* is equally an inflection of the values of *Aufklärung*. The critique of *Geist* offers little advance upon Marx's critiques of Hegel and Feuerbach. The omission of Hegel in Cacciari's early essays is notable given Hegel's attempt to overcome the Kantian, liberal subject.
10. Cacciari, *Architecture and Nihilism*, p. 5.
11. Cacciari, *Architecture and Nihilism*, p. 8.
12. Cited in, Martin Heidegger, *The Fundamental Concepts of Metaphysics: World, Finitude, Solitude*, trans. by William McNeill and Nicholas Walker (Bloomington: Indiana University Press, 2001), p. 5.
13. Cacciari, *Architecture and Nihilism*, pp. 6–9.
14. Citing Nietzsche's *Genealogy*, Karl Löwith writes of this affinity: 'Weber's 'methodological' question as to the value of science is basically the same question that Nietzsche posed in regard to philosophy when he inquired after the meaning and value of 'truth' – for 'what sense could our existence have, if not the sense that within us this urge towards truth has become conscious of itself as a problem?'.' Karl Löwith, *Max Weber and Karl Marx*, trans. by Hans Fantel (London: George Allen & Unwin, 1982), p. 30.
15. Cf. David Owen, *Maturity and Modernity* (London: Routledge, 1994), pp. 84–9.
16. For Weber, positive science, God's murderer, wrests the providence of truth away from God, whereas for Nietzsche this murder is responsible for the equally metaphysical 'will to truth' of positive science itself, that which 'never creates values'. Friedrich Nietzsche, *On the Genealogy of Morality*, trans. by Carol Diethe (Cambridge: Cambridge University Press, 1994), p. 120.
17. 'The fate of our times is characterised by rationalisation and intellectualization and, above all, by the "disenchantment of the world."' Max Weber, 'Science as a Vocation', in *From Max Weber: Essays in Sociology*, trans. by H. H. Gerth and C. Wright Mills (London: Routledge, 1991), p. 155.
18. Cacciari, *Architecture and Nihilism*, p. 28.
19. Max Weber, '"Objectivity" in Social Science', in *Methodology of the Social Sciences*, trans. by Edward A. Shils and Henry A. Finch (New Brunswick, NJ: Transaction Publishers, 2011), p. 81; 112.
20. Weber, '"Objectivity" in Social Science', p. 90.
21. Weber invokes the Goethean image of the stream: 'if the professional thinker has an immediate obligation at all, it is to keep a cool head in the face of the ideals prevailing at the time ... and if necessary, "to swim against the stream".' Max Weber, 'The Meaning of "Ethical Neutrality,"' in *Methodology of the*

Social Sciences, trans. Edward A. Shils and Henry A. Finch (New Brunswick, NJ: Transaction Publishers, 2011), 47. Weber cites Goethe's 'floor of waves beneath me' (*Faust*, Act I, Scene II) in the earlier '"Objectivity"' essay: 'The light of the great cultural problems moves on. Then science too prepares to change its standpoint and its analytical apparatus and to view the streams of events from the heights of thought' (p. 112).

22. Cacciari, *Architecture and Nihilism*, pp. 70–1.
23. Max Weber, *Economy and Society*, ed. by Guenther Roth and Claus Wittich (Berkeley: University of California Press, 1992), ii, p. 1116.
24. Löwith, *Max Weber and Karl Marx*, p. 30.
25. Nietzsche begins to outline his response to the crisis of values in *Human, All Too Human*. This marks a departure from *The Birth of Tragedy*, which remained confined to Schopenhauer's paradigm of tragic fate. The earlier understanding had led to a dualism of 'setting man and fate over against one another as two separate things.' The task of the scientist, today, is to see fate from on high. The 'region ... of torrential streams ... cannot in any way be painted unless one is hovering above it in the air like a bird. Here the so-called bird's eye view is for once not an artistic caprice but the sole possibility.' The stream emerges before the gaze, in the gaze, as the 'sole possibility' of the stream's emergence. Hence, Nietzsche does not merely 'go against the stream' of fate, as in the more modest interventions of Weber (and Foucault?). Nietzsche wants to redirect the stream itself. Friedrich Nietzsche, *Human, All Too Human*, trans. by R. J. Hollingdale (Cambridge: Cambridge University Press, 1996), p. 325; p. 343.
26. Cacciari, *Architecture and Nihilism*, p. 25.
27. Cacciari, *Architecture and Nihilism*, p. 26.
28. Cacciari, *Architecture and Nihilism*, p. 28.
29. Friedrich Nietzsche, *Thus Spoke Zarathustra*, trans. by R. J. Hollingdale, New Impression (Penguin Classics, 2003), p. 198.
30. 'Since Aristotle, there has been a poetics of tragedy. Only since Schelling has there been a philosophy of the tragic.' Peter Szondi, *An Essay on the Tragic*, trans. by Paul Fleming (Stanford, CA: Stanford University Press, 2002), p. 1.
31. "*Trauerspiel* and Tragedy", in Walter Benjamin, *Selected Writings, Vol. 1, 1913–1926*, ed. Howard Eiland & Michael W. Jennings (Cambridge, MA: Harvard University Press, 1997), p. 56.
32. Szondi, p. 16.
33. Arthur Schopenhauer, *The World as Will and Representation*, trans. by E. F. G. Payne (New York: Dover Publications, 1966), i, p. 254.
34. Karl Löwith, *From Hegel to Nietzsche: The Revolution in Nineteenth-Century Thought*, trans. by David E. Green (New York: Columbia University Press, 1991), p. 175.
35. Benjamin appears to overlook the cosmological interpretation of eternal recurrence presented by Löwith, which, as cosmological, Löwith takes to be inconsistent with the 'will to power'. Karl Löwith, *Nietzsche's Philosophy of the Eternal Recurrence of the Same*, trans. by J. Harvey Lomax (Berkeley: University of California Press, 1997).
36. Walter Benjamin, *The Arcades Project*, trans. by Howard Eiland and Kevin McLaughlin (Cambridge, MA: Harvard University Press, 2002), p. 115.
37. Benjamin, *The Arcades Project*, p. 117.

38. Benjamin, *The Arcades Project*, p. 116.
39. Cacciari, *Architecture and Nihilism*, p. 16. Tafuri observes the 'anti-Hegelian rediscovery of the negative' in Bloch and Marcuse. Why not Adorno? Manfredo Tafuri, Architecture and Utopia, p. 59.
40. Patrizia Lombardo, Introduction, in Cacciari, *Architecture and Nihilism*, p. xxv.
41. Their shared critique is that Benjamin's *Schockerlebnis* is not mediated – in art, including architecture. Cacciari, *Architecture and Nihilism*, p. 18.
42. Cacciari, *Architecture and Nihilism*, p. 6.
43. Theodor W. Adorno, *Aesthetic Theory*, trans. by Robert Hullot-Kentor (London: Athlone Press, 1997), p. 54.
44. Adorno, *Aesthetic Theory*, p. 44.
45. Adorno, *Aesthetic Theory*, p. 1.
46. Max Horkheimer and Theodor W. Adorno, *Dialectic of Enlightenment*, trans. by Edmund Jephcott (Stanford, CA: Stanford University Press, 2002), pp. 60–1.
47. 'Within the sphere of Hölderlinian imagery, the domination of nature itself comes close to being the original sin; that is the measure of its complicity with Christianity... Philosophically, the anamnesis of suppressed nature, in which Hölderlin tries to separate the wild from the peaceful, is the consciousness of non-identity, which transcends the compulsory identity of the logos'. Theodor W. Adorno, 'Parataxis', in *Notes to Literature*, ed. by Rolf Tiedemann, trans. by Shierry Weber Nicholsen (New York: Columbia University Press, 1991), p. 241.
48. Adorno, *Aesthetic Theory*, p. 58.
49. Cf. Theodor W. Adorno, 'Functionalism Today', in *Rethinking Architecture: A Reader in Cultural Theory*, ed. by Neil Leach (New York: Routledge, 1997), pp. 5–20.
50. Cacciari, *Architecture and Nihilism*, p. 103.
51. Simmel, p. 237.
52. Martin Heidegger, 'Letter on Humanism', in *Basic Writings*, ed. by David Farrell Krell, trans. by Frank A. Capuzzi and J. Glenn Gray (London: Routledge, 1993), p. 243.
53. Martin Heidegger, *Being and Time*, trans. by John Macquarrie and Edward Robinson (Oxford: Blackwell, 2000), p. 125.
54. Heidegger, *Being and Time*, p. 128.
55. Heidegger, *Being and Time*, p. 138.
56. Cacciari, *Architecture and Nihilism*, p. 107.
57. Martin Heidegger, *Holderlin's Hymn 'The Ister'*, trans. by William McNeill and Julia Davis (Indianapolis: Indiana University Press, 1996), pp. 34–5.
58. Martin Heidegger, 'Building Dwelling Thinking', in *Basic Writings*, ed. by David Farrell Krell, trans. by Albert Hofstadter (London: Routledge, 1993), p. 356.
59. Martin Heidegger, 'Art and Space', in *Rethinking Architecture: A Reader in Cultural Theory*, ed. by Neil Leach, trans. by Charles Siebert (New York: Routledge, 1997), p. 123.
60. Theodor W. Adorno, *The Jargon of Authenticity*, trans. by Knut Tarnowski (London: Routledge, 2002), pp. 43–4.
61. Heidegger, 'Building Dwelling Thinking', p. 349.
62. Cacciari, 'Eupalinos or Architecture', p. 97.

63. "We mean uncanny in the sense of that which is not at home – not homely in that which is homely. It is only for this reason that the un-homely [*das Un-heimische*] can, as a consequence, also be 'uncanny' ['*unheimlich*'] in the sense of something that has an alienating or 'frightening' effect that gives rise to anxiety." Heidegger, *Holderlin's Hymn "The Ister,"* p. 41.
64. Martin Heidegger, '"The Onto-Theo-Logical Constitution of Metaphysics"', in *Identity and Difference*, trans. by Joan Stambaugh, New Edition (Chicago: University of Chicago Press, 2002), pp. 42–76.
65. Massimo Cacciari, *Posthumous People: Vienna at the Turning Point* (Stanford, CA: Stanford University Press, 1996).
66. Cacciari, *Architecture and Nihilism*, p. 169.
67. Cacciari, *Architecture and Nihilism*, p. 172.
68. Cited in, Cacciari, *Architecture and Nihilism*, p. lviii.
69. Michele Bertaggia, 'Prometeo – Conversation Entre Luigi Nono et Massimo Cacciari', in *Programme Luigi Nono* (Paris: Contrechamps, 1987), p. 139.
70. Immanuel Kant, *The Critique of Judgement*, trans. by James Creed Meredith (Oxford: Clarendon Press, 1978), p. 196.
71. 'Time is nothing other than the form of inner sense'. Immanuel Kant, *Critique of Pure Reason*, trans. by Paul Guyer and Allen W. Wood (Cambridge: Cambridge University Press, 1999), p. 163.
72. Ernst Kurth, *Musikpsychologie*, 2nd edn (Bern: Krompholz, 1947), p. 118.
73. Kurth, p. 120.
74. Kurth, pp. 119–28.
75. Kurth, p. 128.
76. G. W. F. Hegel, *Aesthetics: Lectures on Fine Art*, trans. by T. M. Knox (Oxford: Oxford University Press, 1998), p 894; p. 685; p. 893.
77. 'A noble philosopher spoke of architecture as frozen music, and it must have warranted much shaking of the head. We believe this beautiful thought is no better introduced as when we call architecture muted music [*verstummten ... Tonkunst*].' F. W. J. Schelling, *The Philosophy of Art*, trans. Douglas W. Stott (Minneapolis: University of Minnesota Press, 1989), p. 165.
78. L. L. Mackall, 'Goethes "Edler Philosoph"', *Euphorion*, XI (1904), p. 103 f.
79. Georg Lukács, *Theory of the Novel*, trans. by Anna Bostock (London: Merlin Press, 1978), p. 29.
80. Cf. Gershom Scholem, *Walter Benjamin: The Story of a Friendship*, trans. by Harry Zohn (New York: New York Review Books, 2003), p. 97.
81. The second part of The Spirit of Utopia is entitled, 'Karl Marx, Death, and the Apocalypse, Or, the Ways in This World by Which the Inward Can Become Outward and the Outward Like the Inward'. Ernst Bloch, *The Spirit of Utopia*, trans. by Anthony A. Nassar (Stanford University Press, 2000), pp. 233–78.
82. Bloch, p. 55.
83. Cf. Carola Nielinger, '"The Song Unsung": Luigi Nono's Il Canto Sospeso', *Journal of the Royal Musical Association*, 131 (2006).
84. Jürg Stenzl, *Luigi Nono* (Reinbek bei Hamburg: Rowohlt, 1998), p. 63.
85. David Osmond-Smith, *Break-out from the Concert Hall: Luigi Nono and the New Music*, Concert Program (Queen Elizabeth Hall, London, 2005), p. 4.
86. Adorno, *Aesthetic Theory*, p. 138.

87. Cited in, Gerard Pape, 'Nono and His Fellow Travellers', *Contemporary Music Review*, 18 (1991), p. 60.
88. Kurth, pp. 116–36.
89. Stenzl, p. 112.
90. Massimo Cacciari, 'Verso Prometeo', in *Programme Luigi Nono* (Paris: Contrechamps, 1987), p. 153. Translation by Adeline Mannarini.
91. Bertaggia, p. 134.
92. Cited in, Pape, p. 62. Translation amended.
93. Cf. Michel Foucault, 'Of Other Spaces', trans. by Jay Miskowiec, *Diacritics*, 16 (1986).
94. Natalie Bauer-Lechner, *Recollections of Gustav Mahler*, trans. by Dika Newlin (London & New York: Faber & Faber, 1980), p. 40.
95. Adorno, *Aesthetic Theory*, p. 138.
96. Adorno, *Aesthetic Theory*, pp. 225–6.
97. Theodor W. Adorno, *Negativ Dialektik* (Frankfurt am Main: Suhrkamp, 1966), p. 366.
98. Theodor W. Adorno, 'Valéry Proust Museum', in *Prisms*, trans. by Samuel Weber and Shierry Weber (Cambridge, MA: MIT Press, 1981), p. 178.
99. Michel De Certeau, *The Practice of Everyday Life*, trans. by Steven Rendall (Berkeley: University of California Press, 2002), p. 109.
100. Jacques Attali, *Noise: The Political Economy of Music*, trans. by Brian Massumi (Manchester: Manchester University Press, 1985), p. 21.
101. Adorno, 'Valéry Proust Museum', p. 175.
102. But does not music mark the death of tragedy? Monteverdi's 'Tragedy in Music', *Orfeo* – the rebirth of ancient tragedy in modern opera – is baroque melodrama. Opera, Benjamin writes in *Origin of the German Trauerspiel*, is 'the dissolution of *Trauerspiel*' (pp. 211–12). According to George Steiner, in 'the second half of the nineteenth century…opera puts forward a serious claim to the legacy of tragic drama.' In the essay '*Trauerspiel* and Tragedy', Benjamin thus claims that music cancels and includes the tragic: 'just as tragedy marks the transition from historical time to dramatic time, the *Trauerspiel* represents the transition from dramatic time to musical time' (p. 57). George Steiner, *The Death of Tragedy* (London: Faber, 1961), p. 284.
103. Adorno, *Aesthetic Theory*, p. 103.
104. Cacciari, 'Verso Prometeo', p. 152.
105. Karl Marx, 'The Difference Between the Democritean and Epicurean Philosophy of Nature in General', in Norman D. Livergood, *Activity in Marx's Philosophy* (The Hague: Martinus Nijhoff, 1967), p. 62.
106. Theodor W. Adorno, 'Transparencies on Film', in *The Culture Industry: Selected Essays on Mass Culture*, ed. by J. M. Bernstein (London: Routledge, 1991), p. 180.
107. 'At the very beginning Thomas More designated utopia as a place, an island in the distant South Seas. The designation underwent changes later so that it left space and entered time.' Theodor W. Adorno and Ernst Bloch, 'Something's Missing: A Discussion between Ernst Bloch and Theodor W. Adorno on the Contradictions of Utopian Longing', in *The Utopian Function of Art*, trans. by Jack Zipes and Frank Mecklenburg (Cambridge, MA: MIT Press, 1988), p. 3.

5 The Expression of Waiting in Vain

1. Robert Hullot-Kentor, 'Introduction to Adorno's "Idea of Natural History"', in Theodor W. Adorno, 'The Idea of Natural history', trans. by Robert Hullot-Kentor, *Telos*, 1984, p. 103.
2. Adorno, 'The Idea of Natural history', p. 124.
3. Theodor W. Adorno, *History and Freedom*, trans. by Rodney Livingstone (Cambridge: Polity, 2006), p. 124. Hullot-Kentor is thus wrong to suggest, on the basis that it was published posthumously, that Adorno had disowned the lecture.
4. Theodor W. Adorno, *Negativ Dialektik* (Frankfurt am Main: Suhrkamp, 1966), p. 353.
5. Adorno, *Negativ Dialektik*, p. 355.
6. Adorno, *Negativ Dialektik*, p. 359.
7. Theodor W. Adorno, *Metaphysics: Concept and Problems*, trans. by Rolf Tiedemann (Polity Press, 2001), pp. 101, 130.
8. Adorno, *Negativ Dialektik*, p. 15.
9. Adorno, *Metaphysics*, p. 15.
10. Adorno, *Metaphysics*, p. 24.
11. Adorno, *Metaphysics*, pp. 15–16.
12. Cf. Anson Rabinovich, 'Why Were the Jews Sacrificed? The Place of Anti-Semitism in Dialectic of Enlightenment', *New German Critique*, 81 (2000), pp. 49–64.
13. Adorno, *Metaphysics*, p. 33.
14. Adorno, *Metaphysics*, p. 140.
15. Adorno, *Metaphysics*, p. 115.
16. Adorno, *Negativ Dialektik*, p. 354.
17. Adorno, *Metaphysics*, p. 100.
18. Adorno, *Negativ Dialektik*, p. 362.
19. Adorno, *Negativ Dialektik*, p. 355.
20. In notes for his third lecture, Adorno writes, 'The entwinement of metaphysics with thought, inaugurated so emphatically by Aristotle in opposing hylozoism, is irrevocable.' Adorno, *Metaphysics*, p. 14.
21. Adorno, *Negativ Dialektik*, p. 364.
22. Adorno, *Negativ Dialektik*, p. 276.
23. Philippe Lacoue-Labarthe, *Heidegger, Art and Politics: The Fiction of the Political*, trans. by Chris Turner (Oxford: Blackwell, 1990), p. 43.
24. Adorno, *Negativ Dialektik*, p. 372.
25. Adorno, *Negativ Dialektik*, p. 381.
26. Adorno, *Negativ Dialektik*, p. 378.
27. Adorno, *Metaphysics*, p. 58.
28. Immanuel Kant, *Critique of Pure Reason*, trans. by Paul Guyer and Allen W. Wood (Cambridge: Cambridge University Press, 1999), p. 546.
29. Adorno, *Negativ Dialektik*, p. 285.
30. Adorno, *Negativ Dialektik*, p. 288.
31. Adorno, *Negativ Dialektik*, p. 292.
32. Adorno, *Negativ Dialektik*, p. 294.
33. Adorno, *Metaphysics*, p. 144.
34. Adorno, *Metaphysics*, p. 116.

35. Adorno, *Negativ Dialektik*, p. 386.
36. Immanuel Kant, *Groundwork of the Metaphysics of Morals*, trans. by Mary Gregor (Cambridge: Cambridge University Press, 1997), pp. 43–4.
37. Theodor W. Adorno, *Minima Moralia: Reflections on a Damaged Life*, trans. by Edmund Jephcott (London & New York: Verso Books, 1978), p. 175.
38. Adorno, *Metaphysics*, p. 143.
39. Jacob Taubes found Adorno's 'Finale' to *Minima Moralia* 'wonderful, but finally empty'. This forms the basis for Giorgio Agamben's claim, cited in Chapter 1, that 'negative dialectics is an absolutely non-messianic form of thought.' Jacob Taubes, *The Political Theology of Paul*, trans. by Dana Hollander (Stanford, CA: Stanford University Press, 2004), p. 74.
40. Adorno, *Minima Moralia*, p. 247.
41. Adorno, *Negativ Dialektik*, p. 400.
42. Walter Benjamin, 'On the Concept of History', in *Selected Writings, Volume 4*, trans. by Harry Zohn, Howard Eiland, and Michael W. Jennings (Cambridge, MA: Harvard University Press, 2003), p. 389.
43. Martin Heidegger, *The Fundamental Concepts of Metaphysics: World, Finitude, Solitude*, trans. by William McNeill and Nicholas Walker (Bloomington: Indiana University Press, 2001), p. 74.
44. Martin Heidegger, *Being and Time*, trans. by John Macquarrie and Edward Robinson (Oxford: Blackwell, 2000), p. 228. Translation amended.
45. Cited in, Rüdiger Safranski, *Martin Heidegger: Between Good and Evil*, trans. by Ewald Oders (Cambridge, MA: Harvard University Press, 1998), p. 190.
46. Heidegger, *Being and Time*, pp. 72–3.
47. Adorno, 'The Idea of Natural history', p. 112.
48. Cf. Adorno, *Negativ Dialektik*, p. 69.
49. De Beistegui flags-up the central 'tension' of the lecture course, between a concept of existence, whose essence is 'pure time', and one whose essence is already 'subordinated to a task which is historical in nature'. For, 'insofar as *Being and Time* has already identified the "fundamental meaning" of Dasein as temporality...why must we begin to search for the fundamental meaning of our contemporary Dasein?'. De Beistegui acknowledges that 'the solution to this tension...will be found only when Heidegger will reformulate the project of the question concerning the sense of being and transform it into the question concerning the history of being.' The demonstration of this move is ultimately confused, however. As with Löwith's critique of Heidegger, de Beistegui tends to side with the individual and apolitical Dasein of *Being and Time*, against any collective or political Dasein whatever – since such a move must be 'at once too ambitious and naive, too theological and messianic'. In place of messianism, the transition to the history of Being is instead secured for de Beistegui by way of 'the great works and lecture-courses of the 1930s' (including, it should be noted, the 'messianic' interpretations of Hölderlin). These works seek to reawaken the 'wonder' of the Greek Dasein. But such 'wonder' already privileges a particular history in a manner that does not account for this privilege with any philosophy of history. Miguel De Beistegui, 'Boredom: Between Existence and History', in *Thinking With Heidegger* (Indianapolis: Indiana University Press, 2003), pp. 61–82.
50. Heidegger, *Being and Time*, p. 174.
51. Heidegger, *The Fundamental Concepts of Metaphysics*, p. 96.

52. Heidegger, *The Fundamental Concepts of Metaphysics*, p. 114.
53. Heidegger, *The Fundamental Concepts of Metaphysics*, p. 157.
54. Heidegger, *The Fundamental Concepts of Metaphysics*, p. 156.
55. Heidegger, *The Fundamental Concepts of Metaphysics*, p. 134.
56. Heidegger, *The Fundamental Concepts of Metaphysics*, p. 37.
57. Heidegger, *The Fundamental Concepts of Metaphysics*, p. 105.
58. Heidegger, *Being and Time*, p. 231.
59. Heidegger, *Being and Time*, p. 356.
60. Heidegger, *The Fundamental Concepts of Metaphysics*, p. 294.
61. Heidegger, *The Fundamental Concepts of Metaphysics*, p. 96.
62. Heidegger, *Being and Time*, p. 302.
63. Heidegger, *The Fundamental Concepts of Metaphysics*, p. 140.
64. Heidegger, *Being and Time*, p. 318.
65. I have adjusted 'anticipation' to 'anticipatory' in the Macquarrie & Robinson translation of *Being and Time* in order to clarify its distinction from 'expectation'. The English translators themselves use 'anticipatory' in their rendering, 'anticipatory resoluteness'.
66. Heidegger, *Being and Time*, p. 373. Translation amended (see note above).
67. Heidegger, *The Fundamental Concepts of Metaphysics*, p. 145.
68. Heidegger's 1931 lectures on the *Phenomenology* are actually directed against interpretations of 'absolute knowing' as a totality of knowledge, in favour of 'ab-solving'. Heidegger relinquishes Hegelian mediation in a manner that will increasingly become a problem for him. Cf. Martin Heidegger, *Hegel's 'Phenomenology of Spirit'*, trans. by Parvis Emad and Kenneth Maly (Indianapolis: Indiana University Press, 1994).
69. Martin Heidegger, 'The Theory of the Categories and Meaning in Duns Scotus', in *Supplements*, trans. by Roderick M. Stewart and van Buren (New York: State University of New York Press, 2002), p. 68.
70. Theodor W. Adorno, *The Jargon of Authenticity*, trans. by Knut Tarnowski (London: Routledge, 2002), pp. 102–3.
71. Heidegger, *The Fundamental Concepts of Metaphysics*, p. 127.
72. Heidegger, *The Fundamental Concepts of Metaphysics*, pp. 27–34.
73. Heidegger, *The Fundamental Concepts of Metaphysics*, p. 149.
74. Heidegger, *Being and Time*, p. 373.
75. Adorno, 'The Idea of Natural history', p. 116.
76. Adorno, 'The Idea of Natural history', p. 115.
77. Adorno, 'The Idea of Natural history', p. 112.
78. Adorno, 'The Idea of Natural history', p. 115.
79. Adorno, *Negativ Dialektik*, p. 70.
80. Heidegger, *Being and Time*, p. 284.
81. Heidegger, *Being and Time*, p. 344.
82. Theodor W. Adorno, 'Progress', in *Critical Models: Interventions and Catchwords*, trans. by Henry W. Pickford (New York: Columbia University Press, 1998), p. 151.
83. Heidegger, *The Fundamental Concepts of Metaphysics*, p. 177.
84. This can be glanced at from the titles of Heidegger's works during the late 1920s: *Kant and the Problem of Metaphysics* (1928), *The Fundamental Concepts of Metaphysics* (1929–30), and the inaugural lecture, *What is Metaphysics?* (1929).
85. Heidegger, *The Fundamental Concepts of Metaphysics*, p. 30.

86. Heidegger, *The Fundamental Concepts of Metaphysics*, p. 364.
87. Heidegger, *Being and Time*, p. 306.
88. Heidegger, *The Fundamental Concepts of Metaphysics*, p. 94.
89. Walter Benjamin, *The Arcades Project*, trans. by Howard Eiland and Kevin McLaughlin (Cambridge, MA: Harvard University Press, 2002), p. 107.
90. Heidegger, *The Fundamental Concepts of Metaphysics*, p. 124.
91. Heidegger, *The Fundamental Concepts of Metaphysics*, p. 109.
92. Heidegger, *The Fundamental Concepts of Metaphysics*, p. 387.
93. Adorno, *Negativ Dialektik*, p. 116.
94. De Beistegui, p. 74.
95. Cited in, Benjamin, *The Arcades Project*, p. 101.
96. Adorno, *Metaphysics*, p. 143.
97. Adorno, *The Jargon of Authenticity*, p. 107.
98. Adorno, *The Jargon of Authenticity*, p. 131.
99. Heidegger, *Being and Time*, p. 306.
100. Adorno, *Metaphysics*, p. 144.
101. Heidegger, *The Fundamental Concepts of Metaphysics*, p. 163.
102. Heidegger, *The Fundamental Concepts of Metaphysics*, p. 164.
103. The concept of 'fate' was introduced in *Being and Time*. '*Ganzseinkönnen*' is not a contingent, relativist philosophy of history, Heidegger insists, but is rather the greatest possibility of historical Dasein: 'Once one has grasped the finitude of one's existence, it snatches one back from the endless multiplicity of possibilities which offer themselves as closest to one ... and brings Dasein into the simplicity of its *fate* [*Schicksals*]. This is how we designate Dasein's primordial historizing [*ursprüngliche Geschehen*], which lies in authentic resoluteness and in which Dasein *hands* itself *down* to itself, free for death, in a possibility which it has inherited and yet has chosen.' Heidegger, *Being and Time*, p. 435.
104. Adorno, *Metaphysics*, p. 142.
105. Heidegger, *The Fundamental Concepts of Metaphysics*, pp. 69–74.
106. Adorno, *History and Freedom*, p. 4.
107. Theodor W. Adorno, 'Free Time', in *Critical Models: Interventions and Catchwords*, trans. by Henry W. Pickford (New York: Columbia University Press, 1998), p. 171.
108. Martin Heidegger, 'Letter on Humanism', in *Basic Writings*, ed. by David Farrell Krell, trans. by Frank A. Capuzzi and J. Glenn Gray (London: Routledge, 1993), p. 231.
109. Adorno, *Negativ Dialektik*, p. 134.
110. Adorno relies upon a citation of Löwith for the *explicit* connection between Heidegger's decisionism and Hitlerism ('a vulgarly decisive moment'). But as was suggested above, Löwith seems to oppose any and all possible historical determinations of Dasein. He stands by the structural existentialism of *Being and Time*. Adorno does not mean to legitimate Löwith's position here. But the reliance upon Löwith, allied with the absence of a critique of destiny, is notable, given Adorno's own conception of history. Where the younger Adorno had opposed natural history to Hegelianism, the Adorno of *Negativ Dialektik* critically incorporates Hegel. Adorno's deconstruction of Hegelian spirit seeks to retain Hegel's sense of *history in the singular*. Hence the section in *Negativ Dialektik*, 'World-spirit and Natural History'.

111. Heidegger, *The Fundamental Concepts of Metaphysics*, p. 182.
112. Heidegger, *The Fundamental Concepts of Metaphysics*, p. 171. Translation amended.
113. Adorno, *Metaphysics*, p. 68.
114. Theodor W. Adorno, 'Resignation', in *Critical Models: Interventions and Catchwords*, trans. by Henry W. Pickford (New York: Columbia University Press, 1998), p. 293.
115. Martin Heidegger, *The Question Concerning Technology and Other Essay*, trans. by William Lovitt (New York & London: Harper and Row, 1977), p. 35.
116. Heidegger, *The Question Concerning Technology*, p. 42.
117. Heidegger, *The Fundamental Concepts of Metaphysics*, p. 117.
118. Martin Heidegger, 'Only a God Can Save Us', in *Philosophical and Political Writings*, ed. by Manfred Stassen, trans. by Maria P. Alter and John D. Caputo (New York and London: Continuum, 2003), p. 42. Translation amended.

Bibliography

Adorno, Theodor W., *Aesthetic Theory*, trans. by Robert Hullot-Kentor (London: Athlone Press, 1997)

——, *Beethoven: The Philosophy of Music*, trans. by Edmund Jephcott (Cambridge: Polity Press, 1998)

——, 'Die Oper Wozzeck', in *Musikalische Schriften V*, ed. by Rolf Tiedemann, *Gesammelte Schriften* (Frankfurt am Main: Suhrkamp Verlag, 1986)

——, *Dream Notes*, ed. by Christoph Gödde and Jan Philipp Reemsta, trans. by Rodney Livingstone (Cambridge: Polity, 2007)

——, 'Free Time', in *Critical Models: Interventions and Catchwords*, trans. by Henry W. Pickford (New York: Columbia University Press, 1998)

——, 'Functionalism Today', in *Rethinking Architecture: A Reader in Cultural Theory*, ed. by Neil Leach (New York: Routledge, 1997)

——, *Hegel: Three Studies*, trans. by Shierry Weber Nicholsen (Cambridge, MA: MIT Press, 1994)

——, *History and Freedom*, trans. by Rodney Livingstone (Cambridge: Polity, 2006)

——, *In Search of Wagner*, trans. by Rodney Livingstone (London: Verso, 2005)

——, *Kant's 'Critique of Pure Reason'*, trans. by Rolf Tiedemann (Cambridge & New York: Polity Press, 2001)

——, *Metaphysics: Concept and Problems*, trans. by Rolf Tiedemann (Stanford, CA: Stanford University Press, 2000)

——, *Minima Moralia: Reflections on a Damaged Life*, trans. by Edmund Jephcott (London & New York: Verso Books, 1978)

——, 'Music, Language and Composition', in *Essays on Music*, trans. by Susan H. Gillespie (Berkeley: University of California Press, 2002)

——, *Negativ Dialektik* (Frankfurt am Main: Suhrkamp, 1966)

——, 'New Music Today', in *Night Music: Essays on Music 1928–1962*, trans. by Wieland Hoban (London: Seagull Books, 2009)

——, *Notes to Literature*, ed. by Rolf Tiedemann, trans. by Shierry Weber Nicholsen (New York: Columbia University Press, 1991)

——, 'On Some Relationships Between Music and Painting', trans. by Susan H. Gillespie, *The Musical Quarterly* (1995)

——, 'On the Contemporary Relationships of Philosophy and Music', in *Essays on Music*, ed. by Richard Leppert, trans. by Susan H. Gillespie (Berkeley: University of California Press, 2002)

——, 'On the Fetish Character in Music and the Regression of Listening', in *Essays on Music*, ed. by Richard Leppert, trans. by Susan H. Gillespie (Berkeley: University of California Press, 2002)

——, 'On the Relationship Between Painting and Music Today', in *Night Music: Essays on Music 1928–1962*, trans. by Wieland Hoban (London: Seagull Books, 2009)

——, 'Parataxis', in *Notes to Literature*, ed. by Rolf Tiedemann, trans. by Shierry Weber Nicholsen (New York: Columbia University Press, 1991), II

——, *Philosophy of Modern Music*, trans. by Wesley V. Bloomster and Anne G. Mitchell (London: Sheed & Ward, 1973)
——, 'Progress', in *Critical Models: Interventions and Catchwords*, trans. by Henry W. Pickford (New York: Columbia University Press, 1998)
——, 'Resignation', in *Critical Models: Interventions and Catchwords*, trans. by Henry W. Pickford (New York: Columbia University Press, 1998)
——, 'Sacred Fragment: Schoenberg's Moses Und Aron', in *Quasi una Fantasia*, trans. by Rodney Livingstone (London: Verso, 1992)
——, 'The Actuality of Philosophy', trans. by Benjamin Snow, *Telos* (1977)
——, 'The Aging of the New Music', in *Essays on Music*, ed. by Richard Leppert, trans. by Susan H. Gillespie (Berkeley: University of California Press, 2002)
——, 'The Idea of Natural History', trans. by Robert Hullot-Kentor, *Telos* (1984)
——, *The Jargon of Authenticity*, trans. by Knut Tarnowski (London: Routledge, 2002)
——, 'Transparencies on Film', in *The Culture Industry: Selected Essays on Mass Culture*, ed. by J. M. Bernstein (London: Routledge, 1991)
——, 'Valéry Proust Museum', in *Prisms*, trans. by Samuel Weber and Shierry Weber (Cambridge, MA: MIT Press, 1981)
——, 'Vers Une Musique Informelle', in *Quasi una Fantasia: Essays on Modern Music*, trans. by Rodney Livingstone (London & New York: Verso, 1992)
——, 'Vienna', in *Quasi una Fantasia: Essays on Modern Music*, trans. by Rodney Livingstone (London: Verso, 1992)
——, 'Wagner's Relevance for Today', in *Essays on Music*, ed. by Richard Leppert, trans. by Susan H. Gillespie (Berkeley: University of California Press, 2002)
Adorno, Theodor W., and Walter Benjamin, *The Complete Correspondence, 1928–1940*, trans. by Nicholas Walker (Cambridge: Polity Press, 2003)
Adorno, Theodor W., and Ernst Bloch, 'Something's Missing: A Discussion between Ernst Bloch and Theodor W. Adorno on the Contradictions of Utopian Longing', in *The Utopian Function of Art*, trans. by Jack Zipes and Frank Mecklenburg (Cambridge, MA: MIT Press, 1988)
Agamben, Giorgio, *Language and Death*, trans. by Karen E. Pinkus and Michael Hardt (Minneapolis: University of Minnesota Press, 1991)
——, *The Time That Remains: A Commentary on the Letter to the Romans*, trans. by Patricia Dailey (Stanford, CA: Stanford University Press, 2005)
Allison, Henry E., *Kant's Transcendental Idealism* (New Haven: Yale University Press, 2004)
Arditti, Irvine, *Nono's Fragmente-Stille…*, Concert Program (Queen Elizabeth Hall, London, 2007)
Attali, Jacques, *Noise: The Political Economy of Music*, trans. by Brian Massumi (Manchester: Manchester University Press, 1985)
Baudelaire, Charles, *The Painter of Modern Life and Other Essays*, trans. by Jonathan Mayne (Phaidon, 1995)
Bauer, Karin, *Adorno's Nietzschean Narratives: Critiques of Ideology, Readings of Wagner* (Albany, NY: State University of New York Press, 1999)
Bauer-Lechner, Natalie, *Recollections of Gustav Mahler*, trans. by Dika Newlin (London & New York: Faber & Faber, 1980)
De Beistegui, Miguel, 'Boredom: Between Existence and History', in *Thinking With Heidegger* (Indianapolis: Indiana University Press, 2003)

Benjamin, Walter, 'On Language as Such and the Language of Man', in *Selected Writings, Volume 1*, trans. by Jephcott Edmund (Cambridge, MA: Belknap Press, 1996)
——, 'On Some Motifs in Baudelaire', in *Selected Writings, Volume 4*, ed. by Howard Eiland and Michael W. Jennings, trans. by Harry Zohn (Cambridge, MA: Harvard University Press Press, 2003)
——, 'On the Concept of History', in *Selected Writings, Volume 4*, trans. by Harry Zohn, Howard Eiland, and Michael W. Jennings (Cambridge, MA: Harvard University Press Press, 2003)
——, *Selected Writings, Vol. 1, 1913–1926*, ed. by Howard Eiland & Michael W. Jennings (Cambridge, MA: Harvard University Press, 1997)
——, *Selected Writings, Vol. 2, 1931–1934*, ed. by Howard Eiland & Michael W. Jennings (Cambridge, MA: Harvard University Press, 2005)
——, *Selected Writings, Vol. 4, 1938–1940*, ed. by Howard Eiland & Michael W. Jennings (Cambridge, MA: Harvard University Press, 2006)
——, *The Arcades Project*, trans. by Howard Eiland and Kevin McLaughlin (Cambridge, MA: Harvard University Press, 2002)
——, 'The Concept of Criticism in German Romanticism', in *Selected Writings, Volume 1*, trans. by David Lachterman, Howard Eiland, and Ian Balfour (Cambridge, MA: Harvard University Press, 1996)
——, *The Origin of German Tragic Drama*, trans. by John Osborne (London: Verso Books, 1998)
——, 'The Storyteller: Observations on the Works of Nikolai Leskov', in *Selected Writings, Volume 3*, trans. by Harry Zohn (Cambridge, MA: Harvard University Press, 1996)
——, 'The Work of Art in the Age of Its Technical Reproducibility', in *Selected Writings, Volume 3*, ed. by Edmund Jephcott and Harry Zohn (Cambridge, MA: Harvard University Press, 2002)
Bergson, Henri, *Key Writings*, ed. by Keith Ansell-Pearson (London & New York: Continuum, 2002)
Bertaggia, Michele, 'Prometeo – Conversation Entre Luigi Nono et Massimo Cacciari', in *Programme Luigi Nono* (Paris: Contrechamps, 1987)
Blanchot, Maurice, *The Infinite Conversation*, trans. by Susan Hanson (Minneapolis: University of Minnesota Press, 1993)
Bloch, Ernst, *Essays on the Philosophy of Music*, trans. by Peter Palmer (Cambridge: Cambridge University Press, 1985)
——, *The Spirit of Utopia*, trans. by Anthony A. Nassar (Stanford University Press, 2000)
Bowie, Andrew, *Aesthetics and Subjectivity: From Kant to Nietzsche* (Manchester: Manchester University Press, 1990)
Cacciari, Massimo, *Architecture and Nihilism: On the Philosophy of Modern Architecture*, trans. by Patrizia Lombardo (New Haven: Yale University Press, 1993)
——, 'Eupalinos or Architecture', *Oppositions* (1980)
——, *Posthumous People: Vienna at the Turning Point* (Stanford, CA: Stanford University Press, 1996)
——, 'Verso Prometeo', in *Programme Luigi Nono* (Paris: Contrechamps, 1987)
De Certeau, Michel, *The Practice of Everyday Life*, trans. by Steven Rendall (Berkeley: University of California Press, 2002)

Dahlhaus, Carl, *The Idea of Absolute Music*, trans. by Roger Lustig (Chicago & London: University of Chicago Press, 1991)
Debord, Guy, *The Society of the Spectacle*, trans. by Donald Nicholson-Smith (New York: Zone Books, 1994)
Derrida, Jacques, *Of Grammatology*, trans. by Gayatri Chakravorty Spivak (Baltimore: Johns Hopkins University Press, 1998)
Dilthey, Wilhelm, 'Aus Der Zeit Der Spinoza-Studien Goethes', in *Weltanschauung und Analyse des Menschen seit Renaissance und Reformation*, Gesammelte Schriften (Vandenhoeck & Ruprecht, 1991), II
Eisler, Hanns, and Theodor W. Adorno, *Composing for the Films* (London & New York: Athlone Press, 1994)
Felstiner, John, *Paul Celan: Poet, Survivor, Jew* (Yale University Press, 1995)
Feuerbach, Ludwig, *The Fiery Brook*, trans. by Zawar Hanfi (Minnesota: Anchor, 1972)
——, *Thoughts on Death and Immortality: From the Papers of a Thinker, Along With an Appendix of Theological-Satirical Epigrams*, trans. by James Massey (Berkeley: University of California Press, 1980)
Fortune, Nigel, 'Monteverdi and the Secconda Prattica', in *The Monteverdi Companion*, ed. by Nigel Fortune and Denis Arnold (London: Faber and Faber, 1968)
Foucault, Michel, 'Of Other Spaces', trans. by Jay Miskowiec, *Diacritics*, 16 (1986)
Freud, Sigmund, 'Fetishism', in *The Future of an Illusion, Civilization and its Discontents and Other Works*, trans. by James Strachey (London: Hogarth Press, 1964), XXI
——, 'Mourning and Melancholia', in *On the History of the Psycho-Analytic Movement. Papers on Metapsychology and Other Words*, trans. by James Strachey, The Standard Edition of the Complete Psychological Works of Sigmund Freud (London: Hogarth Press, 1964), XIV
Glendinning, Simon, *The Idea of Continental Philosophy* (Edinburgh: Edinburgh University Press, 2006)
Goethe, J. W., *Maxims and Reflections*, ed. by Peter Hutchinson, trans. by Elisabeth Stopp (London: Penguin, 1998)
Greenberg, Clement, 'Towards a Newer Laocoon', in *Art in Theory, 1900–2000*, ed. by Charles Harrison and Paul Wood (Oxford: Blackwell, 2000)
Guerrero, Jeannie Maria, 'Serial Intervention in Nono's Il Canto Sospeso', *Society for Music Theory*, 2006 <http://mto.societymusictheory.org/issues/mto.06.12.1/mto.06.12.1.guerrero.html> [accessed 2 February 2010]
Haar, Michel, *The Song of the Earth: Heidegger and the Grounds of the History of Geing*, trans. by Reginald Lilly (Indianapolis: Indiana University Press, 1993)
Habermas, Jürgen, 'Dialectical Idealism in Transition to Materialism: Schelling's Idea of a Contraction of God and Its Consequences for the Philosophy of History', in *The New Schelling*, trans. by Nick Midgley and Judith Norman (London: Continuum, 2004)
——, *Philosophical-Political Profiles*, trans. by Frederick G. Lawrence (London: Heinemann, 1983)
Hanslick, Eduard, '"Content" and "Form" in Music', in *German Essays on Music*, ed. by Jost Hermand and Michael Gilbert, trans. by Geoffrey Payzant (New York & London: Continuum, 1994)

Hegel, G. W. F., *Aesthetics: Lectures on Fine Art*, trans. by T. M. Knox (Oxford: Oxford University Press, 1998)
——, *Early Theological Writings*, trans. by T. M. Knox (Philadelphia: University of Pennsylvania Press, 1988)
——, *Hegel's Phenomenology of Spirit*, trans. by A. V. Miller (Oxford: Clarendon Press, 1977)
——, *Hegel's Philosophy of Nature: Being Part Two of the 'Encyclopaedia of the Philosophical Sciences' (1830)*, trans. by A. V. Miller (Oxford: Clarendon Press, 1970)
——, *Hegel's Science of Logic*, trans. by A. V. Miller (London: Humanity Books, 1969)
——, *The Difference Between Fichte's and Schelling's System of Philosophy*, trans. by Walter Cerf (New York: State University of New York Press, 1988)
Heidegger, Martin, 'Art and Space', in *Rethinking Architecture: A Reader in Cultural Theory*, ed. by Neil Leach, trans. by Charles Siebert (New York: Routledge, 1997)
——, *Being and Time*, trans. by John Macquarrie and Edward Robinson (Oxford: Blackwell, 2000)
——, 'Building Dwelling Thinking', in *Basic Writings*, ed. by David Farrell Krell, trans. by Albert Hofstadter (London: Routledge, 1993)
——, *Denkerfahrungen* (Frankfurt am Main: Klostermann, 1983)
——, *Discourse on Thinking: A Translation of 'Gelassenheit'*, trans. by John M. Anderson and E. Hans Freund (London & New York: Harper and Row, 1969)
——, *Hegel's 'Phenomenology of Spirit'*, trans. by Parvis Emad and Kenneth Maly (Indianapolis: Indiana University Press, 1994)
——, *Holderlin's Hymn 'The Ister'*, trans. by William McNeill and Julia Davis (Indianapolis: Indiana University Press, 1996)
——, *Kant and the Problem of Metaphysics*, trans. by Richard Taft, 5th edition (Bloomington: Indiana University Press, 1997)
——, 'Letter on Humanism', in *Basic Writings*, ed. by David Farrell Krell, trans. by Frank A. Capuzzi and J. Glenn Gray (London: Routledge, 1993)
——, *Nietzsche: The Will to Power as Art/The Eternal Recurrence of the Same*, trans. by David Farrell Krell (San Francisco, CA: Harper, 1991)
——, *Nietzsche: The Will to Power as Knowledge and as Metaphysics / Nihilism*, trans. by David Farrell Krell (San Francisco: Harper Collins, 1991)
——, 'Only a God Can Save Us', in *Philosophical and Political Writings*, ed. by Manfred Stassen, trans. by Maria P. Alter and John D. Caputo (New York and London: Continuum, 2003)
——, *Schelling's Treatise on the Essence of Human Freedom*, trans. by Joan Stambaugh (Ohio: Ohio University Press, 1985)
——, 'The Age of the World Picture', in *Off the Beaten Track*, trans. by Julian Young and Kenneth Hayes (Cambridge: Cambridge University Press, 2002)
——, *The Fundamental Concepts of Metaphysics: World, Finitude, Solitude*, trans. by William McNeill and Nicholas Walker (Bloomington: Indiana University Press, 2001)
——, '"The Onto-Theo-Logical Constitution of Metaphysics"', in *Identity and Difference*, trans. by Joan Stambaugh, New Edition (Chicago: University of Chicago Press, 2002)

——, 'The Origin of the Work of Art', in *Off the Beaten Track*, trans. by Julian Young and Kenneth Hayes (Cambridge: Cambridge University Press, 2002)
——, *The Question Concerning Technology and Other Essay*, trans. by William Lovitt (New York & London: Harper and Row, 1977)
——, 'The Theory of the Categories and Meaning in Duns Scotus', in *Supplements*, trans. by Roderick M. Stewart and van Buren (New York: State University of New York Press, 2002)
——, 'Words', in *On the Way to Language*, trans. by Peter D. Hertz (London & New York: Harper Collins, 1971)
Heyworth, Peter, *Otto Klemperer: His Life and Times, 1885–1933* (Cambridge & New York: Cambridge University Press, 1996), I
Hodkinson, James, 'The Cosmic-Symphonic: Novalis, Music, and Universal Discourse', in *Music and Literature in German Romanticism*, ed. by Siobhán Donovan and Robin Eliott (Rochester: Camden House, 2004)
Hoffmann, E. T. A., 'Beethoven's Instrumental Music', in *German Essays on Music*, ed. by Jost Hermand and Michael Gilbert (New York: Continuum, 1994)
Hölderlin, Friedrich, *Poems and Fragments*, trans. by Michael Hamburger (London: Anvil Press Poetry, 2003)
Horkheimer, Max, 'Egoism and Freedom Movements: On the Anthropology of the Bourgeois Era', in *Between Philosophy and Social Science: Selected Early Writings*, trans. by G. Frederick Hunter, Matthew S. Kramer, and John Torpey (Cambridge, MA: MIT Press, 1993)
Horkheimer, Max, and Theodor W. Adorno, *Dialectic of Enlightenment*, trans. by Edmund Jephcott (Stanford, CA: Stanford University Press, 2002)
Husserl, Edmund, *On the Phenomenology of the Consciousness of Internal Time*, ed. by Martin Heidegger, trans. by John Barnett Brough (Dordrecht & Boston: Kluwer Academic Publishers, 1991)
Janicaud, Dominique, *The Shadow of That Thought: Heidegger and the Question of Politics* (Evanston, Illinois: Northwestern University Press, 1996)
Jay, Martin, 'The Frankfurt School's Critique of Marxist Humanism', in *Permanent Exiles: Essays on the Intellectual Migration from Germany to America* (New York: Columbia University Press, 1990)
Kant, Immanuel, *Critique of Pure Reason*, trans. by Paul Guyer and Allen W. Wood (Cambridge: Cambridge University Press, 1999)
——, *Groundwork of the Metaphysics of Morals*, trans. by Mary Gregor (Cambridge: Cambridge University Press, 1997)
——, *The Critique of Judgement*, trans. by James Creed Meredith (Oxford: Clarendon Press, 1978)
Kaufmann, Walter, *Nietzsche: Philosopher, Psychologist, Antichrist* (Meridian Books, 1965)
Kepler, Johannes, *The Harmony of the World*, trans. by E. J. Aiton, A. M. Duncan, and Field (Philadelphia: American Philosophical Society, 1997)
Kurth, Ernst, *Musikpsychologie*, 2nd edn (Bern: Krompholz, 1947)
Lachenmann, Helmut, 'Touched by Nono', *Contemporary Music Review*, 18 (1999)
Lacoue-Labarthe, Philippe, *Heidegger, Art and Politics: The Fiction of the Political*, trans. by Chris Turner (Oxford: Blackwell, 1990)
——, *Musica Ficta: Figures of Wagner*, trans. by Felicia McCarren (Stanford, CA: Stanford University Press, 1994)

Lacoue-Labarthe, Philippe, and Jean-Luc Nancy, *The Literary Absolute: The Theory of Literature in German Romanticism*, trans. by Philip Barnard and Cheryl Lester (Albany: State University of New York Press, 1988)

Leibniz, Gottfried Wilhelm, 'Principles of Nature and Grace', in *Philosophical Essays*, trans. by Roger Ariew and Daniel Garber (Indianapolis: Hackett Publishing, 1989)

——, *The Monadology and Other Philosophical Writings*, trans. by Robert Latta (London: Oxford University Press, 1968)

Ligeti, György, and Carl Dahlhaus, 'A Debate on Contemporary Music', in *Contemplating Music: Essence*, ed. by Carl Dahlhaus and Ruth Katz, Source Readings in the Aesthetics of Music (Hillsdale, NY: Pendragon Press, 1992), III

Löwith, Karl, *From Hegel to Nietzsche: The Revolution in Nineteenth-Century Thought*, trans. by David E. Green (New York: Columbia University Press, 1991)

——, *Martin Heidegger and European Nihilism*, ed. by Richard Wolin, trans. by Gary Steiner (New York: Columbia University Press, 1995)

——, *Max Weber and Karl Marx*, trans. by Hans Fantel (London: George Allen & Unwin, 1982)

——, *Nietzsche's Philosophy of the Eternal Recurrence of the Same*, trans. by J. Harvey Lomax (Berkeley: University of California Press, 1997)

Lukács, Georg, *History and Class Consciousness. Studies in Marxist Dialectics*, trans. by Rodney Livingstone (London: Merlin Press, 1971)

——, *Theory of the Novel*, trans. by Anna Bostock (London: Merlin Press, 1978)

Macdonald, Iain, and Krzysztof Ziarek, eds., *Adorno and Heidegger: Philosophical Questions* (Stanford, CA: Stanford University Press, 2008)

Mackall, L. L., 'Goethe's "Edler Philosoph"', *Euphorion*, XI (1904)

Magee, Bryan, *Talking Philosophy: Dialogues with Fifteen Leading Philosophers* (Oxford: Oxford University Press, 2001)

Marx, Karl, *Capital: A Critique of Political Economy*, trans. by Ben Fowkes (London: Penguin, 1976), I

——, *Early Writings*, ed. by Lucio Colletti, trans. by Rodney Livingstone and Gregor Benton (Harmondsworth: Penguin, 1975)

Marx, Karl, and Friedrich Engels, *Basic Writings on Politics and Philosophy*, trans. by Lewis S Feuer (London: Fontana, 1969)

———, *The German Ideology*, ed. by C. J. Arthur (London: Lawrence & Wishart, 1970)

Marx, Karl, and Norman D. Livergood, 'The Difference Between the Democritean and Epicurean Philosophy of Nature in General', in *Activity in Marx's Philosophy* (The Hague: Martinus Nijhoff, 1967)

Mertens, Bram, *Dark Images, Secret Hints: Benjamin, Scholem, Molitor and the Jewish Tradition* (Bern: Peter Lang, 2007)

Metzger, Heinz-Klaus, 'Intermezzo I: Just Who Is Growing Old?' ed. by Karlheinz Stockhausen and Herbert Eimert, trans. by Leo Black, *Die Reihe*, 4 (1960)

Metzger, Heinz-Klaus, and Rainer Riehn, eds, *Luigi Nono* (Munich: Edition text + kritik, 1981)

Murray, Penelope, and Peter Wilson, eds., *Music and the Muses: The Culture of Mousike in the Classical Athenian City* (Oxford: Oxford University Press, 2004)

Nattiez, Jean Jacques, *Wagner Androgyne: A Study in Interpretation*, trans. by Stewart Spencer (Princeton, N.J: Princeton University Press, 1993)

Negri, Antonio, and Michael Hardt, *Empire* (Cambridge, MA: Harvard University Press, 2000)

Nielinger, Carola, '"The Song Unsung": Luigi Nono's Il Canto Sospeso', *Journal of the Royal Musical Association*, 131 (2006)
Nietzsche, Friedrich, *Human, All Too Human*, trans. by R. J. Hollingdale (Cambridge: Cambridge University Press, 1996)
——, *On the Genealogy of Morality*, trans. by Carol Diethe (Cambridge: Cambridge University Press, 1994)
——, *The Birth of Tragedy and The Case of Wagner*, trans. by Walter Kaufmann (New York: Vintage Books, 1967)
——, *The Gay Science*, trans. by Josefine Nauckhoff (Cambridge: Cambridge University Press, 2001)
——, *The Will to Power*, trans. by Walter Kaufmann and R. J. Hollingdale (New York: Vintage Books, 1968)
——, *Thus Spoke Zarathustra*, trans. by R. J. Hollingdale, New Impression (Penguin Classics, 2003)
Nono, Luigi, *Texte: Studien zu seiner Musik*, ed. by Jürg Stenzl (Atlantis, 1975)
Osmond-Smith, David, *Break-out from the Concert Hall: Luigi Nono and the New Music*, Concert Program (Queen Elizabeth Hall, London, 2005)
Owen, David, *Maturity and Modernity* (London: Routledge, 1994)
Pape, Gerard, 'Nono and His Fellow Travellers', *Contemporary Music Review*, 18 (1991)
Phillips, Wesley, 'Adorno on Music, Space and Objectification', *European Journal of Social Theory*, 16 (2013)
——, 'History or Counter-Tradition? The System of Freedom After Walter Benjamin', *Critical Horizons: A Journal of Philosophy & Social Theory*, 11 (2010)
——, 'The Future of Speculation?', *Cosmos and History*, 8 (2012)
Plato, *The Republic*, trans. by Desmond Lee (London: Penguin, 1955)
——, *Timaeus and Critus*, trans. by H. D. Lee (London: Penguin, 1965)
Rabinovich, Anson, 'Why Were the Jews Sacrificed? The Place of Anti-Semitism in Dialectic of Enlightenment', *New German Critique*, 81 (2000)
Rée, Jonathan, *I See a Voice: A Philosophical History of Language, Deafness and the Senses* (London: HarperCollins, 1999)
Rose, Gillian, *Hegel Contra Sociology* (London: Athlone, 1981)
——, *Judaism and Modernity: Philosophical Essays* (Oxford: Blackwell, 1993)
——, *The Melancholy Science: An Introduction to the Thought of Theodor W. Adorno* (New York: Columbia University Press, 1978)
Sachs, Curt, *Rhythm and Tempo* (New York: Dent, 1953)
Safranski, Rüdiger, *Martin Heidegger: Between Good and Evil*, trans. by Ewald Oders (Cambridge, MA: Harvard University Press, 1998)
——, *Nietzsche: A Philosophical Biography*, trans. by Shelley L. Frisch (London: Granta, 2002)
Schelling, F. W. J., 'Philosophical Investigations into the Essence of Human Freedom and Related Matters', in *Philosophy of German Idealism*, ed. by Ernst Behler (New York: Continuum, 1997)
——, 'Stuttgart Seminars', in *Idealism and the Endgame of Theory: Three Essays by F. W. J. Schelling*, trans. by Thomas Pfau (New York: State University of New York Press, 1993)
——, *System of Transcendental Idealism*, trans. by Peter Heath (Charlottesville: University of Virginia Press, 1993)

——, *The Philosophy of Art*, trans. by Douglas W. Stott (Minneapolis: University of Minnesota Press, 1989)

Schlegel, August Wilhelm, *Vorlesungen Über Philosophische Kunstlehre* (Leipzig: Theodor Weicher, 1911)

Schlegel, Friedrich von, *Philosophical Fragments*, trans. by Peter Firchow (Minneapolis: University of Minnesota Press, 1991)

Schmidt, Alfred, *Concept of Nature in Marx*, trans. by Ben Fowkes (London: New Left Books, 1971)

Scholem, Gershom, *Walter Benjamin: The Story of a Friendship*, trans. by Harry Zohn (New York: New York Review Books, 2003)

Schopenhauer, Arthur, *The World as Will and Representation*, trans. by E. F. G. Payne (New York: Dover Publications, 1966), I

Simmel, Georg, 'Metropolis and Mental Life', in *On Individuality and Social Forms*, ed. by Donald Levine, trans. by Edward A. Shils

Snow, Dale E., *Schelling and the End of Idealism: The Horizons of Feeling* (New York: State University of New York Press, 1996)

Stenzl, Jürg, *Luigi Nono* (Reinbek bei Hamburg: Rowohlt, 1998)

Szondi, Peter, *An Essay on the Tragic*, trans. by Paul Fleming (Stanford, CA: Stanford University Press, 2002)

Tafuri, Manfredo, *Architecture and Utopia: Design and Capitalist Development*, trans. by Barbara Luigia La Penta (Cambridge, MA: MIT Press, 1976)

Taubes, Jacob, *The Political Theology of Paul*, trans. by Dana Hollander (Stanford, CA: Stanford University Press, 2004)

Taylor, Ronald, ed., *Aesthetics and Politics: The Key Texts of the Classic Debate Within German Marxism* (London: New Left Books, 1977)

Wackenroder, Wilhelm Heinrich, 'The Marvels of the Musical Art', in *German Essays on Music*, ed. by Jost Hermand and Michael Gilbert (New York: Continuum, 1994)

Weber, Max, *Economy and Society*, ed. by Guenther Roth and Claus Wittich (Berkeley: University of California Press, 1992), II

——, '"Objectivity" in Social Science', in *Methodology of the Social Sciences*, trans. by Edward A. Shils and Henry A. Finch (New Brunswick, NJ: Transaction Publishers, 2011)

——, 'Science as a Vocation', in *From Max Weber: Essays in Sociology*, trans. by H. H. Gerth and C. Wright Mills (London: Routledge, 1991)

——, 'The Meaning of "Ethical Neutrality"', in *Methodology of the Social Sciences*, trans. by Edward A. Shils and Henry A. Finch (New Brunswick, NJ: Transaction Publishers, 2011)

Williams, Alastair, 'New Music, Late Style: Adorno's "Form in the New Music"', *Music Analysis*, 27 (2008), 193–99

Wolin, Richard, ed., *The Heidegger Controversy: A Critical Reader* (MIT Press, 1993)

——, *The Politics of Being: The Political Thought of Martin Heidegger* (New York: Columbia University Press, 1990)

Žižek, Slavoj, and F. W. J. Schelling, *The Abyss of Freedom/Ages of the World* (University of Michigan Press, 1997)

Index

Printed and bound by CPI Group (UK) Ltd, Croydon, CR0 4YY